I0814741

"Near the end of her book, Shively Smith poses the provocative question of what she, as an African American woman, is doing giving an appreciative reading of 1 Peter—a letter that appears to endorse subordination and servitude. Smith offers a fresh, eye-opening interpretation of the letter in the context of Jewish diaspora existence. She argues that 1 Peter 'constructs a double social reality,' fostering a double consciousness that allows the creation and preservation of a strange new fellowship that transgresses social and cultural boundaries, while neither conforming fully to dominant norms nor openly rebelling against them. The letter is a 'writing from the underclass for the underclass, not the overlord.' Smith's comparative sketches of the diaspora visions of Daniel, the Letter of Aristeas, and Philo bring the picture sharply into focus. Strangers to Family is necessary reading for everyone interested in the social history of early Christianity and Hellenistic Judaism, as well as for everyone interested in the theological interpretation of exile and diaspora in the New Testament."

—Richard B. Hays, *George Washington Ivey Professor of New Testament, Duke Divinity School*

"This ambitious, clearly written book first focuses on an exegetical analysis of 1 Peter, then enriches our knowledge of this epistle by contextualizing it within concepts of diaspora found in Hellenistic and Roman Jewish literature. By the end of *Strangers to Family*, the reader better understands how to read 1 Peter as evidence of complex resistance, of negotiations with structures of power, and of a Christian imagination that is rooted in diversity and difference."

—Laura Nasrallah, *Professor of New Testament and Early Christianity, Harvard Divinity School*

"In this stimulating study, Shively Smith examines the constructions of diaspora in 1 Peter as well as its presentation and negotiation in Daniel, the Letter of Aristeas, and Philo. The result is a rich, multidimensional exploration of a versatile and elastic category of importance not only for reading these ancient texts but also for contemporary diaspora peoples."

—Warren Carter, *Professor of New Testament, Brite Divinity School, Texas Christian University*

"Shively Smith provides us with a careful and complex analysis of 'diaspora thinking,' using analytical categories from both 'the ancients' and contemporary scholarship. The text and context of 1 Peter has the primary place in this study, but today's contexts and concerns are not neglected, with the concluding chapter providing significant resonances and resources for our increasingly 'displaced' world."

—Gerald O. West, *Senior Professor in Biblical Studies, University of KwaZulu-Natal*

"Smith brings 1 Peter into dialogue with other 'diasporic texts' in late Second Temple Judaism (the Daniel Tales, Aristeas, and Philo) in ways that not only confirm many of her proposals, but also effectively highlight the crucial conceptual context of 1 Peter in the widespread debates and discussions about the Jewish condition in the late Second-Temple Period throughout the Near East. Smith's concluding reflections promise even more interesting work to come."

—Daniel L. Smith-Christopher, *Professor of Theological Studies, Loyola Marymount University*

STRANGERS TO FAMILY

STRANGERS TO FAMILY

Diaspora and 1 Peter's Invention of God's Household

Shively T. J. Smith

BAYLOR UNIVERSITY PRESS

Cover Design by AJB Design, Inc.
Cover image: Detail from the Arch of Titus, courtesy of iStockphoto/adaniabertil

Library of Congress Cataloging-in-Publication Data

Names: Smith, Shively T. J., author.
Title: Strangers to family : diaspora and 1 Peter's invention of God's household / Shively T.J. Smith.
Description: Waco : Baylor University Press, 2016. | Includes bibliographical references and index.
Identifiers: LCCN 2016009308 (print) | LCCN 2016030225 (ebook) | ISBN 9781481305488 (hardback: alk. paper) | ISBN 9781481306126 (web pdf) | ISBN 9781481306119 (ebook-Mobi/Kindle) | ISBN 9781481305501 (ePub)
Subjects: LCSH: Bible. Peter, 1st—Criticism, interpretation, etc. | Households—Religious aspects—Christianity—Biblical teaching. | Emigration and immigration—Religious aspects—Christianity—Biblical teaching. | Emigration and immigration in the Bible. | Globalization—Religious aspects—Christianity—Biblical teaching.
Classification: LCC BS2795.52 .S65 2016 (print) | LCC BS2795.52 (ebook) | DDC 227/.9206—dc23
LC record available at https://lccn.loc.gov/2016009308

Printed in the United States of America on acid-free paper with a minimum of 30 percent post-consumer waste recycled content.

To my mother, Wenefer Servon White, who named me,
gifted me with my story, and never left my side.

Contents

Preface

The idea for this book was born while I was reading James Scott's *Domination and the Arts of Resistance* and taking doctoral seminars on the book of Daniel and Jewish backgrounds of the New Testament. My colleagues in those seminars proved to be generative conversation partners as the project took shape.[1] I was drawn to the language of diaspora and displacement that saturated our seminar discussions, to Scott's masterful work, and to the social negotiations I discerned from the literary prose of the Daniel court tales. The correlation between particular themes intrigued me. There seemed to be an intrinsic relatedness among terms such as accommodation, assimilation, foreignness, danger, hidden and public transcripts, and double consciousness. Rather than selecting one orientation over the other—such as conformity or resistance, acculturation or difference—all these descriptions for social action and social position, no matter how antithetical, seemed present and active at the same time in Daniel's story and Scott's analysis.

I found myself perusing other writings from the Second Temple period that engaged contexts of dispersion, foreignness, and disenfranchisement. Writings such as the books of Tobit and Esther, the

[1] The robust and intense engagement that took place in the Daniel and Jewish backgrounds doctoral seminars at Emory University set the course of the rest of my doctoral work and research. Indeed, I am indebted to all my colleagues in those seminars because each sharpened my insight and approach and challenged me to revisit biblical texts and themes repeatedly.

Letter of Aristeas, and the works of Philo and Josephus (to name a few) reflected this complicated matrix, conveying to varying degrees a similar set of social negotiations as exhibited in Daniel. From the perspective of these ancient Jewish writings, a displaced or minority community, identifiably different from the cultural environments in which it was situated, at times resisted dominating powers and other times accommodated those same powers. Sometimes the group was outright defiant and deviant and other times compliant, yielding to the status quo without protest, critique, or attack—biding its time for when better conditions, such as social positionality and resources, were in place to challenge the status quo. It appeared to me that the compliance the ancient Jewish writings depicted was not a sign of assent but an act of survival. The social positions the literature highlighted were wide ranging, but all of the Hellenistic Jewish writers imbued their stories of social maneuvering, performance, transition, and change with religious discourse about God's purposeful acts and responses to human agency and faith. These writings entwined social imagining with theological reasoning in forms that were both comparable and different.

As a New Testament scholar, I wondered which writings from that part of the Christian Scriptures also interact with concepts of dispersion, difference, and assimilation. I launched into a thorough rereading of the entire New Testament to see what I could find with such language central to my mind. I encountered a few possibilities. Certainly, the book of Acts emerged as an early candidate. I loved it for all the obvious reasons. First, it was a story. What better way to capture the ambivalent and gray areas of living than in story? Here, the transformations of dynamic characters like Paul and Peter were on display. It offered glimpses into the movement of marginal groups, such as women, the poor, Gentiles, and Jews, from the periphery of their native environments and households to the center of an emerging community situated within that larger society. Certainly, one could read about how incipient Christ-proclaiming communities were forced to abandon their homes and familiar surroundings and scatter to new areas and regions to secure their basic survival. In Acts, I had access to a moving narrative full of subplots and to a diverse cast of characters living as "other" in environments across the ancient Roman world who could respond to vulnerable and peculiar populations with hostility and distrust.

The book of Acts was so compelling, in fact, I almost failed to read the entire New Testament. That would have been disastrous because I would have failed to reach the First Letter of Peter. Not only did 1 Peter display all the terms that caught my attention initially, its sensibility around that experience seemed unique from the other writings I had given a cursory review. It was, in some respects, similar in viewpoint and outlook to the Daniel court tales, the Letter of Aristeas, Acts, and even Philo. Yet, in other respects, 1 Peter was very different. It did not challenge everything my social justice inclinations wanted it to, but the battles against the status quo it did wage were no less significant. In fact, the letter's configuration of the issues forced me to rethink the conceptual and thematic matrix and implications of diaspora and difference at work in diverse ancient texts. First Peter equipped me with a flexible lens by which to think about the life and conditions that Hellenistic Jewish and early Christian texts were shaping as they addressed the realities of their current audiences who often lived on the fringes of societal convention and etiquette. These writers imagined a future not yet realized, but in their minds it was no less real and possible. They charted a path forward, and the First Letter of Peter offered me the eyes to see it.

Acknowledgments

This book is not the product of my singular efforts but represents the fruits of those people, organizations, and communities who have supported me from the moment we encountered each other. For this reason there are many people to acknowledge, but to name each would probably require its own book. So to all who read this book and who have touched my life in some way and encouraged me to read yet another book, write yet another sentence, and ponder a thought for yet an additional moment, I extend my recognition and gratitude to you for that gift.

There are, however, a few people I would be remiss not to mention here as they served as direct catalysts to the production of this work. First, the members of my dissertation committee—Luke Timothy Johnson, Walter T. Wilson, Carol A. Newsom, and Michael Joseph Brown—have been supportive of my research and committed to my development as a scholar and teacher from early in my graduate career. Carol and Walter provided the space for me to read texts and contemplate constructions of diaspora life present in Hellenistic Jewish documents. Their encouragement to pursue my questions and interpretations was critical to my development of this research, and I am thankful for their support, recommendations, and teaching.

I will always be grateful for the mentorship and guidance I received from Michael Joseph Brown. Prior to starting my doctoral research, I worked with him as his research assistant and teaching associate. We dissected my intellectual experiences and perspectives and thought of new and constructive ways forward in pedagogy, research, and writing. It was while working with him as a graduate student and under his supportive guidance that my passion for biblical interpretation and research was solidified. Brown has been a supportive mentor and friend, and I will always be thankful for him.

From my advisor, Luke Timothy Johnson, I learned writing clearly, thinking critically, and stating courageously what I see occurring in texts are difficult, but necessary tasks. I am grateful for all the countless revisions, edits, and conversations he offered during the dissertation process and beyond. He always offered time when I needed it, always spoke candidly about the state of my work, and always supported my emerging insights and scholarly voice. The opportunity to work with him shaped me as a scholar, teacher, writer, and person. In Luke I found a true teacher, advisor, and friend. For that I am grateful.

My work has been supported by several prestigious organizations and fellowships over the course of my doctoral research and beyond: the Fund for Theological Education, the Louisville Institute Foundation, the Ford Foundation, the Black Women in Church and Society Program at the ITC, the Social Science Council, the Mellon Mays Undergraduate Fellowship Program, and Emory University's Laney Graduate School Grant Writing Program. I am grateful for their educative services and financial support. I look forward to working with these organizations in the future to pay forward the support and mentorship I received.

Moreover, I am thankful to the Baylor University Press family and particularly the director, Carey C. Newman. I had the privilege to meet Carey as a fellow of the Louisville Institute during one of its Winter Seminars and I knew then I wanted to work with him and Baylor on this project. I am thankful for all the coaching, editing, and cheerleading he offered me as I transitioned from student to scholar. His vote of confidence and sage wisdom and advice were and are priceless. Carey read and reread chapters until I found the story and my voice within it. Thank you.

I have been gifted with a host of wonderful colleagues, conversation partners, and friends who have read, dialogued, and celebrated my strides in recasting the dissertation into its monograph form. I am thankful for the support, patience, and time the following people extended to me: Angela Sims, Kimberly Russaw, Carla Works, Jill Marshall, Eric Barreto, Thomas Fabisak, Dianne Stewart, Walter Fluker, Gerald West, William Lamar IV, Diana Lewis, Alphonso Saville, Alisa Parker, Stephanie Crumpton, Keri Day, Yolanda Norton, Nyasha Junior, Alexis Wells, Michelle Levan, Julia Buckner, Shanell Smith, Stephanie Crowder, Raedorah Stewart, Ja'el Daniely, Asa Lee, Matthew Williams, and the entire Wesley Theological Seminary community. I am also grateful for the efforts of my teaching and research assistants, Laura Kigweba and Alisha Langhorne, who read, copied, checked, and formatted bibliographical references whenever needed. With colleagues, friends, and students like you, I am excited about the future conversations awaiting us.

I am thankful for my family and the sacrifices that were made and prayers that were offered so I could pursue my dream and become the first person in our family with a Ph.D. and now a book. Words and tears cannot capture my appreciation for my mother Wenefer White, Anthony White, Gwen Thomas, Edward Thomas, Renita Thomas, Brian K. Smith, Claudine Smith, Cheryl Smith, the Clark family, Deborah and Victoria Washington, Winfred Smith, Frank Jackson Sr., Jessie Powell, Dorothy Johnson, Michelle Smith, Syndi Howard, Bridgette and Vance Ross, Toni Belin Ingram and family, Mt. Nebo Church families, Fisk University professors Lean'tin Bracks and Karen Collier, and all those who said, "Shively, you can do it." Thank you. Finally, to my best friend and husband, Brian R. Smith, and our girls, Trinity and Claudia Smith, I love you. This is to remind us that dreams and goals can come to fruition. Thank you for believing in me.

ABBREVIATIONS

AB	Anchor Bible
ABD	*Anchor Bible Dictionary*
Abraham	*On the Life of Abraham* (*De Abrahamo*), Philo
Ad Dem.	*To Demonicus,* Pseudo-Isocrates
Alex.	*Alexander*, Plutarch
Ant.	*Jewish Antiquities*, Josephus
ANTC	Abingdon New Testament Commentaries
BDAG	Bauer, Walter, Frederick William Danker, William F. Arndt, and F. Wilbur Gingrich. *Greek–English Lexicon of the New Testament and Other Early Christian Literature*. 3rd ed. Chicago: University of Chicago Press, 2000
BECNT	Baker Exegetical Commentary on the New Testament
BHGNT	Baylor Handbook on the Greek New Testament
Bib	*Biblica*
B.J.	*Bellum judaicum* (*Jewish War*), Josephus
BJS	Brown Judaic Studies
BTB	*Biblical Theological Bulletin*
CBQ	*Catholic Biblical Quarterly*
Confusion	*On the Confusion of Tongues* (*De confusione linguarum*), Philo
CPJ	*Corpus Papyrorum Judaicarum*. Edited by Victor A. Tcherikover. 3 vols. Cambridge, Mass.: Harvard University Press, 1957–1964
Creation	*On the Creation of the World* (*De opificio mundi*), Philo

CurTM	*Currents in Theology and Mission*
Decalogue	*De decalogo* (*On the Decalogue*), Philo
Dreams	*On Dreams* (*De somniis*), Philo
Embassy	*On the Embassy to Gaius* (*Legatio ad Gaium*), Philo
Ep.	*Epistulae* (*The Letters of Pliny*), Pliny the Younger
ExAud	*Ex Auditu*
Flight	*On Flight and Finding* (*De fuga et inventione*), Philo
HB	Hebrew Bible
HNT	Handbuch zum Neuen Testament
HTR	*Harvard Theological Review*
Husbandry	*On Agriculture* (*De agricultura*), Philo
Hypothetica	*Hypothetica*, Philo
JBL	*Journal of Biblical Literature*
Joseph	*On the Life of Joseph* (*De Iosepho*), Philo
JSNT	*Journal for the Study of the New Testament*
JSS	*Journal of Semitic Studies*
JTS	*Journal of Theological Studies*
LCL	Loeb Classical Library
LD	Lectio divina
Life	*The Life* (*Vita*), Josephus
LNTS	Library of New Testament Studies
LSTS	Library of Second Temple Studies
LXX	Septuaginta/Septuagint
Migration	*On the Migration of Abraham* (*De migratione Abrahami*), Philo
Moses	*On the Life of Moses* (*De vita Mosis*), Philo
NCBC	New Century Bible Commentary Series
NETS	New English Translation of the Septuagint
NIB	*The New Interpreter's Bible*
NIDOTTE	*New International Dictionary of Old Testament Theology and Exegesis*. Edited by W. A. VanGemeren. 5 vols. Grand Rapids: Zondervan, 1997
NovTSup	Supplements to Novum Testamentum
NT	New Testament
NTS	*New Testament Studies*
OTL	Old Testament Library
OTP	*The Old Testament Pseudepigrapha*. Edited by James H. Charlesworth. 2 vols. New York: Doubleday, 1983, 1985

Pol.	*Politica* (*Politics*), Aristotle
Prelim. Studies	*On the Preliminary Studies* (*De congressu eruditionis gratia*), Philo
PW	*Paulys Realencyclopädie der classischen Altertumswissenschaft*. New edition by Georg Wissowa and Wilhelm Kroll. 50 vols. 84 parts. Stuttgart: Metzler & Drückenmuller, 1894–1980
Rewards	*On Rewards and Punishments* (*De praemiis et poenis*), Philo
SBL	Society of Biblical Literature
SBLDS	Society of Biblical Literature Dissertation Series
SBLMS	Society of Biblical Literature Monograph Series
SBLSBS	Society of Biblical Literature Sources for Biblical Study
SBLWGRW	Society of Biblical Literature Writings from the Greco-Roman World
SC	Sources chrétiennes. Paris, 1943–
SCI	*Scripta Classica Israelica*
SNTW	Studies of the New Testament and Its World
TDNT	*Theological Dictionary of the New Testament*. Edited by Gerhard Kittel and Gerhard Friedrich. Translated by Geofrey W. Bromiley. 10 vols. Grand Rapids: Eerdmans, 1964–76
Unchangeable	*That God is Unchangeable* (*Quod Deus sit immutabilis*), Philo
VT	Vetus Testamentum
WBC	Word Biblical Commentary
WUNT	Wissenschaftliche Untersuchungen zum Neuen Testament
YCS	*Yale Classical Studies*

Introduction

Diaspora. Dispersion. Deviancy. Conformity. Foreigner. Resident. Family. The First Letter of Peter has all this in mind from the very beginning when it greets its readers saying, "Peter, an apostle of Jesus Christ; to the elect-foreigners of the Diaspora living in Pontus, Galatia, Cappadocia, Asia, and Bithynia" (1 Pet 1:1; my trans.). From the outset, language of social dislocation and cultural difference saturates 1 Peter's discourse and is interlaced with images of social convention and religious rhetoric. On the first read, the letter appears contradictory and double-minded, prescribing a uniform course of action to its imagined readers without certainty about how the society surrounding them will respond. For instance, it instructs readers to act honorably among the Gentiles but to expect shame (1 Pet 2:12). The letter goes on to prescribe the same medicine again in 1 Peter 2:15—Christians should act honorably and do good among the Gentiles—but then tells them to expect a different outcome—their Gentile adversaries will be silenced. The letter writer appears uncertain about the ramifications or backlash awaiting self-identified Christians living in dispersion who act honorably and "do good," yet the prescribed course of action remains consistent.

The letter is certainly concerned about a vulnerable and scattered population that could respond to their situation a number of different ways. First Peter is, however, advocating a multifaceted approach. On the one hand, it instructs its readers to be compliant residents in the regions they inhabit, yielding willingly to the status quo without protest, critique, or attack. It presumes residents of Pontus will stay put after the letter is read. Likewise, residents of Galatia will remain in Galatia, residents of Cappadocia will remain in Cappadocia, and so forth. Furthermore, it instructs slaves to stay slaves (1 Pet 2:18), women to stay submissive (1 Pet 3:1), and foreigners to remain invisible (1 Pet 2:11). On the other hand, the letter tells readers to be vigilant in "resisting" (1 Pet 5:8) evil and be armed with a formal defense (*apologia*) when confronted publically (1 Pet 3:15).

Indeed, the strategy 1 Peter advances is far from simple. Elements of antithetical social orientations—such as conformity and nonconformity and assimilation and difference—are at work.[1] The challenge with reading 1 Peter is to hold all these terms in tension as necessary components of its vision without diminishing any aspect.[2] While elements of detachment and dissimilarity prevail, the letter begins by asserting a relational unity in the form of a Christian diaspora. Broadly defined, diaspora is a noun that means "a scattering throughout" or "dispersion," which is a state of being spread widely over a region or regions. A diaspora does not necessarily endure uninterrupted indefinitely, and dispersal does not automatically create a diaspora. In sum, diaspora (or dispersion) is a condition, a state, and a discourse of a people that touches spaces and places and includes matters of time, culture, etiquette, and consciousness.[3] By positioning the proper noun form of diaspora after the label elect-foreigner, and before the list of five Roman provinces, 1 Peter appropriates diaspora, with its kaleidoscopic meanings, as the root metaphor and principal

[1] Torrey Seland, *Strangers in the Light: Philonic Perspectives on Christian Identity in 1 Peter* (Biblical Interpretation Series 76; Leiden: Brill, 2005).

[2] Miroslav Volf, "Soft Difference: Theological Reflections on the Relation between Church and Culture in 1 Peter," *ExAud* 10 (1994): 16–17. See also David G. Horrell, "Between Conformity and Resistance: Beyond the Balch-Elliott Debate towards a Postcolonial Reading of First Peter," in *Reading First Peter with New Eyes: Methodological Reassessments of the Letter of First Peter*, ed. Robert L. Webb and Betsy Bauman-Martin (LNTS 364; London: T&T Clark, 2007), 111–43; James C. Scott, *Domination and the Arts of Resistance: Hidden Transcripts* (New Haven, Conn.: Yale University Press, 1990).

[3] Paul Tiyambe Zeleza, "Diaspora Dialogues: Engagements between Africa and its Diasporas," *The New African Diaspora,* eds. Isidore Okpewho and Nkiru Nzegwu (Bloomington: Indiana University Press, 2009), 32.

situation of the addressees.[4] The image of diaspora illustrates how this new ethnoreligious group is to function in its home environment while simultaneously existing separate from it.[5] The letter is an insider correspondence, responding to the needs of a multicultural, scattered, and vulnerable population. It provides a new perspective on their precarious circumstances and a vision of their collective bearing of the stigma "Christian" (1 Pet 4:16). Furthermore, it supplies its readers with a strategy for functioning and surviving in environments prone to violent and aggressive reprisals for cultural difference and social deviance.

First Peter's construction of a diaspora lifestyle or strategy for survival is not new. By the time the letter writer deployed the term "diaspora" as a prevailing image at the end of the first century CE, it already had a rich and varied connotative application. The term grew out of the complex experiences of Hellenistic Judaism, particularly Second Temple Judaism. The first time the proper noun form appears anywhere in writings from the Greco-Roman world is in the Septuagint (the Greek translation of the Hebrew Scriptures, indicated by LXX), occurring there only twelve times (LXX Deut 28:25; 30:4; Neh 1:9; Jdt 5:19; 2 Macc 1:27; Ps 146:2; Pss. Sol. 8:28; 9:2; Isa 49:6; Jer 15:7; 41:17; Dan 12:2).[6] In these cases, diaspora denotes a punitive action

[4] Troy W. Martin, *Metaphor and Composition in 1 Peter* (SBLDS; Atlanta: Scholars Press, 1992). Indeed, the significance of Martin's emphasis on diaspora as the root metaphor of 1 Peter cannot be overstated. This study agrees with his assessment in many ways, but takes an entirely different approach to valuing the diaspora imagery at work in 1 Peter. It diverges from Martin in regard to the assessment of what constitutes the basic metaphors of "diaspora" itself.

[5] Ethnoreligious identity refers to dispersed and diverse people who share common identity markers grounded in traditions, histories, lineage, language, positions, and so forth. For a demonstration of its meaning and use, cf. Michael Joseph Brown, *The Lord's Prayer Through North African Eyes: A Window into Early Christianity* (London: T&T Clark, 2004), xii, xiii, 75, 76, 271–72; Christopher Haas, *Alexandria in Late Antiquity: Topography and Social Conflict*. Ancient Society and History (Baltimore: Johns Hopkins University Press, 1997), 8–9, 14–15.

[6] The verb form, *diaspeirō*, is used by classical Greek writers such as Sophocles and Herodotus. See Soph., *El.* 748 and Hdt., *Hist.* 3.13. For a brief rehearsal of the historical uses of the term "diaspora," see also Stephane Dufoix, *Diasporas* (Berkeley: University of California Press, 2003), 4–5; Robin Cohen, "Diasporas and the Nation-State: From Victims to Challengers," *International Affairs* 72, no. 3 (1996):

taken by God. It is a theological rationale for the geographic displacement and dispersion of Israel across the ancient Mediterranean world. Yet diaspora is not just a term deployed occasionally in the LXX but also an idea or a social construction imagined and offered to readers at particular literary moments. Second Temple writings such as Daniel, Tobit, Esther, the Letter of Aristeas, and Philo's historical treatises narrate moments of diaspora life and consciousness that are similar and distinct in varying ways. Consonant across all these constructions, however, is a concern for displaced communities in need of a clarified group identity. Each writing captures a diaspora context, and each diaspora reference reflects a complicated matrix riddled with aspects of acculturation and difference, assimilation and deviance, and attachment and detachment.

The brilliance of the ancients to describe and theologize dispersion in such a way as to create new frames for living is instructive for contemporary inquisitors of diaspora attentive to matters of immigration, xenophobia, and social class (to name a few).[7] A journey through the early life of diaspora thinking and construction, even within a Judeo-Christian framework, has the potential to show and identify some of the basic features that make diaspora thinking sui generis.

507–20; and Kevin Kenny, *Diaspora: A Very Short Introduction* (Oxford: Oxford University Press, 2013).

[7] Although my language assumes diaspora is being figured and refigured by ancient Jewish sources, it is important to note that I do not think the constructive work-around "diaspora" that the ancients did was specifically in service to creating a formal theory of diaspora. I echo Erich Gruen's position that it does not appear the authors were casting diaspora theory in the way it is now discussed and investigated in contemporary academic discourses. Rather, the ancients were just living and trying to make meaning of their existential realities and concerns that involved a praxis of double aims and social, regional, and cultural attachments. Thus, what has been left to us are disparate literary artifacts of that thinking that now appear to be answering, engaging, and imagining the very issues resonant in diaspora discourses and constructions of the current day. The ancients left behind letters, narratives, and treatises that the modern reader now has an opportunity to examine as a form of diaspora thinking and consciousness taking place at the inchoate stages of the conception of "diaspora." Gruen, *Diaspora: Jews amidst Greeks and Romans* (Cambridge, Mass.: Harvard University Press, 2002), 243; John M. G. Barclay, *Negotiating Diaspora: Jewish Strategies in the Roman Empire* (LSTS 45; New York: T&T Clark, 2004), 2.

One should not presume that the conception of diaspora has only recently been critically examined and re-visioned as a versatile and elastic category useful for describing a variety of contemporary population movements, community experiences, and peripheral sociopolitical locations.[8] Diaspora actually *began* as a flexible and adaptable category and is not just an innovation of postmodern and postcolonial (and other) ruminations.[9] Among Hellenistic Jews, from a diversity of backgrounds and embracing a variety of allegiances, diaspora was conceived various ways, albeit within a theological frame. Both nontheological and religious studies of diaspora can benefit from an investigation of the "early life" of diaspora imaginings. It can even be said that there is nothing new under the sun when it comes to diaspora conception and construction.

The Basis of Diaspora Conception

The first step toward appreciating the diaspora thinking at work in 1 Peter and other select Hellenistic Jewish writings is defining the semantic range of meanings and the sociocultural concerns pertinent to diaspora conception in general. Early Greek Jewish (LXX) conceptions of diaspora are different from Hebrew Bible (HB) conceptions of

[8] The year 1991 brought the first publication of the journal *Diaspora: A Journal of Transnational Studies* as well as the popular article by William Safran called "Diasporas in Modern Societies: Myths of Homeland and Return," *Diaspora* 1, no. 1 (1991): 83–99, which garnered much discussion and theorizing around the defining characteristics of diaspora as a definitive pattern of population movement. From this time, diaspora studies bloomed in academic circles of all sorts as an actual dimension of historic population movements across the world. See Robin Cohen, *Global Diasporas: An Introduction* (London: UCL Press, 1997); and Jane Evans Braziel and Anita Mannur, *Theorizing Diaspora* (Malden, Mass.: Blackwell, 2006).

[9] Leslie R. James, "The African Diaspora as Construct and Lived Experience," in *The Africana Bible: Readings Israel's Scriptures from Africa and the African Diaspora*, ed. Hugh R. Page Jr. et al. (Minneapolis: Fortress, 2010), 11–18; Stuart Hall, "Cultural Identity and Diaspora," in *Identity: Community, Culture, Difference*, ed. Jonathan Rutherford (London: Lawrence & Wishart, 1990), 223–37; Joseph E. Harris, ed., *Global Dimensions of the African Diaspora* (2nd ed.; Washington, D.C.: Howard University Press, 1993); Paul E. Lovejoy, "The African Diaspora: Revisionist Interpretations of Ethnicity, Culture and Religion and Slavery," *Studies in the World History of Slavery, Abolition, and Emancipation* 2, no. 1 (1977).

exile and wandering. While the latter notions existed alongside language and ideas of diaspora in the Hellenistic period, they should not be confused as synonymous with diaspora. Indeed, the Greek Jewish Scriptures maintain these as two distinct situations. To be a nomadic community or an exiled community is not the same as being counted as a diaspora people.

Despite this difference, diaspora is commonly associated with the Babylonian captivity and correlated to Hebrew words for exile and imprisonment (e.g., *galut*).[10] Julius Wellhausen is credited as the first biblical scholar to make "diaspora" an English word in the 1881 ninth edition of the *Encyclopaedia Britannica*, where he wrote the essay on "Israel."[11] Here, Wellhausen defined diaspora as a synonym for the Jewish Dispersion, which he limited to the period between the Babylonian captivity of 587 BCE and the end of the Roman Empire.[12] This definition gained momentum in academic discourses in the twentieth century among scholars researching the ideological importance of "diaspora" to Jewish history.[13] Other renderings designated the period after the destruction of the Second Temple in 70 CE onward as the period of diaspora. Still other definitions extended the period

[10] Erich Gruen presents an example of this understanding. Although he recognizes that in antiquity diaspora and exile were not equivalent, he still considers them closely related, even synonymous in biblical and Hellenistic Jewish writings, which he claims frequently exhibit a "characterization of diaspora as exile." Gruen, *Diaspora*, 235, 342n21.

[11] Howard Wettstein, "Coming to Terms with Exile," in *Diasporas and Exiles: Varieties of Jewish Identity*, ed. Howard Wettstein and Catherine Soussloff (Berkeley: University of California Press, 2002), 39n20. Julius Wellhausen's original 1881 Encyclopaedia Britannica article, "Israel," was reprinted in his 1885 monograph: Julius Wellhausen, *Prolegomena to the History of Israel: With a Reprint of the Article "Israel" from the "Encyclopedia Britannica,"* trans. J. Sutherland Black and Allan Menzies (Cambridge: Cambridge University Press, 2013 [1885]), 500, 514, 516, 542, 543.

[12] Specifically, Wellhausen says, "Something still remains to be said with reference to the diaspora. We have seen how it began; in spite of Josephus (*Ant.* 11.5, 2), it is to be carried back not to the Assyrian but merely to the Babylonian captivity; it was not composed of Israelites, but solely of citizens of the southern kingdom. It received its greatest impulse from Alexander, and then afterwards from Caesar." Wellhausen, *Prolegomena to the History of Israel*, 542.

[13] Daniel Smith-Christopher, *A Biblical Theology of Exile* (Minneapolis: Fortress, 2002), 9–10; Daniel Boyarin and Jonathan Boyarin, "Diaspora: Generation and the Ground Jewish Identity," *Critical Inquiry* 19 (1993): 723.

of the Jewish diaspora from the close of the Roman Empire in the fifth century to the constitution of the independent nation-state of Israel in 1948.[14] Moreover, social and cultural intellectual circles broadened the meaning of diaspora to encompass the migration and dispersal patterns of contemporary migrating populations (e.g., Africans, Armenians, Hispanics, Turks), not just Jews.[15] By the close of the twentieth century, notions of diaspora, immigration, exile, deportation, and so forth were often used uncritically as interchangeable terms and concepts.

Because of the conceptual merging of emigration, exile, and diaspora, modern studies in both diaspora theory and biblical interpretation have demonstrated a degree of semantic slippage. From the perspective of the biblical text, there is no counterpart in the HB to the technical word "diaspora" in the LXX.[16] There are a number of other Greek cognates for the Hebrew words that connote exile and captivity (*golah*, *gala*, and *galut*), such as *paroikia* (permanent resident foreigner), *apoikia* (forced resettlement far from home, a colony),[17] *metoikesia* (removal or captivity of the Jews),[18] *aichmalōsia* (captivity),[19] and *apokalypsis* (an uncovering).[20] These are used as markers of the community's identity abroad or as descriptions of the situation at the site of mass dislocation and imprisonment. The term "diaspora," however, is not used to translate those Hebrew words denoting exile and captivity. It also does not describe the tangible political and militaristic circumstances that gave rise to it like foreign conquests and mass

[14] Yael Zerubavel, *Recovered Roots: Collective Memory and the Making Israeli National Tradition* (Chicago: University of Chicago Press, 1995); Giusto Traina, *428 AD: An Ordinary Year at the End of the Roman Empire* (Princeton, N.J.: Princeton University Press, 2009), 9; Donald Kagan, *The End of the Roman Empire: Decline or Transformation* (3rd ed.; Lexington, Mass.: D. C. Heath, 1992), 139–42.

[15] See Safran, "Diasporas in Modern Societies"; Michael Gomez, *Reversing Sail: A History of the African Diaspora* (Cambridge: Cambridge University Press, 2005).

[16] "διασπορά," *TDNT* 1:156.

[17] LDS, 98.

[18] LDS, 506.

[19] LDS, 24.

[20] LDS, 99; Dufoix, *Diasporas*, 4; Erich Gruen, "Diaspora and Homeland," in Wettstein and Soussloff, *Diasporas and Exiles*, 58n1.

deportations. It is, rather, a conception born in the imagination of the Greek translators of the HB that conveys divine prerogatives and human interactions.

Furthermore, diaspora is not used to depict the Israelites as a wandering people who often voluntarily emigrate, as in the case of Abraham (LXX Gen 9:18; 12:4, 10).[21] When biblical Hellenistic Jewish writings depict wandering, other Greek terms are used to describe it, including *planaō* (LXX Gen 37:15; Exod 14:3), *paroikeō* (LXX Deut 26:5), *dierchomai* (LXX Ps 104:13), *diaskorpizō* (LXX Zech 11:16), and *xeniteia* (LXX Wis 18:3). When the noun form of "diaspora" is deployed, in contrast, the notion of rootlessness and wandering is absent. The LXX depicts the diaspora condition as created, controlled, and remedied by God, which has implications for the social situation and movements of God's people. The movements of diaspora people, therefore, are never without purpose, direction, or aim. When the ancient Jewish writers portray Israel as a "wandering people," "diaspora" is not the term used.

As the Hellenistic Jewish interpreters reconceived Hebrew ideas and history in light of Greek culture, they distanced exilic and wandering experiences from diaspora experience and crafted their message about diaspora as a new situation and attitude communicable in Greek, not Hebrew. Thus "diaspora" appears to be not simply a word originating in the Greek language but, more importantly, a worldview that emerges as an innovation of Greek culture and history working on Judaism, which is imported into the Greek Jewish Scriptures and integrated with ideas already present and dominant in the HB. Yet, diaspora is not merely absorbed as one of many notions about displacement and disenfranchisement operative in Jewish Scriptures. It emerges in the LXX as its own distinct condition, worldview, and theological rationale meriting careful study and elucidation.

[21] This is the point on which Troy Martin and I disagree. Martin argues that the image and language of diaspora, within both 1 Peter and the LXX, denote a "wandering people" and represent "a journey to be undertaken," which is also "a dangerous place where assimilation to paganism and defection from the true faith takes place." However, the word for diaspora is never used to connote the rootless wandering of God's people as set out in the HB. Martin, *Metaphor and Composition*, 150, 159–60.

As such, a need exists for descriptive analysis of the different forms of diaspora construction and thinking evident in a select group of texts. This book fills that void in a unique way, producing not the typical tradition-history narrative of diaspora conception and construction some have come to expect from formal biblical studies but an appreciative reading of diaspora thinking present in the New Testament and other Second Temple Jewish writings. There is much insight to be gained from a literary comparative analysis of diaspora as an ideological and social construction, not dependent on a chronological mapping of source and reception history. Much is made clear about the diversity and features of diaspora constructions circulating in its early life—especially when that conversation is broached from the vantage point of 1 Peter. By analyzing 1 Peter alongside other Hellenistic Jewish writings that have similar concerns about the survival of a disadvantaged community, one gets a sense of the different options available to people who are forced to negotiate survival as a dislocated and scattered body. Still, 1 Peter's idea of diaspora does not merely imitate the diaspora ideas of others but establishes a distinctive, even subversive, understanding to minimize the degree of harm Christians experienced due to their atypical social routines and novel spiritual confession.

Nontheological academic discussions about diaspora have focused on the cultural and historical movements of specific populations.[22] A population movement is designated a diaspora (or not) based on the degree to which elements of the quintessential Jewish diaspora appear operative in the sociohistorical circumstances and geographic movements of the specific transitory population under investigation. Using the Jewish diaspora as a starting point, such studies have focused on issues related to kinship, citizenship, disenfranchisement, immigration, xenophobia, and even apartheid-type regimes. This scholarship has increased awareness of the different cultural and historical forms of diasporic populations and variously conceived of the basic characteristics of diaspora. One schema put forward nine elements as the

[22] Safran, "Diasporas in Modern Societies," 83–99; Khachig Tölölyan, "Rethinking Diaspora(s): Stateless Power in Transnational Moment," *Diaspora* 5 (1996): 3–36.

"common features of a diaspora."[23] Collectively, these nine features, outlined to put forward the precise issues, focuses, and features at stake in sociological academic study of diaspora, constitute a diaspora experience:

1. Dispersal from an original homeland, often traumatically, to two or more foreign regions;
2. Alternatively, the expansion from a homeland in search of work, in pursuit of trade or to further colonial ambitions;
3. A collective memory and myth about the homeland, including its location, history and achievements;
4. An idealization of the putative ancestral home and a collective commitment to its maintenance, restoration, safety and prosperity, even to its creation;
5. The development of a return movement which gains collective approbation;
6. A strong ethnic group consciousness sustained over a long time and based on a sense of distinctiveness, a common history and the belief in a common fate;
7. A troubled relationship with host societies suggesting a lack of acceptance at the least or the possibility that another calamity might befall the group;
8. A sense of empathy and solidarity with co-ethnic members in other countries of settlement; and
9. The possibility of a distinctive yet creative and enriching life in host countries with a tolerance for pluralism.[24]

This list introduces language and concerns that are vital to contemporary constructions and examinations of prospective diaspora contexts. Ideas and terminology that dominate the discourse include homeland departure, collective memory and myth, allegiance and attachment, return and restoration, collective ethnic group identity, local and global kinships, host environments, trauma and alienation, resettlement and tolerance, acculturation and difference, and common history and shared fate. While these features are insightful and necessary categories from which to study and theorize diaspora, this schema is too rigid to be particularly helpful in describing the

[23] Cohen, "Diasporas and the Nation-State," 515.
[24] Cohen, "Diasporas and the Nation-State," 515.

diaspora constructions outlined by Second Temple Jewish and early Christian writers.

Instead of being wedded to a fixed set of defining features, this examination of early literary constructions of diaspora leverages an analytical framework focused on "specific processes" that occur. By starting with questions rather than a taxonomy of features, this reading of ancient diaspora literature creates room for a variety of diaspora perspectives and modes to manifest from the texts.[25] There are seven questions guiding this literary investigation of diaspora thought and construction in Hellenistic and early Christian writings:

1. What reasons for and conditions of dispersal does the text exhibit?
2. Is the homeland real or mythical (possibly even theological), and what sort of relationship to it does the text advance?
3. What sort of relationship to the host land does the text prescribe?
4. What are the intracommunity dynamics and practices that it assumes and advocates?
5. Does the text evince a sense of multiple centers of belonging for the diaspora community being discussed and what is the nature of those connections?
6. Where is there evidence of a double consciousness in which aspects of acculturation and difference, or conformity and resistance are both at work?[26]

[25] Kim D. Butler, "Defining Diaspora, Refining a Discourse," *Diaspora* 10, no. 2 (2001): 193–94.

[26] The concept of "double consciousness" is borrowed from W. E. B. Du Bois. However, I am not using it here to refer to the racial and cultural differences of African Americans from dominant white American culture. Rather, I find it useful as a theory related to the experience of minorities and outsiders who juggle and embody multiple ways of being. The opportunity to use Du Bois' twentieth-century concept of double consciousness to describe a first-century historical location demonstrates the connection between ancient and contemporary contexts of diaspora experience and thinking. The correlation between ancient and modern contexts hints at the importance of returning to and rereading ancient texts as diasporic accounts, especially given our current world in which an outcome of globalization is that more populations are resettling into new forms of diasporic living. Du Bois, *Souls of Black Folk*, 8; Zeleza, "Diaspora Dialogues," 31–34.

7. What roles do God, Jesus, the Holy Spirit, Satan, and the entire cosmic organism play in the diaspora context being described?

While the questions leverage the language and concerns of standard lists of common features of diaspora, they offer a different way forward in examining how ancient texts construct diaspora situations and envision daily life. Rather than exegeting diaspora discourses for historical background and value or the presence or absence of certain commonalities, the focus is on the complex social and ideological projects these texts reflect in their final form. The questions leave room for these issues to be considered in a variety of ways and do not require conformity to a set pattern. This book builds on diaspora studies, demonstrating that diaspora is not just a historical phenomenon but also a literary trope that signifies cultural ideals, conjures specific social relationships and positionalities, and represents constructive dialogues on difference, deviance, and assimilation. It does not reconstruct plausible historical diaspora settings and conditions per se but examines the early life of "re-presenting" diaspora in literature.[27]

This book, moreover, is the product of a larger, growing trend in biblical studies that examines the ways in which difference, conformity, cultic commitment, and cultural lifestyles intersect.[28] To see how these four topics cohere in the form of the pliable metaphor of "diaspora" requires an interdisciplinary approach to the Bible and an eclectic blend of methodological perspectives. Thus, the book combines the insights of historical criticism, literary criticism, diaspora studies, and theological and ideological analyses to illuminate the varied

[27] It is important to reinforce that this project is not a historical reconstruction of diaspora events in biblical antiquity per se. Many scholars have undertaken such a historiographical task and succeeded to varying degrees. For such studies, see Victor Tcherikover, *Hellenistic Civilization and the Jews* (New York: Atheneum, 1970); Smith-Christopher, *Biblical Theology of Exile*; John M. G. Barclay, *Jews in the Mediterranean Diaspora: From Alexander to Trajan (323 BCE–117 CE)* (Edinburgh: T&T Clark, 1996); Gruen, *Diaspora*.

[28] Benjamin Harrison Dunning, *Aliens and Sojourners: Self as Other in Early Christianity* (Philadelphia: University of Pennsylvania Press, 2009); Richard Horsley, ed., *Hidden Transcripts and the Arts of Resistance: Applying the Work of James C. Scott to Jesus and Paul* (Semeia Studies 48; Atlanta: SBL, 2004).

constructions of diaspora life evident in a selection of biblical writings. The ideas and constructions of diaspora that are readily available to the informed modern reader of biblical and intertestamental writings occupy the study. The impression of diaspora ideas and lifestyles left after reading the writings is of interest. What is at stake here is how the writings imagine and shape diaspora into a livable situation is what is at stake here, not whether those ideas were historically viable, accurate, or manifested.

Drawing connections between conformity and nonconformity, assimilation and resistance, resident and alien, local and global, the writers of the texts examined here were constructive cultural anthropologists, social scientists, and theologians working with the conventional structures of society of their day and the imperatives of their cultic and cultural identities. They developed tailored bodies of knowledge about social order, disorder, and change that they were convinced would enable their target audiences to navigate the difficult terrain of social deviance and presence in environments that could and did view those communities with great suspicion and skepticism. These authors were innovative in their use of a metaphor that had the ability to evoke a range of contradictory but complementary responses in their audiences, and they were masterful in crafting imagery that was adaptable enough to generate new interpretations as new situations arose and time passed in the communities.

Part I

Diaspora through the Lens of 1 Peter

The first three chapters are focused strictly on the New Testament First Letter of Peter and its construction of a diaspora-Christian identity and praxis. The letter leverages diaspora to cast a unique understanding of existing as a distinct people of God living throughout the world. The contemporary reader faces the challenge of understanding the letter afresh in light of its peculiar image of diaspora, rather than simply its canonical placement or its historical misinterpretation in service to social institutions such as American slavery and patriarchy. What is diaspora in the thought-world of 1 Peter? How does it shape and inform the worldviews and practices of the people who subscribe to its proposal? Moreover, what benefit is the image of diaspora to the larger sociopolitical and theological vision the letter conveys? Diaspora creates a world of duality, even plurality, rather than singularity, and 1 Peter leverages that to empower readers with a new vision of the world and their agency within it as the people of God, or, in the vernacular of their environs, as "Christians" (1 Pet 4:16). The image of dispersion as the chosen state of God's people infiltrates all aspects of the letter.

1

Chosen Kinship
Imagining Christian Diaspora

One benefit of narrative is its capacity to shape stories, be they fictional or actual, into new ways of knowing—into new stories. Sometimes those stories are for mere entertainment, providing readers an escape from their reality and introducing them to new worlds, new characters, unexpected events, and alternate story lines that appear odd, deviant, bewildering, and even enticing. Other times stories are educational, imparting information and knowledge previously out of the grasp of its audience as well as animating or corroding its audience's moral center and good judgment. In addition to stimulating a reader's imagination and offering something "other" than the world one knows and recognizes, stories can also make propositions. Narratives can bestow new frames upon readers for reconsidering old facts. Narratives can construct new trajectories and bring shape and definition to cloudy dreams and unmapped plans.

While 1 Peter is not a narrative in a formal sense, it leaves a similar indelible mark on its readers, even in its epistolary form.[1] First

[1] The notion of the narrative quality of New Testament letters has been addressed, quite generatively, by scholars such as Katherine Grieb in *The Story of Romans: A Narrative Defense of God's Righteousness* (Louisville, Ky.: Westminster John Knox, 2002); Bruce W. Longenecker et al., in *Narrative Dynamics in Paul: A Critical Assessment* (Louisville, Ky.: Westminster John Knox, 2002); M. Eugene Boring, "Narrative Dynamics in First Peter: The Function of Narrative World," in *Reading First Peter with New Eyes: Methodological Reassessments of the Letter of First*

Peter is an ancient letter written by someone called "Peter, the apostle of Jesus Christ," to variously located and mixed Jewish Gentile audiences (although predominantly Gentiles) located elsewhere and at a distance from the author.[2] Specifically, 1 Peter is a paraenetic letter, written to encourage a troubled, vulnerable, and scattered readership.[3] Its aim is to embolden the group's commitment to their confession and community and equip them with practical advice on how to endure and prepare for the inevitable attacks to come.

Like narratives, 1 Peter casts a new vision of readers' immediate circumstances and imminent future. An important dimension of its paraenetic shape is the constructive work of its rhetoric. It is not just stating facts and addressing concerns with abstract "feel-good" language. Rather, the letter proposes an entirely new way of thinking about events and situations that is self-evident and real to its intended audience. The letter imagines a different course of action in familiar and precarious times. It is an invitation to "switch stories" and enter

---

Peter, eds. Robert L. Webb and Betsy Bauman-Martin (LNTS 364; London: T&T Clark, 2007), 8–40.

[2] Church tradition assigns the historical Peter, one of Jesus' twelve apostles, as the author of the letter, but historical and literary data does not support such claims. It is more likely the letter was written after Peter's martyrdom in Rome under Nero (64 CE) by a follower (or followers) of Peter writing under the cover of his name, which was a common literary practice in the ancient world that did not necessarily discredit the authority and authenticity of the writing. Thus, 1 Peter was likely pseudonymously written around the time of sporadic local persecutions in Asia Minor under Domitian (81–96 CE), and before the Asia Minor persecutions attested in the Pliny–Trajan correspondences in the early second century (ca. 111–112 CE). As such, the name Peter will not be referenced, although the letter represents the "theological heritage and social vision of the great apostle-martyr." It is to the specifics and content of that vision and heritage the book is most preoccupied. John H. Elliott, *Conflict, Community, and Honor: 1 Peter in Social-Scientific Perspective* (Eugene, Ore.: Cascade, 2007), 25–26.

[3] S. Snyder, "Participles and Imperatives in 1 Peter: A Re-examination in the Light of Recent Scholarly Trends," *Filologia Neotestamentaria* 8 (1995): 187–98; Travis B. Williams, "Reconsidering the Imperatival Principle in 1 Peter," *Westminster Theological Journal* 73 (2011): 59–78; David Hill, "'To Offer Spiritual Sacrifices' (1 Peter 2:5): Liturgical Formulations and Christian Paraenesis in 1 Peter," *JSNT* 16 (1982): 45–63; Lauri Thuren, *Argument, and Theology in 1 Peter: The Origins of Christian Paraenesis* (Sheffield: Sheffield Academic, 1995); Steven J. Kraftchick, "1 Peter," in *Theological Bible Commentary*, ed. David L. Petersen and Gail R. O'Day (Louisville, Ky.: Westminster John Knox, 2009), 457.

into a new life orientation and a new way of being "God's own people" (1 Pet 2:9).[4] It is a sort of "love offering" to its intended readers (and beyond) who dare to consider that their life story transcends their immediate situation. For those with hopes that there is something more to the Christian confession and story than just membership in a local body that convenes regularly in spite of the threat of extirpation, 1 Peter gifts them with a new image, diaspora.

It is that imaginative work or storytelling around the notion of diaspora that requires focused investigation and deep appreciation. In addition to asserting theological propositions, what the letter imagines as possible in the world and what it envisions as the core identity and makeup of the people of God is essential to appreciating 1 Peter fully and its place among other diaspora-focused writings from the Hellenistic Jewish world. The image of diaspora expresses a core belief that no body constitutes merely a group of isolated strangers striving to make it on their own in a world known for responding with great cruelty, disregard, and violence for the unrecognizable "other." Diaspora in 1 Peter reminds readers they are members of a diverse and vast kinship requiring only acknowledgment and embrace. First Peter constructs a new reality in which readers "can see how to fit their own stories" into a larger narrative that surpasses them.[5] There is value to be gained from reading 1 Peter as a kind of diaspora consciousness and narrative that imagines something so new it requires innovation in semantic definition and social construction.

[4] Walter Brueggemann uses this language when he says, "I assume that the biblical text is not a handbook for morality or doctrine as it is often regarded, nor on the other hand, is it an historical record, as many are wont to take it. Rather the biblical text is the articulation of imaginative models of reality in which 'text-users,' i.e., readers in church and synagogue, are invited to participate." Brueggemann, *Biblical Perspectives on Evangelism: Living in a Three-Storied Universe* (Nashville: Abingdon, 1993), 8; quoted in Grieb, *Story of Romans*, xxi.

[5] Grieb, *Story of Romans*, xxii.

Imagining Diaspora as 1 Peter Imagines

The first image of diaspora 1 Peter communicates is kinship.[6] The term "diaspora" is situated strategically in 1 Peter's opening greeting (1 Pet 1:1). Here, the letter assigns the recipients the distinct identity of "the elect-foreigners of the Diaspora."[7] The letter's salutation illustrates its complex vision of the world and the Christian kinship that extends across it. The word "diaspora" appears in the form of a genitive of apposition and gives further definition to the preceding head noun, which is the conjoined substantive "elect-foreigner" (*eklektois parepidēmois*).[8] As the head phrase, elect-foreigner depicts a large category that is ambiguous and unspecific. Exactly which group of elect-foreigners is the letter addressing, and where are they located?

Diaspora clarifies the identity and location of the addressees, yet alone this grammatical construct is too broad to be particularly helpful.[9] Both the Greek Dispersion and Jewish Dispersion are too

[6] Luke Timothy Johnson, "Imagining the World Scripture Imagines," *Modern Theology* 14 (1998): 165–80.

[7] Reinhard Feldmeier argues the first verses in the letter serve a unique purpose, which is to establish foreignness as a mark of Christian identity. His conclusion is based on the assertion that the term for foreigner (*parepidēmos*) and the term for dispersion (*diaspora*) signify the same thing—namely, the addressees' status as "minorities and outsiders" in the broader society. He says specifically, "More unusual than this expansive address (which also appears elsewhere in early Christian literature) is its addressing the addressees as 'foreigners of the dispersion [diaspora].' The double reference to the status of the recipients as minorities and outsiders, which is strengthened by the designation 'foreigners,' points to the special agenda of this writing to interpret this foreignness as a mark of the essence of being Christian." Feldmeier, *The First Letter of Peter: A Commentary on the Greek Text*, trans. Peter H. Davids (Waco, Tex.: Baylor University Press, 2008), 1. While I agree that difference and foreignness are central themes in 1 Peter, I think the significance and innovation around diaspora merits more singular attention.

[8] The scribal addition found in the middle fourth century Codex Sinaiticus as well as the entire Syriac textual tradition (א, sy) is instructive for understanding the relationship between the two terms, elect and foreigner. Both textual traditions add the coordinating conjunction *kai* after *eklektois* and before *parepidēmois*, indicating an equivalent correspondence. My hyphenated phrase, "elect-foreigner," attempts to maintain that correlation as an essential characteristic of 1 Peter's novel construction of diaspora Christianity.

[9] Paul Achtemeier, *1 Peter* (Hermeneia; Philadelphia: Fortress, 1996), 81; Karen H. Jobes, *1 Peter* (BECNT; Grand Rapids: Baker, 2005), 75; Mark Dubis, *1 Peter: A*

vast and ubiquitous in geography and chronology for the mere use of the Greek word to effectively delimit them. The letter provides additional details in the form of a catalog of provinces. This resolves the ambiguity of elect-foreigner in the opening and anchors the image of diaspora in geographic places and among particular sets of peoples, though scattered and disparate. Organized from broad to narrow, elect-foreigner, diaspora, and the catalog collectively project the literary imagination of the letter writer. Those regions and the people whom 1 Peter addresses are just segments of a larger population dispersed across the Roman world. The letter uses the proper noun form of diaspora, therefore, to heighten its readers' awareness of their larger kinship and collective consciousness.

It is important to note that from the perspective of the epistle, decisive and volitional consent induce the diaspora condition, not divine compulsion and peremptory command. In other words, diaspora is not the creation and action of God against the people. Rather, diaspora life is the product of people's faithful response to God's action through Christ as they embrace their newfound identity and kinship, now called "Christian" (1 Pet 4:16). The paraenetic quality of the letter constantly encourages readers to a common future action, which implies choice. First Peter encourages readers, as diaspora Christians, to make three different social choices. It exhorts them to choose how they will relate to the outside world, to each other within the community, and to God and God's created order.

Choosing to Relate Globally

While 1 Peter opens with a focus on the territory of Asia Minor, it portrays the scale and reach of Christian relationships surpassing those boundaries. The letter envisions other diaspora communities alongside its intended recipients and crafts a vision of a Christian relational matrix readers have yet to fully realize or leverage. From the letter's vantage point, the addressees constitute independent local communities who have a responsibility and connection to other independent Christian communities located elsewhere. In fact, the letter

---

Handbook on the Greek Text (BHGNT; Waco, Tex.: Baylor University Press, 2010), 2.

itself demonstrates this connection and responsibility as it implies that the author wrote it from Rome for circulation among multiple Christian communities in Asia Minor.[10] The final greeting in 5:13, in which "the sister church in Babylon . . . sends you greetings," signals a kinship and bond. It is an acknowledgment that there are others in the world similar to the letter's addressees (1 Pet 5:9) to whom they are accountable and attached.

Moreover, each time the designation "us" appears in the body of the letter, whether in 1 Peter 1:3, "By his great mercy God has given *us* a new birth into a living hope," or in 4:17, "for the time has come for judgment to begin with the household of God; if it begins with *us*," readers are reminded they are part of a larger interregional body. The "us" of Christianity includes all those who belong to the household of God locally and abroad. Consistently throughout 1 Peter, diaspora functions as a literary and conceptual mechanism for crafting a new dyadic identity. It nurtures a collective awareness around being "Christian" in which a fundamental characteristic is choosing to be part of a larger body that is not limited to the recipients' local environs.

For the letter, the voluntary aspect of diaspora becomes a factor when people choose to operate as "Christian." Christians are a unified but diverse body of members who are obedient to Jesus Christ (1 Pet 1:14) and hope in God (1 Pet 1:21). They can choose to be obedient to the revelation of God that is revealed through Christ's resurrection (1 Pet 1:3; 3:21) or not (1 Pet 1:14). The repetitive use of the conditional conjunction "if" (*ei*) signals the volitional nature of their diasporic situation. For instance, 1 Peter 1:17 says, "If you invoke as Father the one who judges. . . ." Likewise, 1:20 says, "But if you endure being beaten for doing good and suffer for it. . . ." The conditional component in these verses arises from the possibility that the readers can choose to not call on God as Father or not endure being unduly punished and attacked. Indeed, historical sources postdating 1 Peter indicate the author's intuition was correct. Some Christians would eventually choose to abandon the faith and community altogether.

[10] Catherine Gunsalus Gonzalez, *1 & 2 Peter, and Jude* (Belief: A Theological Commentary on the Bible; Louisville, Ky.: Westminster John Knox, 2010), 152; M. Eugene Boring, *1 Peter* (ANTC; Nashville: Abingdon Press, 1999), 38.

The Pliny–Trajan correspondence of 112 CE, in which Pliny inquires about Emperor Trajan's preferences regarding how to handle the Christian problem in his territory, confirms what the letter writer feared could happen more than twenty-five years earlier. Pliny's letter states that he ferreted out some former Christians, who have demonstrated their "repentance" in the form of public obeisance to the emperor's image and prayers to Greco-Roman gods. Instead of being private devotees of a monotheistic faith, they have allegedly willingly participated in public acts of emperor worship and polytheism. Former Christians' public display of polytheistic practices is significant because, as Pliny states, committed Christians refused to perform such observances. Pliny states, "For, whatever the nature of their admission, I am convinced that their stubbornness and unshakable obstinacy ought not to go unpunished" (*Ep.* 10.96).[11] The account of Pliny's formal interrogation, where the threat of physical punishment and execution was real, highlights the degree to which "choice" is a factor in Christian identity and allegiance. Christianity, particularly diaspora Christianity, is a volitional social location and group identity that can thrust invisible people and classes into the spotlight of Roman governance and local suspicion.

A brief canonical survey of other instances of diaspora in the NT reveals that by the end of the first century, when 1 Peter along with the bulk of the NT writings had been written, conceptions of diaspora had evolved from a prohibitive and forced condition to notions of voluntary group departure and permanent settlement elsewhere. Across the NT literature, the word "diaspora" represents liberating and deliberate mass emigration and the formation of new social bonds, both inside and outside the immediate Jewish and Christian communities. For instance, in Acts 8:1, Jewish Christians in Jerusalem are said to disperse (*diaspeirō*) to Judea and Samaria out of fear of impending persecution at the hands of a fanatical Jewish Pharisee, Saul.[12] Acts

[11] Radice, LCL.

[12] The term "diaspora" appears only three times across the entire NT (John 7:35; Jas 1:1; 1 Pet 1:1). In all three cases, the Jewish diaspora outside of Palestine and its activity among Greco-Roman peoples is the focus. Likewise, the verb form of diaspora (*diaspeirō*) appears three times, in Acts 8:1, 8:4, and 11:19. All three occurrences highlight the scattering of Jewish Christians at pivotal points in the story of Acts.

8:4 details what the dispersed Jewish Christian populations did upon their arrival to their new locations—they evangelized people while simultaneously resettling among them. Again, in Acts 11:19 the Jewish Christians respond to the possibility of persecution, as exhibited in the execution of the Hellenist Stephen, by scattering (*diaspeirō*) to even farther-flung areas and resettling among established Greek Jewish communities in Phoenicia, Cyprus, and Antioch.[13] Although these passages define diaspora as a departure from a geographic place, rather than a departure from a normative Greco-Roman lifestyle, they nonetheless lead to an act of group preservation, which rarely results in total withdrawal and isolation from the larger surrounding environment.

In contrast, earlier Hellenistic Jewish writers characterized the origin of diaspora as God's punishment of the Jews for their disobedience. Punishment took on the form of involuntary displacement, disenfranchisement, and marginal "othering" (LXX Jer 15:7; Jdt 5:19; Deut 28:15-25).[14] In biblical Jewish writings, diaspora signals a strained relationship between God and the people in the form of forced population movement and resettlement outside Israel's proclaimed homeland. For instance, Nehemiah summarizes God's own words from LXX Deuteronomy 30:1-5 when he says, "Remember now the word that you commanded your servant Moses, saying, 'You, if you are faithless, I will scatter you among the peoples, and if you return to me and keep my commandments and do them, if your dispersion is to the farthest skies, from there I will gather them and lead them to the place where I have chosen my name to encamp there.'" (Neh 1:8-9 NETS). Likewise, in LXX Jeremiah 41:17, God says, "You have not obeyed me by calling for a release, each pertaining to his fellow. Behold, I am calling for a release for you to the dagger and to death and to the famine, and I will give you as a dispersion to all the kingdoms of the earth." These passages represent the scriptural position that God is responsible for the Israelites' dislocation from their "home," while

[13] Narry F. Santos, "Diaspora in the New Testament and Its Impact on Christian Mission," *Torch Trinity Journal* 13, no. 1 (2010): 6.

[14] Erich Gruen, *Diaspora: Jews amidst Greeks and Romans* (Cambridge, Mass.: Harvard University Press, 2002), 5–7.

foreign rulers are merely instruments God uses to accomplish the task (LXX Jer 41:18; 28:25).[15]

The NT writers, however, characterize the act of dispersal as a voluntary population movement from a central location to another with the aim of avoiding social, political, and physical persecution. Likewise, 1 Peter projects dispersal as a period of volitional and mixed interaction and relationships. It is never characterized in the epistle as forced withdrawal, separation, and dislocation. Instead of being passively moved from a specific geographic point of origin, the letter depicts readers as actively moving toward being established as their own social community in their own land (1 Pet 1:13-15; 3:8-12). They are actually seeking and embracing a new peoplehood and family that transgress conventional territorial borders.

Language about sharing a collective experience of suffering (1 Pet 2:21; 3:14, 17-18), embracing the title "Christian" (1 Pet 4:13-14, 16) as a collective name, and cultivating a normative ethos of mutuality and selflessness within the community (1 Pet 1:22; 2:1; 4:8-10) supports the author's vision.[16] Diaspora Christians are a newly constituted people (1 Pet 2:9-10; 4:16; 5:2) living as foreigners and strangers (1 Pet 1:17; 2:11; 4:1-4) in their ancestral homeland or place of residence. Its configuration suggests that the diaspora experience does not always require a community's physical movement and resettlement. Diaspora does not indicate God's people leaving a place to which they hope to return. That bidirectional movement is absent in 1 Peter. Instead of being passively moved from a specific geographic point of origin, the letter depicts the readers as actively moving toward establishment of their own social community in their own land (1 Pet 1:4; 3:22; 5:10) with a global and celestial reach and kinship.

[15] The English translation of the LXX that dominates going forward is the NETS.

[16] David Horrell, "The Label Χριστιανός: 1 Peter 4:16 and the Formation of Christian Identity," *JBL* 126 (2007): 361–81; Martin Hengel, "Early Christianity as a Jewish-Messianic, Universalistic Movement," in *Conflicts and Challenges in Early Christianity*, ed. Donald A. Hagner (Harrisburg, Pa.: Trinity International, 1999), 6; Paul A. Holloway, *Coping with Prejudice: 1 Peter in Social-Psychological Perspective* (WUNT 244; Tübingen: Mohr Siebeck, 2009), 226–28.

First Peter, therefore, re-creates the whole diaspora situation. It asserts that diaspora should be embraced, rather than remedied. In this epistle, the image of diaspora is not one of judgment, condemnation, and negative consequences. Diaspora is also not a potential avenue for avoiding persecution, suffering, and censure. Here, diaspora fosters a collective sense of belonging and obedience that persists. From the moment the epistle opens with the statement that the readership are "elect-foreigners of the Diaspora" to its closing when it declares that their "brothers and sisters are experiencing the same types of suffering" (1 Pet 5:9) along with those in so-called Babylon (1 Pet 5:13), the epistle maintains that Christians are a unified body in both faith and experience, albeit a collective that is diverse and distributed across the Roman world. The innovative contextual imaginings of 1 Peter cultivate a collective awareness and appreciation of a global confession (1 Pet 2:9).

Local Realities of a Christian Diaspora People

The shared kinship with communities elsewhere is only one dimension of the diaspora reality the letter casts. The letter presents two other dimensions in the form of local membership relations (1 Pet 4:7-11) and how they present themselves as a unified community to their outside local environs (1 Pet 3:15; 5:19). From the perspective of the letter, diaspora comes about because people choose to embrace their identity as scattered yet related kinship groups, who exist on the fringes of their provincial neighborhoods. Local members of Christian communities are situated within and interact with outsiders who do not share and are potentially intolerant of their core beliefs, values, and practices. By calling readers a diaspora people, the letter affirms their identity as "people of God" against accusations of illegitimacy (1 Pet 2:10; 4:14, 16) and prepares them for the loss of social place in their specific locales (1 Pet 1:17; 2:12; 4:4). In this way, the letter expresses a keen awareness of the perils accompanying a disenfranchised and marginal diaspora existence and does not shy away from concretely addressing concerns of danger, difference, and ostracism.

Starting with the term for election (*eklektos*) in 1 Peter 1:1, the letter establishes that a characteristic of diaspora-Christian identity is a divinely sanctioned social distinction. Language of election, which appears elsewhere in the letter (1 Pet 2:4, 6, 9; 5:13), echoes notions of election present within Jewish diaspora discourses. Throughout Jewish literature, election is a distinguishing characteristic and experience of an unconventional, and often marginal, group of people. While election connotes the experience of being God's chosen, it also signifies the experience of being identifiably distinct from *others*. A foundational text in the conception of election is LXX Deuteronomy 7:6-9:[17] "For you are a people holy to the Lord your God, and the Lord your God has chosen (*proaireō*) you to be for him an exceptional people . . . the Lord brought you out with a strong hand and with a high arm and redeemed you from a house of slavery, from the hand of Pharaoh king of Egypt." As this passage reveals, the notion of Israel's election often occurs alongside discourse about captivity, foreignness, and liberation.[18] Divine election does not automatically include social power or affluence. On the contrary, the passage reasons that to be designated an elect people generally means a period (long or short) of existing as a subculture among a larger dominant one. Although God's liberating activity is always reaffirmed as a certainty,[19] to be chosen as an exclusive insider group does not eliminate the possibility that God's people may still have to live on the fringes of another culture and society (LXX Deut 7:8; Isa 45:22-23).[20] The theme of election

[17] Joel Lohr, *Chosen and Unchosen: Conceptions of Election in the Pentateuch and Jewish-Christian Interpretation* (Siphrut 2; Winona Lake, Ind.: Eisenbrauns, 2009), 148; T. Mann, *Deuteronomy* (WBC; Louisville, Ky.: Westminster John Knox, 1995), 62–69; Émile Nicole, "בחר," *NIDOTTE* 1:640–41.

[18] While LXX Deut 7:6-9 represents discourse about election and captivity, notice the passage does not address the condition of diaspora. Indeed, the immediate literary context of Deut 7–8 depicts images of punitive wandering (8:2-6) and guided possession of another's land (7:17-24; 8:7-10). It does not offer any images of God dispersing the people to foreign lands.

[19] See LXX Exod 19:4-5. James Cone describes the correspondences between the elect people of God and their temporal oppressed condition this way: "Certainly this means, among other things, that God's call of this people is related to its oppressed condition and to God's own liberating activity already seen in the exodus." James Cone, *A Black Theology of Liberation* (20th anniv. ed.; Maryknoll, N.Y.: Orbis Books, 2001 [1970]), 2.

[20] As Joel Lohr's work has pointed out, there is another side to discourse on election in LXX Deut 7 and other texts, and that is the situation of the unchosen.

in 1 Peter appears to ratify what LXX Deuteronomy states—that even as foreigners, the community can still live as free people (1 Pet 2:16) because of their intimate connection to God.

Other examples of the correspondences between the themes of election, captivity, and freedom appear in prophetic writings such as Isaiah and Jeremiah.[21] The prophetic writings, in contrast to LXX Deuteronomy 7, frequently make the correspondence between election and diaspora more explicit and fixed. For instance, in LXX Isaiah 65:9 the prophecy that the chosen shall inherit and settle in God's holy land implies that at the time of the prophecy this inheritance had not yet occurred. God's elect people were temporarily living as strangers and outsiders among other peoples. Prior to this prophecy, Isaiah repeatedly declares that even though God manufactures minority conditions, scattering them to foreign lands, he also remedies that condition by liberating the people (LXX Isa 49:6, 24:1, 56:8).

The First Letter of Peter appears to fully adopt the traditional notion of election from the Jewish Scriptures. Nevertheless, while it recalls God's election of Israel, it connects election to the figure of Jesus Christ and reestablishes mass dispersion as a condition that accompanies election. According to 1 Peter, Jesus marks the beginning of a new people and a new mode of election. The Greek term for election, *eklektos*, appears five times in the letter, more often than in any other NT writing. Four instances occur in the first two chapters alone (1 Pet 1:1; 2:4, 6, 9). In 2:4-9, the usage echoes the theme of election taken from Isaiah and Psalms. Here, the author rewrites LXX Psalms 117:22 and LXX Isaiah 28:16 designating Israel's historic experience of sociopolitical rejection and physical dislocation axiomatic to Christian identity and life. Moreover, the image of the stone is understood as a metaphor for Jesus Christ.

Just as Jesus is chosen by God (*de theō eklekton*, 1 Pet 2:4) and rejected by humankind, so too the new Christian communities are

It is beyond the scope of this immediate project to explore that here, although I am fully aware that my current discussion is one-sided. For information on the relationship between chosen and unchosen, see Lohr, *Chosen and Unchosen*, 1–2, 92–114, 161–74.

[21] LXX Isa 41:8-9, 43:10-15, 44:1-2, 45:13; LXX Jer 26:27-28; 30:10-11.

chosen by God (*hymeis de genos eklekton*, 1 Pet 2:9) and anticipate rejection by others in the near future (i.e., 1 Pet 1:7; 2:12). Yet their chosenness and rejection occur not individually but within the context of a newly established family (*genos*, 1 Pet 2:9). The letter's reinterpretation of the process of divine election concludes with a series of declarations that fashion the Christian community as an unprecedented and binding collective. By pronouncing readers "a chosen kindred, a royal priesthood, a holy nation, and a people owned by God" (2:9, 10), the letter asserts believers share an ancestral background that is rooted in the realities of Jesus Christ's election and in the shared experience of existing as a scattered conglomerate of minorities. God is presented as the chief actor and decision maker in election, not diaspora. God manufactures divine election, but God's people manufacture and embrace diaspora while accepting their new relational proximity to those who were at one time "strangers" to them.

First Peter is not, however, a supersessionist document, in that Israel's concept of election has not now passed "without remainder to Christianity."[22] Rather, 1 Peter expands the originally exclusive self-designation. The new *genos*, or family of God, is based on a shared belief (1 Pet 2:7) rather than an ancestral bloodline. Jesus Christ, as the cornerstone, becomes the new organizing entity that holds the chosen and eclectic family (*genos*) together as its own insulated community. It does not refute the validity of Jewish election, nor does it offer any explanation of how Jews and Christians are to relate to each other. Rather, 1 Peter simply appropriates the notion of election as foundational for the Christian way of life.[23] The first four instances of election indicate that the Christian addressees are a people who,

[22] Achtemeier, *1 Peter*, 69.

[23] Peter has no explicit discourse on Jewish-Christian relations like that found in Rom 9–11. Peter's silence on Jewish-Christian relations and his appropriation, without recognition, of Israel's language and images has led to a debate among scholars. Some scholars have argued that the silence indicates that Peter sees Israel as the model forerunner to Christian identity and practice. See Ernest Best, *1 Peter* (NCBC; Grand Rapids: Eerdmans, 1982), 46. Others, like Achtemeier, argue it represents the Christian trend of co-opting Israel's language, images, and identity and refiguring them as wholly Christian in kind and origin. See Betsy Bauman-Martin, "Speaking Jewish: Postcolonial Aliens and Strangers in First Peter," in Webb and Bauman-Martin, *Reading First Peter with New Eyes*, 144–77.

as a group, exist on the fringes of their local environments (1 Pet 1:1; 2:4, 6, 9), while the last instance in 1 Peter 5:13 explicitly expands the kinship group beyond just its local borders. The term *syneklektos* is a Greek neologism meaning "elected together." This fifth occurrence of the word for election establishes that believers both locally and abroad constitute a single body who share in a common experience of not just election but also dispersion and foreignness. Although they are a mixed body of Messianic Jews and Gentiles who continue to live among other non-Christian Jews and Gentiles, their status as the elect of God supersedes their original cultural identity markers (1 Pet 4:2-5). Opening and closing the letter with the conception of election, therefore, signifies a definitive group identity, which involves social distance from the surrounding world. It does not necessarily mean conflict with or a departure from traditional Judaism, especially diaspora Judaism. The term "election" places in opposition the Christian community and the larger society, not Christianity and Judaism.

What election suggests in terms of social difference, 1 Peter makes explicit and complicates further with the second Greek term in the greeting (1 Pet 1:1), *parepidēmos*, meaning "wandering foreigner." This term appears three times in the NT and twice in the LXX.[24] Each time *parepidēmos* appears in the LXX it is accompanied by the Greek term meaning "permanent resident foreigner" (*paroikos*, LXX Gen 23:4; LXX Ps 38:13), which also appears in 1 Peter 1:17; 2:11.[25] Historically, the term *paroikos* indicated a permanent foreign resident in a particular locale who possessed limited legal protection but not the privileges and status of full citizenship. This is visible within the Jewish law (e.g., LXX Exod 12:45; Lev 22:10-11; 25:6, 35, 39-43; Num 35:15). *Parepidēmos* signaled visiting strangers who were viewed as total outsiders of the local privileges, protections, and way of life of the local environment. They were not "a class of people," but were simply viewed as temporary or sojourning residents in a particular environment.

[24] Outside of 1 Peter, *parepidēmos* ("wandering foreigner") appears only one other time in the NT, Heb 11:13 (cf. 1 Pet 1:1; 2:11).

[25] Achtemeier, *1 Peter*, 173. For studies, see Hans Shaefer, "Paroikoi," *PW* 18, no. 4 (1949): 1695–1701; William Barclay, *New Testament Words* (Philadelphia: Westminster, 1974), 284; Torrey Seland, *Strangers in the Light: Philonic Perspectives on Christian Identity in 1 Peter* (Biblical Interpretation Series 76; Leiden: Brill 2005), 39–78.

In the LXX, the *paroikos–parepidēmos* pairing exhibits a dual attachment or sense of belonging to both a current place of residence as well as a place of origin located elsewhere. In Genesis, the Jewish patriarch Abraham asks his Hittite neighbors for a burial site for the matriarch Sarah. Abraham identifies himself as "a permanent resident foreigner (*paroikos*) and wandering foreigner (*parepidēmos*) living among you." Abraham, thereby, expresses two identities—he is both one who resides among and one who remains different from the people with whom he lives. Likewise, in LXX Psalms 38:13, *paroikos* and *parepidēmos* appear in a prayer to God.[26] The psalmist calls himself both a permanent resident foreigner (*paroikos*) as well as a wandering foreigner (*parepidēmos*) in the land that belongs to God (cf. LXX Lev 25:23). The LXX passages reflect multiple local attachments and allegiances.[27] Consequently, foreignness in these LXX passages does not amount to voluntary withdrawal or even martyrdom. Foreignness

[26] There appears to be some inconsistency between the Greek translation and the HB regarding the relationship between the Greek terms *paroikos* and *parepidēmos* and the Hebrew terms *toshav* and *gēr* in LXX Gen 23:4 and LXX Ps 38:13. Outside of these passages, the Greek term *paroikos* is used interchangeably for *toshav* (LXX and HB Exod 12:45; Lev 22:10; 25:6, 23, 35, 40, 45, 47) or *gēr* (LXX and HB Gen 15:3; 23:4; Exod 2:22; 18:3; Deut 14:21; 23:7; 2 Sam 1:13; Jer 14:8), which roughly denotes a foreign servant who lives permanently among foreigners. Since both HB terms can be translated by the Greek *paroikos*, the difficulty is identifying which term *parepidēmos* is actually translating and what it means when the two Greek terms appear together in LXX Gen 23:4 and LXX Ps 38:13. Indeed the juxtaposition of permanent residence and transient residence is a common topos in the HB (Num 35:15; 1 Chr 29:15). The Greek term *parepidēmos*—meaning wandering or temporary foreigner—translates *toshav* in Gen 23:4 and Ps 38:13 while *paroikos* translates *gēr*, and these verses reflect the common literary strategy of juxtaposing permanent foreigners to wandering foreigners.

[27] John M. G. Barclay, *Negotiating Diaspora: Jewish Strategies in the Roman Empire* (LSTS 45; New York: T&T Clark, 2004), 2. Barclay says that a primary characteristic of diaspora life exhibited in Jewish literature and modern diaspora contexts is "multi-local attachments of diaspora." He says, "Diaspora communities are, by definition 'not-here to stay.' They retain a sense of belonging elsewhere (in memory, myth, or longing to return), but also typically develop strong attachments to their present place of belonging. In this sense 'diaspora' is a much more complex—and perhaps more interesting—phenomenon than 'migration,' since a diaspora community is neither a wandering body of people, nor simply a community of 'immigrants' absorbed into a new home."

is about fashioning a modus vivendi for living within while remaining different from a larger dominant culture and society.

Although the double phrase has a rich linguistic history in the LXX, in 1 Peter "resident foreigner and wandering foreigner" function as auxiliary metaphors to diaspora, providing descriptive pictures for how addressees live into their diaspora condition. The terms intimate that although Christians may now be considered culturally different and distinct, they are nonetheless neighbors to others outside the community. The double construction, *paroikos kai parepidēmos*, moreover, illustrates the diaspora way of life (1 Pet 2:12, *anastrophē*)—in terms of practices and behaviors believers are to assume "among the Gentiles." Consequently, an inescapable reality of diaspora-Christian life is the practice of moving between two domains, a Christian and non-Christian, together with balancing two distinct expectations about social etiquette and compliance.

From 1 Peter 2:11 forward, the author provides more specific directives regarding how readers are to live as both present among and distinct from a larger society that does not share their values (1 Pet 4:3-4, 16) and has proven to be hostile (1 Pet 2:12, 20; 3:14-15, 16; 4:14). It says, "Beloved, I encourage you as resident-wandering foreigners to abstain from fleshly lusts, which war against the soul." Like the double construction elect-foreigner (*eklektos kai parepidēmos*) in 1 Peter 1:1, the construction resident-wandering foreigner (*paroikos kai parepidēmos*) in 1 Peter 2:11 advances the idea that Christians' immediate lifestyle involves "a contradiction of double aims."[28] On the one hand, they exist as a distinct community that the larger public can observe as different from themselves; but on the other hand, they embrace normative lives, existing as contributing members of the social structures within which they find themselves. The phrase "resident-wandering foreigner" does not evoke an existing social situation as much as it *shapes* the readers' future social behavior and heightens their awareness of how they will be perceived.[29]

[28] W. E. B. Du Bois, *The Souls of Black Folk* (New York: Dover, 1994), 13; Zeleza, "Diaspora Dialogues," 31–33.

[29] There are several indicators in the immediate literary context of 2:11 that the focus is on the addressees' future action. The presence of the comparative conjunction

Analyzed separately, the notions of election and foreignness in 1 Peter make compelling claims about Christian difference and presence in the broader society. On their own, election and foreigner carry a sense of duality and hybridity.[30] Whether as elect ones or foreigners, the letter depicts the condition of Christian readers as one in which they live here—in their current provincial residence—and belong elsewhere—as people of the Christian diaspora.[31] Although the notion of election sits in primary position, it is not intended to eclipse the notion of foreignness any more than the double construction elect-foreigner eclipses the letter's conception of diaspora. If the letter designates election and foreignness as the essence of Christian identity, then diaspora is the modality that brought it about and the quality of life through which that particular Christian identity is practiced. In short, the opening adjectival phrase elect-foreigner sets competing versions of the same reality side by side.[32]

---

hos, coupled with the conventional paraenetic catchword *parakaleō* (lit. "to urge" or "exhort"), frames the discourse surrounding language of resident-wandering foreigner in terms of expectations, not present reality. In terms of *parakaleō*, the first-person present indicative appears within NT epistles as a means of making a personal appeal and moral exhortation for a future action. For instance, in 2 Cor 2:8 Paul appeals to the Corinthians to reconcile his offender with the community. The request ("So I urge you . . .") is for an immediate future action (2 Cor 10:1). Likewise, Paul appeals directly to Philemon to accept Onesimus back (Phlm 9–10). Here, again, it is a request for immediate future action.

[30] John Elliott, for example, says, "This initial designation of the addressees expresses at the letter's outset their paradoxical situation: they are *strangers* in society, yet *elected* by God." Elliott, *1 Peter: A New Translation with Introduction and Commentary* (AB 37B; New York: Doubleday, 2000), 312; emphasis original. Likewise, Feldmeier says, "Election and foreignness correlate: 'Election' designates separation by God, which finds its social form in integration into the people of God. On the other hand, societal exclusion as a 'foreign body' results from this. On this basis, then, in a type [of] reverse conclusion 1 Peter can assure the oppressed Christians of their belonging to the people of God and his race, house, priesthood, etc." Feldmeier, *First Letter of Peter*, 54–55.

[31] Here, I have paraphrased a popular characterization of a diaspora condition, originally quoted by James Clifford called "living here and belonging elsewhere." Clifford, "Diasporas," *Cultural Anthropology* 9, no. 3 (1994): 311; Zeleza, "Diaspora Dialogues," 32.

[32] Joel B. Green, "Living as Exiles: The Church in the Diaspora in 1 Peter," in *Holiness and Ecclesiology in the New Testament*, ed. Kent E. Brower and Andy Johnson (Grand Rapids: Eerdmans, 2007), 313, 317.

Although not found in the immediate context of foreigner language in 1 Peter (1:1; 1:17; 2:11; *parepidēmos* and *paroikos*), imagery related to strangers and strangeness in the form of the Greek term *xenos* is closely associated with these terms and also appears in the letter (1 Pet 4:4, 12).[33] Whereas foreigner language (*paroikos* and *parepidēmos*) is deployed to heighten the readers' awareness that they live a "double-conscious" diaspora existence characterized by belonging both here and there, the image of strangers or strangeness (*xenos*) helps to bring awareness to how Christians are perceived by non-Christian outsiders.[34] First Peter introduces the condition of being strange in 4:4 with the use of the present verb form of *xenos* (*xenizō*): "Wherein they perceive as a stranger you who no longer run with them into the same flood of dissipation." This passage articulates perception and implies continued future changes in social behavior. Their Gentile neighbors experience Christians differently because they no longer act like them. In 1 Peter 4:12, two forms of the root word, *xenos*, connoting some form of strangeness or difference are operative (a verb and an adjective form). The verse states, "Beloved, do not consider it strange (*xenizethe*) the fiery trials among you coming as a test for you, as a strange thing (*xenou*) happening to you." The verse captures believers' initial impressions about the opposition and skepticism they face and normalizes it. They have, so to speak, become "strangers in their own land." Yet, within the body of people who embrace the identity of "Christian," *the diverse membership has transformed itself from being a group of strangers to being a family.*

[33] The word *xenos*, meaning "strange" or "stranger," is a topos that often occurs in conversations around foreignness in the LXX. Frequently, *xenos* is the characterization attributed to those in "exile" caused by humans, not necessarily diaspora caused by God (LXX 1 Macc 11:38; 2 Macc 5:9; Ps 68:9; Wis 19:14). It also appears in the context of discussions around Israel's status as strangers and foreigners (*allotrios*) and Gentile perceptions that their rites and customs were odd and conflicted with Gentile customs and rites (see Josephus, *Ant.* 9.136; Josephus, *Ant.* 20:39; cf. LXX Lam 5:2; Philo, *Confusion* 82).

[34] Du Bois, *Souls of Black Folk*, 8.

The Relationship between God and the Diaspora People

First Peter acknowledges, even assumes, the coethnicity of its readers. The letter never encourages Galatians to uproot from Galatia and desist from identifying as Galatians or at least residents of Galatia.[35] At best, it encourages them to embrace their newfound identity as "Christian" while holding onto those aspects of their Galatian culture and social location that do not pose an overt threat to their Christian identity. Since a common physical natal origin is not shared among the diverse Christian groups, the letter leverages something else in order to hold together its constructed Christian diaspora. It cements the proposition that its readers are a distinct ethnoreligious people by issuing a theological myth. The primary function of the myth is to bind readers—who have mixed backgrounds and different originations—together with a common story that imbues their new "Christian" identity with meaningful continuity.[36]

A persistent theme in Jewish diaspora discourses is the belief that God enacted the Israelites' physical dislocation as punishment for their disobedience. As religious writings, discourses about God and the community's relationship are common, even expected. After all, the purpose of religious writings is to communicate perspectives about ultimate reality and the implications of religious experience and convictions "for life in the community and world."[37] Texts from Hellenistic Judaism substantiate why the people of God experienced misfortune in the form of foreign conquest, defeat, and displacement. The rationale offered is simple and direct—God did it.

First Peter characterizes diaspora reality as a relational distance God will close in the near future. It assigns the label "diaspora

[35] Debates continue regarding which part of the Roman Galatian province actually identifies or carries the name "Galatian." One helpful study to consult is: Brigitte Kahl, *Galatians Re-imagined: Reading with the Eyes of the Vanquished* (Minneapolis: Fortress, 2010).

[36] David G. Horrell, *Becoming Christian: Essays on 1 Peter and the Making of Christian Identity* (LNTS 394; London: T&T Clark, 2013).

[37] Luke Timothy Johnson, *The Writings of the New Testament* (3rd ed.; Minneapolis: Fortress, 2010), 6, 9.

people" to readers because of where they are situated in the larger cosmic organism and how they relate to God, the supreme authority. Diaspora-Christian existence is a relational cosmology,[38] which transgresses spatial and chronological boundaries and advances christological and theological claims.[39] As such, the letter compels readers "to examine their own understanding of reality and indirectly" invites "them to live their lives in the world" it projects.[40] The letter constructs its theological narrative by depicting a cosmic system complete with its own cast of actors, multiple settings, and historical chronology.[41]

Peter's Literary Construction of the Cosmos

Three locations compose 1 Peter's cosmic system: earth, heaven, and hell. No word for "earth" appears in the epistle. However, the word

[38] By "cosmology" I am referring to "the worldview of a particular age," broadly speaking. Donald K. McKim, *Westminster Dictionary of Theological Terms* (Louisville, Ky.: Westminster John Knox, 1996), 63; Letty M. Russell and J. Shannon Clarkson, eds., *Dictionary of Feminist Theologies* (Louisville, Ky.: Westminster John Knox, 1996), 57; Michelle Voss Roberts, *Dualities: A Theology of Difference* (Louisville, Ky.: Westminster John Knox, 2010), 59, 68.

[39] Paul Avis describes the role spatial and chronological features serve in biblical literature by acknowledging that these writings construct realities as much as they reflect them. He says, "In saying the Bible is not a history book but a mythology, I am not arguing that the events it records could not possibly have happened in real time. It is simply that spatial and chronological relations within biblical texts always have symbolic significance whether or not they happen to correspond to reality as ordinarily understood. The patterning is determined by literary-aesthetic considerations rather than by historical or geographical facts." Avis, *God and the Creative Imagination: Metaphor, Symbol and Myth in Religion and Theology* (London: Routledge, 1999).

[40] Boring, *1 Peter*, 85; Boring, "Narrative Dynamics in First Peter," 7-40. See also Steven J. Kraftchick, "Reborn to a Living Hope: A Christology of 1 Peter," in *Reading 1–2 Peter and Jude: A Resource for Students*, ed. Eric F. Mason and Troy W. Martin (Atlanta: SBL, 2014), 83.

[41] The standard definition offered by scholars like Oscar Cullmann and Martin Hengel remains instructive, which is that salvation history is "the series of episodes in human history through which God works outs [his] saving purpose for the world." Murray Rae, *History and Hermeneutics* (London: T&T Clark, 2005), 33–34; Cullmann, *Salvation in History* (London: SCM Press, 1967), 24–25; Hengel, "Salvation History," in *Reading Texts, Seeking Wisdom: Scripture and Theology*, ed. David Ford and Graham Stanton (Grand Rapids: Eerdmans, 2003), 229–44.

kosmos appears several times (1 Pet 1:20; 3:3; 5:9) and has a specific meaning: a vast physical and tangible space, created by God (1 Pet 1:2), inhabited by humans (1 Pet 2:4), and traversed by a variety of other actors, such as Jesus Christ (1 Pet 1:1, 2, 3, 7, 11), the Holy Spirit (1 Pet 1:2, 11, 12), the OT prophets (1 Pet 1:10), Christian missionaries (1 Pet 1:12), angelic beings (1 Pet 1:12), and the devil (1 Pet 5:8). First Peter calls Christians' time in the physical world time lived "in the flesh," which frequently parallels life "in the spirit" (1 Pet 1:24; 3:18; 4:6). These verses, however, reflect more than just literary convention. They illustrate the essential space-time realities that constitute 1 Peter's cosmology. On the one hand, the community's current life in the physical world corresponds with their future life awaiting them in the spirit world because of their relationship to God and Christ's example (1 Pet 3:18; 4:1-2). On the other hand, the letter's vision of the tangible "cosmos" is restricted to the regions around and between the five Roman provinces (1 Pet 1:1), the city of Rome (1 Pet 5:13), and anywhere in the world that houses Christians (1 Pet 5:9). Although the physical, concrete space is important, in the thought-world of the epistle it forms only a portion of the larger expanse serving as the stage upon which the events of divine history occur.

While their physical reality is the created world, the readers' diaspora existence is determined by where they are situated in relation to hell and heaven. First Peter alludes to the existence of a hell or a netherworld of some sort in 3:19-20 and 4:6, although the word "hell" never appears in the discourse. Notions concerning its existence contribute to the letter's construction of diaspora in a unique way. First, 3:19 and 4:6 are ambiguous passages that mention "spirits in prison" and "the dead ones" without clarifying their identity.[42] This is because the specific

[42] These passages are some of the most difficult in the entire NT. In 1 Peter 3:19 the identity and location of "spirits in prison" remain ambiguous and contested. In terms of the location, the NT tradition (Matt 12:40; Acts 2:27; Rom 10:7; Eph 4:8-10) and other early Christian sources (Clement of Alexandria, *Strom.* 6.6.45-46; Origen, *Frag. Joan.* frag. 79:20-23; Athanasius, *Ep. Epic.* 5:26-27; Justin, *Dial.* 72.4) understand Christ's descent into hell as referring to Christ's presence among the dead. Francis W. Beare, *The First Epistle of Peter: The Greek Text with Introduction and Notes* (3rd ed.; Oxford: Blackwell, 1970 [1947]), 172. Even if this is the case and 1 Peter is in fact referring to "hell," Hades (some minuscules add *tōi hadē* for *phylakē*

identity of these imprisoned spirits or dead ones is less important than the identity and action of Jesus as the resurrected Christ and God, as the prime orchestrator and cosmic judge of all creation (1 Pet 3:17-18, 22; 4:5-6). First Peter 3:19 literally says, "[Christ] having gone (*poreuomai*), he made proclamation to the spirits in prison." In like manner, the author describes Christ's ascent into heaven ("having gone into heaven"; 1 Pet 3:22), using the exact form of *poreuomai* ("having gone") to indicate Christ's movements between the nether place and heaven. By duplicating the word, the letter projects a positive correspondence between the spirits' prison as a domicile visited by Christ and heaven as Christ's current location. Although the specific location of "hell" is unclear, it appears to be a place that Christ traverses.

Heaven is an intangible, but no less real, place in the epistle. It is the abode of God and Jesus (LXX 1 Kgs 8:30), where God is enthroned (LXX Isa 66:1; Exod 24:9-11), and where one finds the provenance of the Holy Spirit (1 Pet 1:12; 3:22). Heaven is constantly present and intervening in the affairs of the physical world. On earth "the Devil walks around like a roaring lion" (1 Pet 5:8-9); people malign and slander their innocent neighbors (1 Pet 2:12; 3:14, 16); and murders, crime, and mischief occur (1 Pet 4:15). Yet forces from heaven—specifically the Holy Spirit (1 Pet 1:12)—are present, animating believers' lives and uniting the entire community under one banner—the elect people of God (1 Pet 1:1-2). Although believers do not live there currently, they are nonetheless affiliate members (1 Pet 4:17) with a heavenly inheritance (1 Pet 1:4). The physical inaccessibility of heaven is what designates them a displaced people who must live as temporary foreigners in another land (1 Pet 1:17). The addressees of the letter constitute a diaspora not only because they are a dispersed people but also because they have yet to arrive as a complete collective at their destination, heaven.

While the letter names multiple settings and a variety of actors on the cosmic and earthly stage, God remains the chief protagonist.

---

in this verse), or some sort of imprisoned afterlife, the passage remains unclear where precisely this is located. It could be housed in the earth itself as in Enoch's accounts, below it, or somewhere else entirely. See also Meghan Henning, *Educating Early Christians through the Rhetoric of Hell: Weeping and Gnashing of Teeth as Paideia in Matthew and the Early Church* (WUNT 2; Tübingen: Mohr Siebeck, 2014).

It states five characteristics about God that indicates the addressees' current dispersion from God is temporary. God is the Creator of the world (1 Pet 4:19) and the divine Father of all creation (1 Pet 1:2, 3, 17). God is the one who chose Jesus to be the chief cornerstone before the creation of the world (1 Pet 1:20) and determined Christ's presence and activities in the physical world (i.e., 1 Pet 1:2, 7, 21; 3:17-18; 4:1-2). God is the one who occupies the central seat of power and authority in heaven, and Jesus sits "at the right hand" (1 Pet 3:22). God sends forth His Spirit to testify to God's accomplishments (1 Pet 1:12; 4:6, 14). Finally, and most importantly, it is God whom the Christians ultimately come to know through belief and understanding in the revelation of Jesus Christ, not Jesus alone (1 Pet 1:21; 2:5, 12, 16, 19; 3:5, 18; 4:6, 16; 5:12). While 1 Peter has a strong Christology, it ultimately projects a theological worldview in which God is the transcendent sovereign of heaven, earth, and even hell.

Time Markers of the Theological Diaspora Narrative

First Peter portrays the Christian diaspora as an aspect of a larger unfolding cosmic pageant. Time is what moves that cosmic drama forward. Consequently, the letter unfolds as a progressive sequence of events in which dispersion plays a temporal role. Grammatical analysis is instructive here because it illustrates how the letter underscores the temporal nature of Christian existence abroad.

The first mention of "time" occurs in 1 Peter 1:5 in the form of the word *kairos*. At the outset, the author uses *kairos* to make a future eschatological claim that the fullness of the believer's salvation "will be revealed in the last time." This raises a question: if the last time is the fullness of salvation, what is the function of the present? The letter provides an answer by deploying *kairos* in another passage, saying, "For the time (*kairos*) has come for judgment to begin with the household of God, if it begins with us what will be the end of those who do not obey the gospel of God?" (1 Pet 4:17). For believers, the present time is a moment of both corporate identity and collective "judgment." To be Christian does not mean salvation is complete, judgment is averted, and humility is unnecessary. On the contrary, the present time for believers is a time of waiting for vindication from inevitable suffering (1 Pet 1:6), growing as a Christian family (1 Pet 2:2), and anticipating God's judgment on the actions of all creation (1 Pet 4:17).

Language of foreignness and strangeness is woven together with another temporal noun for "time," *chronos*, in order to depict Christians' behavioral change and fortify their position as atypical residents within their original contexts. According to 1 Peter 1:17, the recipients live during a time of corporate foreignness. The epistle's notion of corporate difference recalls the episodes of foreignness depicted in Jewish tradition. For instance, LXX Genesis 12:10 narrates Abraham's journey into Egypt as a resident-immigrant (*paroikeō*) during a period of famine. LXX Genesis 15:13 describes an immigrant period (*paroikos*) in which Abraham's progeny is said to live in Egypt for four hundred years. Likewise, LXX Exodus 2:22 explicitly connects the imagery of immigrant or foreigner (*paroikos*) to landlessness by defining "Gershom," the name of Moses' son, as "a permanent resident foreigner (*paroikos*) in the land of another" (cf. LXX Exod 18:3). Moses gave his son the name Gershom as an expression of his own displacement and alien status, being one who fled out of fear for his life from his place of birth, Egypt.[43]

Yet the experience of 1 Peter's addressees are unlike the geographic dislocation experienced by the Israelite captives in Egypt, Babylon, and so forth. First Peter's representation of the time of living as a permanent resident foreigner is one of strangeness or difference without a change of residence (1 Pet 1:17). They have become foreigners within their original communities because they embody a new social norm. Their present actions differ from their former actions, and thus they are subjected to living as resident strangers in familiar surroundings and upon people who once viewed them as ordinary. The letter anticipates that Christians' bold proclamation will put them in a precarious relationship with their surroundings, particularly when the content of the proclamation is communicated more through actions

[43] Interestingly, underneath Moses' reference seems to be the yearning for what Moses identifies, at least at this point in the Exodus account, as his native land, Egypt. LXX Exod 2:22 potentially represents an early expansion of Israelite notions of homeland and native environments. Israelite experiences of alienation are not restricted to just displacement from ancient Palestine but involve dislocation from any site in which Israelites have created their own community.

than words (1 Pet 4:1–6). Periods of residential deviance and difference serve a grand purpose in the life of the believing community and in the period of diaspora. They establish the relationship between God and God's people and fuel their public proclamation, which could draw prospective converts to the faith (1 Pet 2:9, 12).

First Peter connects the congregants' current acts of social deviance to a vivid recollection of the past by using another temporal adverb, "now" (*nyn*, 1 Pet 1:12; 2:10, 25; 3:21). The letter recalls the time of the Jewish prophetic tradition (1 Pet 1:10) and summarizes the content of the prophecies as revelatory projections of a future time, which the Christians now live within and embody ("which now [*nyn*] were announced to you through the ones having preached the gospel to you"; 1 Pet 1:12). Likewise, 1 Peter 2:10 deploys the *nyn* to juxtapose past expectation to present realities of diaspora Christianity, saying, "who once were not a people but now (*nyn*) are a people of God." Here, the author condenses three verses from Hosea (LXX Hos 1:6, 9; 2:25) into one verse. The original LXX passage from Hosea is focused on the marriage of the minor prophet Hosea to an unfaithful wife, Gomer (LXX Hos 1:2). The nature of the relationship between Hosea and Gomer is often thought to be an analogy for God's relationship to Israel and Israel's unfaithfulness. God instructs Hosea to name his second son Lo-Ammi, or "Not My People," as a representation of Israel breaking its covenant (LXX Hos 1:9). During the time of Hosea's prophecies, Israel is characterized as an unfaithful people who do not become God's people (LXX Hos 2:1), although reconciliation remains possible (LXX Hos 2:7, 21–23). The future relationship Hosea foretold 1 Peter 2:10 depicts as a present reality for its Christian congregations when it says "but now you are God's people."

The chronological narrative about God looks backward and forward. It tells what God revealed through the prophets, what the patriarchs and matriarchs did out of faith in God, and God's choice of Jesus to be the first among many (1 Pet 1:3, 20–21). Moreover, the chronological markers depict the sequence of events in First Peter's relational cosmology and give Christian diaspora existence a definitive beginning and conclusion as well as purpose in the current moment.

Conclusion

By now it should be clear that in 1 Peter the notion of diaspora is central to properly understanding the letter's purpose and impact. Diverging from more traditional Hellenistic scriptural notions concerning diaspora, 1 Peter does not define it as a geographic dislocation from a physical and human place of origin. The distinguishing characteristic of diaspora in the epistle is that it is the consequence of a vertical relationship to God the Father and Christ Jesus together with a horizontal relationship among the Christian sisterhood and brotherhood, both locally and globally. The letter writer has creatively manipulated diaspora discourse—and related topics such as foreignness, strangeness, and suffering—to sensitize readers to kinship dynamics and prepare them for the backlash they will inevitably face from outsiders. Fundamentally, the letter's construction of diaspora existence encodes and transmits foundational ideas about Christian identity and reality.

The cosmology of 1 Peter functions as a narrative of knowledge in which diaspora is transformed from a punitive and embarrassing situation to a condition of being the legitimate people of God. Instead of titles such as "foreigner" and "Christian" being pejorative and limiting, the letter tells them to embrace these as markers of the diaspora-Christian situation. The letter characterizes the Christian situation as momentary existence in a world that does not recognize the God of all creation. Ultimately, the author of 1 Peter appreciates the gravitas of appearing illegitimate, different, and out of place in the world and responds by deploying diaspora as a legitimating category of respectability.

Moreover, the letter considers suffering as an unavoidable feature of diaspora life. Through reference to the devil (1 Pet 5:8), its theological storyline assigns a face to evil and personal attacks. Diaspora Christians can bring about unnecessary suffering if they are ethically out of step with the expectations and regulations of society, but also if they are out of step with their own community's moral code (1 Pet 3:13-17; 4:15). The letter warns them to be morally above reproach, doing and embodying good, not bad, deeds and behaviors (1 Pet 2:12, 15, 20; 3:13-14). More importantly, suffering is inevitable in the Christian diaspora because that positionality carries the experience of difference and oddity. The suffering the letter anticipates is the kind that comes from any group viewed as deviant and suspicious in the Roman world. In addition to adopting and adapting diaspora in order to construct a novel Christian identity, the letter also describes the everyday dealings of the Christian way of life. Even though diaspora is temporary, 1 Peter asserts that a particular set of behaviors and attitudes characterizes diaspora-Christian life in the present.

2

THE CULTIC LIFE

Practices of the Christian Diaspora

The previous chapter demonstrates that the image of diaspora shapes the entire First Letter of Peter. The fundamental proposition 1 Peter puts forward to readers is that they are the people of God living temporary existences of dispersion and distance. The letter blends the ancient Jewish diaspora conception with a theocentric and christocentric narrative, portraying its intended readers as segments of interdependent communities variously positioned and engaged in their respective locations but unified by their relationship with God. Diaspora unites rather than separates members of its kinship. By wielding its image and corresponding labels (i.e., foreigner, elect ones, peoplehood, etc.), 1 Peter distinguishes the Christian way of life from that of the non-Christian. Additionally, the letter constructs diaspora Christianity as a double-duty routine. It exhorts Christian readers to balance the precepts of the Christian community with the imperatives of civil society.[1] Instead of distinguishing Christian life as a posture of either withdrawing or opposing the world, 1 Peter envisions Christianity—particularly diaspora Christianity—as a balancing act between integration and segregation, presence and difference, conformity and distinction.

[1] Arnold T. Monera, "The Christian's Relationship to the State according to the New Testament: Conformity or Non-conformity?" *Asia Journal of Theology* 19 (2005): 120.

The letter is fundamentally a strategy of "best practices" for diaspora Christians navigating three social institutions of the Greco-Roman world: cult, citizenship, and household relations.[2] In each case, 1 Peter prescribes, in paraenetic fashion, a double consciousness, in which its addressees observe two distinct cultural systems and oscillate between two parallel realities—namely, living under human authority and living under God's sovereignty.[3] According to the letter, diaspora-Christian communities hold dual resident citizenship, function as members of two households, and privilege the monoreligiosity of Christianity over the polyreligiosity of the broader pagan world in which they exist.[4] Rather than the previous chapter's question of how 1 Peter defines diaspora, the focus going forward is on answering this question: "What does 1 Peter say its readers should do as diaspora people in the present moment?"[5]

[2] John M. G. Barclay, *Jews in the Mediterranean Diaspora: From Alexander to Trajan (323 BCE–117 CE)* (Edinburgh: T&T Clark, 1996), 400–401.

[3] My working definition of double-consciousness resembles Du Bois' perspective. It is also greatly influenced by the historian John Winkler, who provides a working definition of his own in his short essay titled "Double Consciousness in Sappho's Lyrics." He says double consciousness is "a kind of cultural bi-lingualism on our part, for we must be aware of and fluent in using two systems of understanding." Winkler, *The Constraints of Desire* (New York: Routledge, 1990), 162.

[4] By "polyreligious," I am referring to a mix of religious practices and orientations. See Luke Timothy Johnson, *Among the Gentiles: Greco-Roman Religion and Christianity* (Anchor Yale Bible Reference Library; New Haven, Conn.: Yale University Press, 2009); Rogers Brubaker, *Nationalism Reframed: Nationhood and the National Question in the New Europe* (Cambridge: Cambridge University Press, 1996), 3.

[5] In some respects, my work is reminiscent of a similar query made by Wayne Meeks in his watershed text, *The First Urban Christians: The Social World of the Apostle Paul* (2nd ed.; New Haven, Conn.: Yale University Press, 2003), 142. In the opening of his chapter on "Ritual," Meeks says, "The appropriate question, as we undertake to describe the rituals mentioned in the Pauline letters, is 'what do they do?'" Meeks' question is, ultimately, my question for this chapter. I, however, do not limit it to just the ritual behaviors addressed in 1 Peter. I expand Meeks' original question to also encompass the moral, civil, and behavioral postures the letter details.

The Point of No Agreement: Cultic Practice

One of the three major prescriptions the letter puts forward revolves around cultic practices. It envisions a particular set of cultic activities and champions them as essential components of a thriving diaspora Christianity. Some are obvious, stated outright, and familiar to present-day readers of the letter. Others are less obvious but no less important in 1 Peter's imaginings of the daily life of diaspora Christians.

No Idol Worship

First Peter characterizes Christian religious practices as a distinct ritual lifestyle (1 Pet 1:15; 2:12), which departs from conventional polyreligious practice and observance in some clear and definitive ways. One of the most distinctly Christian activities the letter advances is monoreligious practice and monotheistic belief (1 Pet 1:17; 4:19). It contrasts the intended recipients' current Christian worship of God to their former life as idol worshippers.[6] The letter depicts idolatry as the physical worship of something other than God. Idolatry is an act readers abandoned once they joined the Christian community. 1 Peter 1:18 says, "For you know what caused you to no longer be enslaved, knowing that not with perishable things like silver or gold were you redeemed from your vain (*mataios*) manner of life handed down from your ancestors."[7] By naming silver and gold, using the adjective *mataios* ("vain"), and then relating both to pagan ancestral tradition

[6] 1 Peter's emphasis on monotheism reflects the influence and, indeed, evinces the symbolic world of Israel even though Israel is not explicitly mentioned. Statements such as "according to the foreknowledge of God, the Father" (1 Pet 1:2) and "Blessed be God and Father" (1:3) are reminiscent of the theological proposition of Israel's Shema in HB Deut 6:4: "Hear, O Israel! The Lord is Our God, the Lord alone." Moreover, the Shema's prohibition against idolatry constitutes the thought-world and position of 1 Peter. Just as HB Deut 6:13-14 says, "You shall not follow other gods, such as those of the surrounding nations," Peter directs readers not to participate in "lawless idolatry" (1 Pet 4:1-4).

[7] Daniel C. Arichea and Eugene A. Nida, *Handbook on the First Letter from Peter* (New York: United Bible Societies, 1980), 40.

(*patroparadotos*),[8] the letter characterizes the addressees as the descendants of idol worshippers as well as former practitioners themselves.

In addition to the indirect prohibition against idol worship in 1:18, 1 Peter heightens readers' awareness of their new reality by deploying the Greek word for idolatry (*eidōlolatria*) as the culminating term in its list of Gentile vices in 4:4. The letter lists six vices to avoid: sensuality (*aselgeia*, e.g., Eph 4:18-22), desire (*epithymia*, e.g., Col 3:5), drunkenness (*oinophlygia*, e.g., 1 Tim 5:13),[9] carousing (*kōmos*, e.g., Rom 13:13), drinking parties (*potos*, e.g., Jdt 6:21), and idolatry (*eidōlolatria*, e.g., 1 Cor 10:14). With the exception of *potos*, these terms appear in other Jewish and Christian vice lists (e.g., Rom 13:13; Col 3:5; Gal 5:19-21; Wis 14:23, 26) as representative of "the desires of the Gentiles" (1 Pet 4:3).[10] They appear often in the literary setting of a pagan feast or festival, akin to Bacchaic rites.[11] While it may be difficult to know for certain whether the author of 1 Peter had an actual drinking party in mind when he penned the list, it is clear these terms had currency in Greco-Roman discourses on ritual festivals and were used by Jewish and Christian writers as derogatory descriptions of conventional polyreligious practices.[12] The linguistic register of the letter (*mataios, eidolon;* 1 Pet 1:18; 4:3), then, specifies which circumstances and spaces from the socioreligious milieu of the broader pagan culture are inappropriate and prohibited for those honoring the one God.

[8] BDAG, πατροπαράδοτος, 789.

[9] Compound word is nonexistent, but *phlygarō* as "gossipy, talkative" does exist.

[10] Ramsay MacMullen and Hans-Josef Klauck offer a variety of examples of Roman cult practice in the empire. Some of the practices they document include public festivals, sacrifices, establishment of cult statues and shrines, dances and music performances, and intimate encounters. First Peter appears to be familiar with that environment and is attempting to respond directly to it. MacMullen, *Paganism in the Rome Empire* (New Haven, Conn.: Yale University Press, 1981), 146–67; Klauck, *The Religious Context of Early Christianity: A Guide to Graeco-Roman Religions* (Minneapolis: Fortress, 2003), 12–42.

[11] Johnson, *Among the Gentiles*, 33; Euripides, *Bacchae* 64–169. See Josephus, *Ant.* 20:112 for *aselgeia*; 2 Macc 6:4, *Letter Aristeas* §113, Wis 14:23, and Sibyl 5:394 for *kōmos*; LXX Gen 19:3, 40:20, Judge 14:10, 1 Sam 25:36 for *potos*.

[12] Plutarch, *Mor.* 612–748; J. Davidson, *Courtesans and Fish-Cakes: The Consuming Passions of Classical Athens* (New York: St. Martin's, 1998); P. A. Harland, *Associations, Synagogues, and Congregations: Claiming a Place in Ancient Mediterranean Society* (Minneapolis: Fortress, 2003), 55–88.

In addition to listing practices that no longer constitute their religious and ritual life, 1 Peter also details the response they should anticipate from their neighbors. It makes statements such as "They are surprised that you no longer join them" (1 Pet 4:3), "Beloved, do not be surprised by the fiery ordeal" (1 Pet 4:12), and "even if you suffer for doing what is right" (1 Pet 3:14). The letter calibrates the expectations of its addressees and alerts them to the strong possibility that their absence from conventional religious spaces (which is primarily a social space) and their modified social attitudes will garner attention and elicit specific responses of inquiry (1 Pet 1:6), skepticism (1 Pet 4:4), and antagonism (1 Pet 2:12).

Within the context of the larger Greco-Roman world, the link between physical worship, religious orientation, and social location is demonstrated in discourses from Plutarch and Aristides. Plutarch, a Roman historian and philosopher living around the time of some of the earliest Christian writers and followers (50–120 CE), repeatedly connects civil activity and attitude to belief and service to the gods. In many ways, these two orientations represent two sides of the same coin. In his critique of the Epicureans, a Roman philosophical movement, Plutarch makes his sensibility clear: "If oracles and divination and divine providence and the affection and love of parent for child and political activity and leadership and holding office are honorable and of a good report, so surely those who say there is no need to save Greece, but rather eat and drink so as to gratify the belly without harming it, are bound to suffer in repute and to be regarded as bad men."[13] First Peter reflects this widespread cultural sensibility Plutarch expresses. The legitimacy of a group that does not participate in the very public social life of the broader society because of the requirements of their religious identity makes them definite targets of suspicion and critique. Just as the letter writer of 1 Peter is not disillusioned about the inevitable backlash that comes with embracing an alternative value system (1 Pet 3:15), he demands that his readers recognize that their religious orientation affects their social standing.

[13] Plutarch, *Pleasant Life*, 19; *Colotes* 2. Quoted and translated in Johnson, *Among the Gentiles*, 106.

There is, however, benefit to worshipping the one God solely. First Peter suggests that, while the letter recognizes its addressees suffer the loss of social place and acceptance that void is not left unfilled. Christian worship provides a degree of accessibility to the divine that is beyond the reach of non-Christians, particularly pagan non-Christians. Aelius Aristides, a Greek orator and writer who flourished in the second century (117–181 CE), repeatedly connects his zealous worship of Asclepius with his professional successes in the field of oration and his struggle with physical illness.[14] Unlike Aristides, for whom salvation secures professional success and degrees of physical healing, salvation in 1 Peter means divine protection (1 Pet 1:5) and the security of knowing that the believer's life will continue on in the future (1 Pet 1:4-5, 23-25; 4:18-19).[15] When the letter makes statements such as "Through him [Jesus Christ] you have come to trust in God" (1 Pet 1:21, cf. 1:21) and "you are . . . God's own people" (1 Pet 2:9), it reaffirms the distinct worship life of Christians. Christians worship the one God because this God is revealed to them through Jesus' death and resurrection (1 Pet 1:3). Idol worship, therefore, is "worthless" or "empty" because it cannot offer that guarantee. Consequently, the words *mataios* and *eidōlon* encourage believers' ongoing distance from their former lives as idol-worshipping Gentiles and fortifies their new monotheistic belief and worship of the one God against aggressive social opposition.

In short, 1 Peter does not encourage believers to participate in the religious life of the Gentile world. Instead, the letter differentiates the ritual life of believers from that of nonbelievers and designates them as two irreconcilable alternatives. The letter is clear: Christians cannot worship and comingle with the Gentiles in non-Christian cultic settings. Here, double-conscious existence is not about participating in both a Christian cult and a pagan cult; rather double-conscious diaspora living entails embracing what are distinctly Christian practices,

[14] Aelius Aristides' work called *Sacred Tales* provides some useful insight into the link between embodied worship and religious sensibility. Aristides sees his embodied obedience and professional work as an orator as visible examples and affirmations of his singular devotion to Asclepius. For some examples, see Aristides, *Sacred Tales* 4:15, 7, 38.

[15] Johnson, *Among the Gentiles*, 63.

while being aware of how Gentile outsiders perceive Christians' physical absence from normative religious spaces. Their absence from pagan cultic spaces adds another layer of meaning to the letter's working notion of diaspora.

Baptism and Creeds

Baptism is an important theme in 1 Peter. The Greek term for baptism, *baptisma*, is used explicitly in 1 Peter 3:21 alongside other allusions to baptism (i.e., "born again," 1 Pet 1:3, 22; "newborn babies," 1 Pet 2:2).[16] While its importance for shaping the tradition of Christian baptism should not be minimized, baptism is just one ritual practice among several the letter represents as part of Christian life in the diaspora.

The letter portrays baptism as a watershed moment that distances Christians' past life or first birth from their present and future life or second birth. By making declarative statements such as "He has given us a new birth" (1 Pet 1:3), "Now that you have purified your souls by your obedience" (1 Pet 1:22), and "You have been born anew" (1 Pet 1:23), the letter renders baptism an authentic turn from one existential posture to another. Instead of their former ways of idolatry (1 Pet 1:18), "they commit themselves to a trustworthy Creator" (1 Pet 4:19). Instead of ignorant conformity to human norms (1 Pet 1:14), Christians now live disciplined lives that are aligned to the will of God (1 Pet 4:2, 7). Instead of doing evil, they do good (1 Pet 3:11). According to the thought-world of 1 Peter, baptism signifies a heightened awareness of God. Such consciousness of God is both a virtuous (1 Pet 2:19) and practical necessity when facing slander and abuse (1 Pet 3:16).

In addition to its spiritual (consciousness of God) and practical (offense against attack) functions, baptism also plays a confessional role in the life of diaspora Christianity. It signifies both a public and an active proclamation of their new orientation. The reference to baptism as a type (*ho . . . antitypon*) of saving act in 1 Peter 3:21 is similar to the

[16] For a thorough rehearsal of the baptismal language and traditions extant in 1 Peter and the scholarly debates surrounding such readings, see John Elliott, *1 Peter: A New Translation with Introduction and Commentary* (AB 37B; New York: Doubleday, 2000), 32–35.

act of saving in the story of Noah.[17] Salvation, water, and mindfulness of God are intertwined in the baptism moment as a public "pledge to God from a good conscience." Closely related to the baptism imagery is a christological pattern of suffering and exaltation. The claim that Christians have received a "new birth into a living hope through the resurrection of Jesus Christ from the dead" is repeated throughout the letter as the content of the baptismal confession (1 Pet 1:23; 2:2; 3:20-22). It rings with the sound of the gospel's multiple christological formulations and creedal confessions that associate "new birth" with baptism (i.e., John 3:3-5, 16). First Peter is constantly, in various ways, declaring to readers their right standing or relationship to God because of what was accomplished in Jesus Christ, not what they face as persecuted individuals in the world.

Baptism in 1 Peter, therefore, specifies a distinctly Christian understanding of salvation and is not just a recapitulation of baptism as a Jewish cleansing ritual. Salvation means a shift from a former life of polytheistic belief and a corrupt conception of God to a keen awareness (1 Pet 3:18).[18] Consequently, the purpose of baptism in the life of the community is to solidify Christians' new identity as a people in good standing and close kinship with God (1 Pet 3:21; 4:19). Baptism marks the beginning of a confessional life—in both word and deed—that announces the nature of the believer's relationship with God, which is brought about because of Christ's sacrificial death and resurrection (1 Pet 2:21-25; 3:18-19; 5:1). This perspective suggests that the importance of baptism lies in its capacity to produce a single confessional identity that unifies Christians both locally and abroad despite threats of violence and pain.

[17] We see the connections between salvation, water, and mindfulness of God in other places in the NT, specifically Heb 10:22 and Qumran texts such as 1QS V 8–10, CD XVI 7. For more information on these connections, see Elliott, *1 Peter*, 681.

[18] Indeed, 1 Peter contains atonement language regarding what Christ accomplished through suffering, death, and resurrection (2:24; 3:18). In addition to atonement, the letter also claims that Jesus' passion and resurrection served the purpose of providing an "example" that future believers could follow (1 Pet 2:21). The language of atonement and model is woven together in the letter as two inextricable strands, which clarify the meaning and purpose of Jesus' suffering. There is no wonder that Luther designated this letter one of the jewels of his reformed theology.

Preaching

In addition to asserting that monotheism, baptism, and creedal confession are essential to shaping a Christian-diaspora ethos, 1 Peter asserts that preaching is necessary. Preaching, in the form of spreading the gospel to others through word and/or conduct, is one of the first practices the letter assumes as active in the Christian community. First Peter 1:12 reminds the congregants that they have already benefitted from hearing the good news of Jesus Christ. Because the letter's readers first received the preached or oral gospel (*euangelizō*, 1 Pet 1:12, 25), they in turn are expected to make a similar kind of proclamation to other non-Christians.

First Peter delineates two components of the Christian preacher's content. First, preaching discloses that Jesus Christ both suffered greatly and reigns mightily (1 Pet 1:11). Repeatedly the letter specifies the content of Christian proclamation as a balance between retellings of Jesus' suffering and death (1 Pet 1:18a; 4:1; 2:21-24) and declarations of Christ's resurrection, heavenly exaltation, and imminent return (1 Pet 1:18b; 3:21-22). The letter claims that the gospel (*euangelion*) of Jesus Christ entails an existential awareness that believers are the possession of God (1 Pet 2:9; 3:18). When the letter labels believers as members of the household of God, it makes a statement not just about their membership but also about God's *ownership* of believers (1 Pet 4:17). Such a paradox, the existence of defeat and victory in one divinely blessed body, remains the obscure truth that Christians are expected to accept and to which the good news refers.

Second, preaching is a mechanism for spreading the movement. In addition to informing believers of the content of their faith, it attracts new believers to the community. The letter sketches the potential impact Christians can have by continuing to live among non-Christians and preaching to them through word and conduct. In 1 Peter 4:11, speech (*laleō*) and service (*diakoneō*) are highlighted as two aspects of proclaiming and glorifying God "in all things through Jesus Christ." Although speech can be used for deceit (1 Pet 3:10), the letter instructs the audience to use speech as a means of drawing and not repelling. Both speech and ministerial service represent approaches to "preaching" to others about God (cf. 1 Cor 10:31).

Proclamation also accords with the confessional life Christians practice among non-Christians who can respond positively or negatively. The purpose of a Christian "manner of life" (*anastrophē*) or a Christian "ethic of doing" (*poieō*) is to draw prospective members to the community. The letter frequently juxtaposes "doing bad things" (*kakopoios*) and "doing good things" (*agathopoios*, 1 Pet 2:14; 3:17) as a strategy for turning detractors toward God and producing a favorable opinion of Christians living among them. First Peter is adamant that readers should opt for doing good (1 Pet 2:15, 20; 3:6, 17; 4:19),[19] which has the benefit of silencing opponents (1 Pet 2:12) and earning God's approval (1 Pet 2:20; 3:11-12). The drawback to this strategy, however, is that even with good behavior the addressees can and will suffer for operating as "Christian" (1 Pet 4:16, 19; cf. Acts 11:26; 26:28). The letter, nonetheless, asserts that what Christians do is as important as what they say while spreading the gospel.

Prayer

Prayer is another communal practice that the letter espouses as a common and persistent ritual in the cultic life of its readers. The letter never instructs readers to pray but presumes they already do so (*proseuchē*, 1 Pet 3:7; 4:7) and even offers up its own literary form of prayer as encouragement to continue (1 Pet 1:3-12; 4:11; 5:1).

No details regarding the frequency of prayer are offered in 1 Peter, but it portrays prayer as a practice that is both personal and communal in nature. While speaking directly to husbands, the letter instructs them to treat their wives as coheirs so as not to hinder the efficacy of their prayers (1 Pet 3:7). This points to the fact that inappropriate Christian kinship interaction can either amplify or hamper one's

[19] The letter asserts what Christians do determine whether they are truly a people of repute or disrepute. It underscores the various types of moral or immoral action by augmenting the Greek root word for "to do," *poieō*, and transforming it into multiple compound words. Although the letter uses the basic root of *poieō* three times (2:22; 3:11-12), it also transforms it into a set of compound words, most of which occur only in the NT. These terms are *agathopoios* and *agathopoieō* (2:14; 2:15, 20; 3:6, 17; 4:19), *kakopoios* and *kakopoieō* (2:12, 14; 3:17; 4:15), *peripoiēsis* (2:9), and *zōopoieō* (3:18).

individual prayer life. Here, 1 Peter depicts prayer as a component of an autonomous Christian identity and practice. Before an individual believer engages in corporate cultic practices, a proper understanding and observance of internal Christian social relationships is necessary. Prayer, while clearly important to the letter, is not enough in and of itself.

The second reference to prayer gives a rationale for its necessity. First Peter's addressees are to pray because the end is near (1 Pet 4:7). Prayer is designated then as the essential practice that the Christian community performs as a corporate body, which anticipates the return and judgment of Jesus Christ. The letter envisions the act of "invoking" or "calling upon" God as a cooperative, not individual, action (1 Pet 1:17). It is a generative context for the vertical relationship between believer and God, as well as a formative context for the horizontal relationship between individual believers. The letter imagines that prayer is a site for the group to find solidarity and unity.[20]

In addition to naming the act of prayer, the letter also models prayer in several places. In fact, it opens by modeling a prayer of blessing that celebrates the essence of God and identity of the community (1 Pet 1:3–12). Later, in 1 Peter 4:11b, prayer appears again, but this time as a demonstration of how and what to pray: "To him belong the glory and the power forever and ever. Amen." Similar to the celebratory prayer of 4:11 in which the power of God is affirmed, 1 Peter 5:11 says, "To him be the power forever and ever. Amen." Moreover, in a scriptural quotation from LXX Psalms 34:13–17, the letter names prayer as a practice of the faithful Christian committed to doing good (*ean tou agathou zēlōtai genēsthe*, 1 Pet 3:12).

Through such modeling of prayer, the creedal and confessional life of the church is revealed. Prayer is about proclaiming the restoration of God's kingdom, not asking for things. Prayer involves the confession of Jesus Christ as the agent of God the Father and creator of all things. At the center of this confession is the recognition that God the Father is the primary agent and actor in the larger cosmic scheme. Yet Jesus remains the point of access to God and others in the

[20] Arichea and Nida, *Handbook on the First Letter from Peter*, 38.

diaspora community. Moreover, prayer, according to 1 Peter, involves the conscious actions of members of the Christian kinship in healthy, affirming, and unified relationships with each other.

Hospitality and Staying Sober

First Peter names two other practices as proper religious habits of diaspora Christians: hospitality and sobriety. Although these are not typically ascribed to religious practices, they are in the context of 1 Peter. Unlike the practices laid out previously, hospitality and sobriety are prescribed more often than assumed. They do not appear to be practices as indigenous to the worship life of the community as the others. As such, the letter writer adds hospitality and sobriety to the set of practices he champions as Christian activities meriting immediate incorporation into the worship life of the provincial communities.

The letter constantly reminds readers that they are to show genuine hospitality to all members of the community.[21] In 4:9, the letter instructs them, "Be hospitable to one another without fussing." Although the Greek word form behind "hospitality" in 1 Peter 4:9 is an adjective, the syntax intimates that the letter's imperative force demands a culture of hospitality among the Christian members—particularly traveling Christians. Here the word for hospitality, *philoxenos*, is actually a compound word constituted by the root words for love and stranger.[22] The letter is literally instructing addressees to welcome Christian strangers or travelers to their midst. This practice of extending hospitality to familial strangers is common in the ancient world. Josephus labels Taricheae, a land belonging to his

[21] Lucien Richard suggests that communal hospitality is one of the ways the church lives out the life Scripture imagines. In describing hospitality and God's sovereignty, Richard says it "encourages a diaspora ethics of itinerancy, detachment, dispossession, solidarity, and endurance in suffering, rather than a homeland ethics of stability, engagement, acquisition, and human fulfillment in the present life." Richard, *Living the Hospitality of God* (New York: Paulist Press, 2000), 79; Luke Timothy Johnson, "Imagining the World Scripture Imagines," *Modern Theology* 14 (1998): 165–80; idem, *Sharing Possessions: What Faith Demands* (2nd ed.; Grand Rapids: Eerdmans, 2011).

[22] The language of hospitality, particularly the word *philoxenos*, occurs in 1 Tim 3:2 and Titus 1:8 as a distinguishable trait of bishops.

fellow country people, as a region with the reputation of being hospitable and welcoming to both compatriots as well as foreigners (Josephus, *Life* 142). In contrast, the Stoic philosopher Epictetus insinuates that the act of hospitality is a means of self-preservation rather than ruin when he says, "Now the ruin of Alexander was when he lost the character of modesty, fidelity, regard to hospitality, and to decency."[23]

Similarly, 1 Peter designates hospitality a necessary *religious practice* for nurturing and solidifying the collective identity and fellowship of Christians abroad. Within the community, hospitality takes on the form of mutuality, support, and affirmation (1 Pet 3:8; 4:8-10; 4:14). It is a mechanism for addressing the diverse and dispersed nature of the community's membership. The community is transient and therefore welcoming, and appreciating the stranger in their midst is necessary for the fellowship, both locally and abroad, to remain intact and survive their temporary dispersion.[24] Hospitality is depicted as a distinct Christian practice because it has a narrow focus; the maintenance and preservation of the scattered Christian communities that the letter suggests are linked to one another (1 Pet 1:1; 5:9, 12, 13).

First Peter addresses the issue of sobriety differently than hospitality. Whereas it actually deploys rhetoric of hospitality and mutuality in order to state what diaspora Christians should do, in regard to sobriety it takes a prohibitive stance by deploying rhetoric regarding what they should *not* do. The letter instructs addressees to not participate in "the same excessive debauchery" as the Gentiles (1 Pet 4:4), which translates into living a self-controlled, disciplined, and sober life (*nēphō*, 1 Pet 1:13; 4:7; 5:8). The terms 1 Peter deploys to signify "excessive debauchery" (*anachysis* and *asōtia*) appear rarely in the LXX and NT and do not function as common scriptural vernacular.[25] Typi-

[23] Epictetus, *Discourses* 1.28; translation from Epictetus, *Enchiridion and Selections from the Discourses of Epictetus*, trans. George Long (Stilwell, Kans.: Digireads, 2005), 38.

[24] See also *1 Clem.* 12, where the story of Rahab is rehearsed as evidence of the link between extending hospitality to God's people and receiving salvation.

[25] The term for "excessive" or "outpouring," *anachysis*, does not appear anywhere else in the NT, LXX, or Josephus' works. It appears only in some of Philo's writings, but not in a negative sense. Philo does not use it to designate excessive and out-of-control phenomena. It typically represents an effusion of something natural, such as

cally, when biblical authors address the issues of drunkenness, excessive debauchery, or pagan feasts, some form of the words *methē* or *methyō* is used (LXX Jdt 13:15; Tob 4:15; Prov 20:1; *Pss. Sol.* 8:14). These terms do not appear at all in 1 Peter. The linguistic register of the letter, which demands temperance in matters of communal and casual drinking, deviates from conventional rhetoric. Yet it establishes for the entire diaspora-Christian community a social decorum and communal orientation akin to what is specified for the offices of elders and bishops in the pastoral letters (Titus 1:6-7; cf. 1 Tim 3:2-3).

Complementing its prohibitions against intemperance, 1 Peter delineates, with some specificity, a broader register of unethical behaviors that signify idolatry and insobriety as well as violate conventional requirements of social behavior and Greco-Roman jurisprudence. The letter includes both a stylized vice list (1 Pet 4:3) and an abbreviated commandment list (1 Pet 4:15). Both echo Jewish moral discourses in form and content. They recall the simple vice lists found in LXX Jeremiah 7:9 and Hosea 4:2 as well as lists extant in later Hellenistic Jewish writings (e.g., Wis. 14:22-26; 2 Enoch 10:4-5; Philo *Posterity* 82; *Confusion* 163). Moreover, 1 Peter's miniature commandment and vice catalogs are reminiscent of the Decalogue in LXX Deuteronomy 5:6-21 and LXX Exodus 20:1-17 (cf. Mark 10:19; Luke 18:20; Philo *Decalogue* 36). Together, these two literary forms constitute the crux of Christian prohibitions. They represent actions that Christians just cannot do because they conflict with the essential orientation of being in relationship with God, God's people, and the world at large. For bad or good, 1 Peter's ethical catalogs of vices and commandments alert Christians and their neighbors to Christian peculiarities and distinctions abroad and accompany directives about hospitality and sobriety. These are not just issues concerning internal piety

light, which ultimately has a positive impact (Philo, *Abraham* 159; *Moses*, 1:212; *Creation* 57). This is in stark contrast to 1 Peter where *anachysis* represents a destructive type of excess that is antagonistic to God and the way of life of God's people. See also BDAG, ἀνάχυσις, 75. Similarly the term for debauchery, *asōtia*, appears only two other times in the NT (Eph 5:18 and Titus 1:6) and in each instance it is represented as a prohibitive action that is consigned to a non-Christian or non-Jewish way of life (cf. 2 Macc 6:4; Prov 28:7).

and spiritual disposition. Instead, 1 Peter casts them as religious acts that are essential to the social, structural, and institutional life of the community.

Conclusion

First Peter portrays diaspora Christianity as an active, robust, and diverse cultic life. Its authorization of a specific set of religious practices for Christian observance is also an injunction against pagan cultic convention. Whereas Christian rituals serve as solidifying and unifying acts of Christian life and faith, the ritual life of pagan communities is inappropriate and incompatible with Christianity. What is even more striking is that based on the tone of the letter, it appears most of the practices the letter names were occurring already in the community by the time it was written. First Peter does not, for the most part, outline these practices but assumes they are familiar to and common among diaspora-Christian communities located in the provinces.

The cultic life of the communities reinforces the differences between Christians and non-Christians, rather than bridging them. Here, more so than with issues related to household relations or citizenship, one encounters practices that have no counterpart in the pagan world. Christians cannot worship both God the Father and idols; nor can they pray to other gods or participate in pagan festivals. The double-conscious valence of Christian cultic practice is that it distances the Christian from the non-Christian and distinguishes "us" from "them." As such, 1 Peter provides a realistic and honest assessment about the addressees' situation. While they exist as Christian practitioners, they also must exist as targets of a society that does not subscribe to their Christian way of life.

3

Provinces and Households

The Relational Matrix of the Christian Diaspora

Although 1 Peter makes it clear that diaspora Christians cannot participate in both Christian and pagan cultic customs, the letter encourages them to observe both Christian and non-Christian forms of civic interaction and household arrangement. It characterizes diaspora Christianity as a web of social relations that demands members cultivate a double-duty civil persona and household interaction in order to survive in spite of imperfect circumstances. An essential component of Christian life, especially as conceived in diaspora terms, is the practice of Christian responsibility and allegiances on multiple fronts.[1] Consequently, 1 Peter is not just re-visioning Christian identity and kinship in terms of diaspora but also recasting the social ethics of the community in light of their scattered, yet no less settled, existence.

For the most part, 1 Peter depicts its addressees as predominantly people from marginal and dominated classes. The letter identifies its recipients as slaves and foreigners as well as freeborn and freed people living legally as husbands and wives in provincial households.[2]

[1] Arnold T. Monera, "The Christian's Relationship to the State according to the New Testament: Conformity or Non-conformity?" *Asia Journal of Theology* 19 (2005): 123.

[2] It is significant to note that by specifically addressing some hearers as slaves and others as wives and husbands, 1 Peter implicitly also provides a broad snapshot of the diverse social status of its readership. For some to be addressed as "slaves" while others are addressed as "wives" and "husbands" reveals the different sociopolitical

These Christians are not masters, governors, or kings. The latter are the powerful people 1 Peter is describing to readers (1 Pet 2:13-17), but those it addresses directly exist as targets and even expendable classes under hegemonic regimes (1 Pet 2:11, 18; 3:1, 7). First Peter does not gloss over the realities of a social location characterized by subjectivity, servility, subordination, and invisibility, nor does it endorse that existence as ordained by God. It is a reality that must be maneuvered and managed, not subscribed to. One thing is clear, 1 Peter does not champion hegemonic arrangements and regulations of daily life as God's preferred order.

Relating to Authorities: Kings, Governors, and the Lord

First Peter 1:1 names five places—Pontus, Galatia, Cappadocia, Asia, and Bithynia—as the whereabouts of the intended recipients and the letter's destinations in the order of its geographic circulation.[3] In addition to mapping the route for the dissemination of the letter, 1 Peter's opening situates its readers in regions that are subject to the Roman provincial system.[4] The letter names two common political positions

---

locations of the church members. Legally, only freeborn or freed men and women could be married and actually assume the legal status of husband or wife to another under Roman law. For a survey and description of these social classes, see John H. Elliott, *A Home for the Homeless: A Social-Scientific Criticism of 1 Peter, Its Situation and Strategy* (2nd ed.; Minneapolis: Fortress, 1990); David Balch, *Let Wives Be Submissive: The Domestic Code in 1 Peter* (SBLMS 26; Atlanta: Scholars Press, 1981); Carolyn Osiek and David L. Balch, *Families in the New Testament World: Households and House Churches* (Louisville, Ky.: Westminster John Knox, 1997).

[3] Given the history of travel patterns and conquest in Asia Minor, it is likely that the list of five provinces in 1:1 actually reflects the travel pattern of the letter's courier, as it seems to have made a circular route around Asia Minor starting in Pontus and ending in Bithynia (Strabo, *Geography* 12.3.1–2; 12.4.1).

[4] Jeffers describes the provinces as "the basic unit of administration in the Roman Empire." James S. Jeffers, *The Greco-Roman World of the New Testament Era: Exploring the Background of Early Christianity* (Downers Grove, Ill.: InterVarsity, 1999), 110. "One primary source documents Julius Caesar's rationale for establishing the provincial system in places that he conquered: [Julius Caesar] thought priority must be given to organizing the provinces and districts into which he had just come so that they would be free from internal disturbances, would adopt laws and judicial procedures, and would cease to fear external enemies." Caesar, *Alexandrian War*

in the provinces, kings and governors (*basileus* and *hēgemōn*), and portrays them as municipal authorities over its addressees (1 Pet 2:13, 14). According to the letter, civil powers provide essential services to residents at the local level—they punish wrongdoers and praise the righteous. As such, the letter directs Christian readers to respond to these authorities in specific ways.

By conjoining two agents of Roman civil authority and decision making—kings and governors—the letter provides a strikingly accurate description of the Roman authoritative matrix active in the provinces. When 1 Peter states "Submit . . . to every human institution be it a king . . . or to the governors" (1 Pet 2:13-14), it avows that diaspora Christians are still subject to Roman hegemonic power, even though they have experienced a "new birth" (1 Pet 1:3, 23) and baptism (1 Pet 3:21). First Peter casts the provincial system in terms similar to other NT and Greco-Roman sources (cf. Mark 13:9; Luke 21:12). Notable is the mention of governors and kings as Paul is being interrogated from region to region on his way to Rome. In Acts 23:33–24:2, Paul is brought before the Roman governor of Judea, Felix. As the story unfolds, the case against Paul escalates and he eventually appears before both Governor Felix and King Agrippa II: "Then the king and governor got up along with Bernice and those who had been seated with them" (Acts 25:13-27).[5] From Luke's description of Paul's interrogation, one gets the sense that the Roman authority of primary concern for provincial residents is the governor of the jurisdiction. First Peter reports this structure when it depicts the emperor-appointed governors ("having been sent by the king," 1 Pet 2:14) as the imperial authority whom Christians in Asia Minor (present-day western Turkey) will likely face if charged as wrongdoers (*kakopoios*, 1 Pet 2:14, 16) or accused of not submitting to civil institutions and powers (1 Pet 2:13).

65, quoted by Jeffers. See Josephus for other descriptions of the provincial system directly impacting diaspora Jews; Josephus, *Ant.* 18:53.

[5] Agrippa II was king around 52 CE. *ABD* 1:98; K. C. Hanson, "The Herodians and Mediterranean Kinship, Part 3," *BTB* 20, no. 1 (1990): 10–21.

Outside the NT, Greco-Roman sources testify to the fact that the immediate Roman authority in the provinces was governors.[6] These governors, as well as the central imperial power, were generally distrustful of provincials, considering them potentially noncompliant residents of Roman-controlled territories. Roman sources that both predate and postdate 1 Peter show that the governor's foremost concern was controlling political volatility and protecting imperial interests, more than ensuring the welfare of locals.[7] A fourth-century legal document states that the basic duties of the governor are to ensure the province remains "peaceful and quiet" by hunting down and freeing the province of bad men who are described as "sacrilegious people," robbers, kidnappers, thieves, and all their known associates.[8] Likewise, Cicero, a Roman statesman of the first century, wrote a letter to the governor of Asia in 54 BCE, describing provincial residents as a class of unethical and politically dangerous people: "But in the province itself, if you have found someone who had entered deeply into your intimate acquaintance, and who was not known to us before, be careful how much you trust him."[9] Cicero expresses a common sentiment among imperial rulers, assuming that provincial residents are

[6] There are several accounts of provincial governors refusing to hear cases about Roman citizens and opting instead to send them on to Rome. Even in these cases, provincial governors provided the first legal encounter with Roman authority. See Tacitus, *Ann.* 16:10.2; Pliny, *Ep.* 6:31.

[7] Jeffers describes the interest of Rome in provincial governance this way: "Rome did not care how local cities and regions in the provinces were governed, so long as the taxes were collected and allegiance to Rome remained firm . . . even the more efficient governments of the senatorial provinces did not make providing justice to the people their first priority. Their purpose was to maintain the imperial system. The very limited interest of governors in local affairs, which did not threaten the stability of the society, is illustrated in the account of Gallio and Paul in the book of Acts [18:12-16]." Jeffers, *Greco-Roman World*, 115.

[8] Justinian, *Digest of Law* 1.18.6, 13; Jo-Ann Shelton, *As the Romans Did: A Sourcebook in Roman Social History* (2nd ed.; Oxford: Oxford University Press, 1998), 270.

[9] Translation from David Cherry, *The Roman World: A Sourcebook* (Malden, Mass.: Blackwell, 2001), 157–58; Cicero, *Letters to His Brother Quintus* 1.1.15, 18; translation: Marcus Tullius Cicero, *Cicero on Oratory and Orators: With His Letters to Quintus and Brutus*, trans. John Selby Watson (Bohn's Classical Library; London: R. Clay Printer, 1855), 8.

people with questionable integrity and immoral behavior. They are, for the most part, unworthy of imperial recognition, service, and trust.

Around 112 CE, Pliny, the governor of Bithynia and Pontus, exchanged a series of letters with the Roman emperor, Trajan (not to be confused with the exchange of letters about Christians in the territory discussed in chapter 1). This particular series of Pliny–Trajan correspondences offers another glimpse into the chain of command from king to governor in the provinces and conveys their mutual concerns about mass sedition and resistance in the region. In a letter to the emperor, Pliny requests permission to form a firefighter *collegium* in Bithynia-Pontus (Pliny, *Ep.* 10.33)—an area the First Letter of Peter is addressing over twenty-five years earlier. Trajan denies the request outright, citing the possibility of provincial unrest as his reason.[10] Although Pliny would have full control of a firefighter organization and there was precedent in other regions, the group was not permitted to form because of concerns, even paranoia, about opportunities for political rebellion in Asia Minor.[11] Consequently, one sees the empire denying basic social services to areas it deems volatile and prone to unwarranted aggression and rebellion. What is significant to recognize is that these so-called incorrigible, unruly, and recalcitrant territories are the stomping grounds of the Christians the letter is addressing and instructing.

As the sources suggest, the emperor and the provincial governors worked closely together in monitoring and maintaining Roman order and control in the provinces. Just as the Pliny–Trajan correspondence demonstrates this close relationship and joint governing, so too does 1 Peter when it says to submit to human institutions, to the king as the ultimate authority, and to the governors sent by the king to both punish and praise (1 Pet 2:13, 14). The term for king, *basileus*, was used for the Roman Caesar or emperor (cf. Jos. *B.J.* 5.563; John 19:15;

[10] Mark Reasoner, *Roman Imperial Texts: A Sourcebook* (Minneapolis: Fortress, 2013), 144–45.

[11] Pliny the Younger, *Ep.* 10.34; Shelton, *As the Romans Did*, 286; Neil Elliott and Mark Reasoner, *Documents and Images for the Study of Paul* (Minneapolis: Fortress, 2011), 283–84.

Acts 17:7; Rev 17:9, 12).[12] The letter's explicit acknowledgment of both the Caesar-king and governor roles in the provinces reinforces the inescapable reality that all the provincial Christians of the diaspora are subject to: "The rulers of the Roman Empire with the Caesar at the top."[13]

Thus, 1 Peter does not encourage its readers to evade the power structure or ignore the hierarchal matrix of the Roman-occupied provinces in which they live. Rather, the letter urges readers to recommit themselves to those structures. In addition to honoring everyone, loving the Christian family, and fearing God, the letter tells the addressees to "Honor Caesar" (lit. *basileus*, 1 Pet 2:17) to avert undue Roman attention, not because the empire represents the proper social ordering of the world. What appears to be esteem for the Roman provincial system in 1 Peter is actually a response to the system's capacity for inhumane cruelty, attack, and mass extermination. The letter writer commands readers to "honor Caesar" because Caesar will not hesitate to rid the region of the community entirely if it poses a challenge to the empire. It is not just one life that is in danger if any single Christian in the diaspora acts in a socially disruptive or deviant manner; the survival of the entire membership is compromised.

The letter forbids Christians from drawing undue attention to themselves that can lead to martyrdom. According to 1 Peter, Christ has already served as martyr, "suffering for you" (1 Pet 2:21). It wields the image of dispersion and Christ's suffering as a strategy for living, not dying, as Christians. This is even more intriguing given that 1 Peter was likely written immediately before the rise of early Christian martyrologies such as *The Passion of Perpetua and Felicitas* and *Martyrdom of Polycarp*. First Peter never encourages opposition leading to martyrdom; rather it advocates compliance and obedience as a strategic measure to avoid execution.[14]

[12] Reinhard Feldmeier, *The First Letter of Peter: A Commentary on the Greek Text*, trans. Peter H. Davids (Waco, Tex.: Baylor University Press, 2008), 158.

[13] Feldmeier, *First Letter of Peter*, 159.

[14] Candida Moss, *The Myth of Persecution: How Early Christians Invented a Story of Martyrdom* (New York: HarperCollins, 2013); Daniel Boyarin, *Dying for God: Martyrdom and the Making of Christianity and Judaism* (Stanford: Stanford University Press, 1999).

First Peter defines civic conduct as a social act that establishes Christians as a compliant group of provincial residents. As a remedy to the negative opinions of imperial powers in the region, the letter prescribes assimilation and preparedness: "Having good conduct among the Gentiles so that though they slander you as evildoers; seeing your good works, they may glorify God when he comes to visit" (1 Pet 2:12).[15] Here the letter highlights the reality that diaspora Christians exist in a context of honor. Although the conventional word for honor (*timē*) does not appear in this particular verse, the notion of cultivating a particularly positive form of public recognition persists.[16]

The close parallel between "good works" (*kalos*) and honorable conduct (*timē*) in service to larger Greco-Roman social convention and power structures is attested in other sources from early Christianity, Hellenistic Judaism, and the Greco-Roman world. For instance, Matthew 5:17 says, "Let your light shine before others, so that they may see your good works and give glory to your Father in heaven." In Matthew 26:10, Jesus questions the disciples: "Why do you trouble the woman? She has performed a good work for me." In each case, good works represent noble actions that can draw people to God, compelling onlookers to "glorify God," or actions that can shame onlookers who do not value or discern God's presence (see also John 10:32).[17] Likewise, Jewish wisdom literature proffers similar notions about the social function and necessity of being deemed "honorable" as opposed to shameful. For instance, LXX Proverbs 3:35 states, "The wise will inherit glory, but the ungodly have exalted dishonor." LXX Sirach 5:13 states, "Glory and dishonor are in speaking, and a person's tongue is his/her disaster" (cf. LXX Sir 3:10; 29:6). Similarly, Greco-Roman moralistic discourses designate social values of honor or glory and dishonor or shame as components of a person's social activity and an indicator of a person's social character and status. The Greek rhetorician

[15] My translation.

[16] The BDAG renders one particular meaning of *kalos* as "of moral quality . . . good, noble, praiseworthy" action. BDAG, καλός, 504.

[17] The terms *timē* and *doxa* often appear together in the NT (1 Pet 1:7; 1 Cor 6:20; see also Josephus, *Ant.* 12.118). In 1 Peter, it is *kalos* and *doxa* that appear side by side, yet the same meaning is in effect. For further discussion about the connection between *timē* and *doxa*, see Johannes Schneider, "*timē*," *TDNT* 8 (1972): 172–75.

Isocrates points to honor and shame as a major component of ethical behavior. He exhorts Demonicus to honor the gods (*Ad Dem.* 1.13), honor one's parents (*Ad Dem.* 1.16), and avoid doing and even speaking of shameful action (*Ad Dem.* 1.15).[18]

Language for dishonor appears in the form of shame (*kataischunō*, 1 Pet 2:6; 3:16), blaspheming, (*blasphēmeō*, 1 Pet 4:1), maligning (*katalaleō*, 1 Pet 2:12; 3:16), and scandal (*skandalon*, 1 Pet 2:8). The letter presents shame as a quality the addressees can and should avoid, even when others accuse them of being shameful. Moreover, the letter instructs the addressees to anticipate attacks from shameful people or those who lack honor. It refers to these antagonists as blasphemers (1 Pet 4:4) who malign (1 Pet 2:12; 3:16) Christians because they no longer participate in typical social events and conventional practices.

On a first reading, 1 Peter's command to respect human institutions appears so decisive, one is left to wonder if it offers any sort of objection to Roman authority and imperial structures. The letter does offer such a critique in the form of a second power chain: the Lord–slave (*kyrios–doulos*) relation. First Peter frames Christian civility in terms of a Lord–slave (*kyrios–doulos*) dichotomy that runs concurrent to the king–governor (*basileus–hēgemōn*) power chain. The letter asserts that the best way for Christians to properly understand the king–governor chain and its power over them is to first recognize Jesus as the Lord over even human power (1 Pet 2:13, 16). 1 Peter downgrades the force of Roman authority by establishing God as the supreme being (1 Pet 4:19) and Jesus as the direct agent of that power (1 Pet 3:22). Instead of Caesar reigning supreme the letter insists God is sovereign. Although it dilutes Roman imperial authority, it does not dismiss it. The letter affirms that Christians must observe the existing social hierarchy even as they wait for the return of the Lord, who governs all the cosmos (1 Pet 3:22).

[18] DeSilva summarizes Pseudo-Isocrates' perspective of honor and shame, saying, "Honor and dishonor played a dominant part in moral instruction as well. In his collection of advice *To Demonicus* [*Ad Dem.*], Isocrates repeatedly uses the phrases 'it is disgraceful' and 'it is noble' (rather than 'it is right' or 'wrong,' 'profitable' or 'unprofitable') as sanctions for behavior." David A. deSilva, *Honor, Patronage, Kinship and Purity: Unlocking New Testament Culture* (Downers Grove, Ill.: InterVarsity, 2000), 24.

Verse by verse, from 1 Peter 2:14 to verse 17, human authority is juxtaposed to divine authority. Verse 13 juxtaposes human institutions and the emperor to the Lord Jesus. Verses 14 and 15 juxtapose the decisions of the governors (and by extension the king) to the will of God. Verse 16 juxtaposes the realities of living as slaves and subordinates of Rome to existing as slaves and subordinates of God. Last, verse 17 makes the chief juxtaposition between fearing God and honoring the king. Intrinsic to the very structure of 1 Peter 2:14-17 is a critique and recasting of the affluence and power of human institutions as compared to God's order. Its structural arrangement suggests two sets of social values, one that functions within the larger Roman provincial system, and the other that functions within the smaller Christian community.

Located in 2:17 is 1 Peter's strongest articulation of the double-duty civil persona it deems essential to Christian survival in the diaspora. With four plural imperatives, 1 Peter outlines the conventional values of the Roman provinces as well as the novel values of diaspora Christianity. Civil conventions are positioned as bookends to the two interior imperatives, which express core tenets of Christian life and belief. As such, verse 17 evinces a small chiasmus.[19] The arrangement below demonstrates visually the rhetorical force of this verse.

A. You all honor everyone! *(v. 17a, Public Roman provincial lifestyle)*
    B. You all love the brotherhood! *(v. 17b, Insider Christian lifestyle)*
    B. You all fear God! *(v. 17c, Insider Christian lifestyle)*
A. You all honor the king! *(v. 17d, Public Roman provincial lifestyle)*

The interior commands deal with Christian fellowship. The second imperative directs Christians to love the brotherhood/sisterhood. The

[19] The chain of four imperatives appears in other Greco-Roman moralistic discourses. A prime example is Ps.-Isocr., *Ad Dem* 1.16, "Fear the gods, honor your parents, respect your friends, obey the laws." Translation from George Norlin, *Isocrates with an English Translation in Three Volumes* (Cambridge, Mass.: Harvard University Press, 1980).

act of "loving" is characteristic of Christianity because the community is to love Jesus (1 Pet 1:8), love one another deeply (1 Pet 1:22; 2:17), and even love the Christian life (1 Pet 3:10). The third imperative exhorts the addressees to fear or reverence God. The letter continually designates fearful reverence for God intrinsic to the Christian community and practice. Fear of God carries a particular monotheistic quality (1 Pet 1:17; 3:14, 16), which distinguishes it from common pagan polytheistic belief and practice (1 Pet 1:18; 4:3-4). Consequently, the second and third imperatives capture key aspects of a particularly Christian lifestyle and reaffirm the value of the distinct ritual life of Christianity.

In contrast, the first and last imperatives relate daily existence in Roman-ruled provinces to life in a context of honor. The first command is to "honor everyone," without qualifier (v. 17a). Just as they are members of a Christian community that esteem each other, they are also members of the Roman provinces that esteem honor among residents, citizens, and authorities. The last imperative drives the point home: "Honor the king" (v. 17d). Just as Christians are to reverence their chief authority, God, they are also to honor the chief authority of the Roman provinces, the Caesar-king. Deference to the Caesar-king is a strategic maneuver intended to preserve Christian life and extend Christian presence, rather than throw it into antagonism and peril. The Lord–slave relationship, then, projects an authority chain that flows downstream from God as the supreme authority to Jesus Christ as God's agent and finally to Christians as the beneficiaries. Every reader is a participant in the Lord–slave relationship and one of "the elect ones" (1 Pet 1:1), a member of the household of God, and a subordinate to Caesar and his governors (1 Pet 4:16-17).

Master–Slave Relations

At the center of 1 Peter, in 2:11–3:7, is a stylized Greco-Roman household code that some later interpreters misused, misinterpreted, and misappropriated in order to underwrite power hierarchies between husbands and wives, masters and slaves, and state and citizens.[20]

[20] David Balch, "Household Codes," in *Greco-Roman Literature and the New Testament: Selected and Forms and Genres*, ed. David E. Aune (SBLSBS 21; Atlanta:

Unfortunately, such readings often stray far from what the letter is actually asserting, ratifying the hierarchies and inequities specified in the letter as the work of flawed human institutions, not the prophetic and revelatory work of Christ. The letter addresses a series of domestic bonds in the form of slavery relations (1 Pet 2:18-25), marriage relations (1 Pet 3:1-7), conjugal family relations (1 Pet 5:1-5), and extended family relations (1 Pet 3:8; 5:9). The letter specifies some of those relationships—marriage and slavery—in their conventional Greco-Roman form, others—conjugal and extended family—as novelties of Christianity.

First Peter's household arrangement reflects what should happen ideally within the confines of the private home and conjugal family in order to ensure the dispersed communities are safe (or at least as safe as one can hope for) in those spaces. One of the ways it does this is by leveraging Aristotle's model, which begins with master–slave relations as the smallest part of the household (and in turn the city [*polis*]), although the other NT household codes begin with husband–wife relations.[21] First Peter 2:18 states, "Household servants, accept the authority of your masters with all deference, not only those who are kind and gentle but also those who are harsh." The sentence in verse 18 begins with the vocative plural form of the word *oiketēs*, meaning household servants, whom 1 Peter addresses directly. It represents a shift from verse 13, where the letter uses the vocative plural form of *agapētos*, meaning "Beloved," to address its entire readership. The root word of *oiketēs* is *oikos*, meaning "house" or "household," indicating that the household is the central location for a significant segment of the letter's constituency. This means there are without question household servants in the Asia Minor churches who are under the authority of (lit. "submissive/subordinate to") non-Christian household masters

Scholars Press, 1988), 25–50; Clarice J. Martin, "The *Haustafel* (Household Codes) in African American Biblical Interpretation: 'Free Slaves' and 'Subordinate Women,'" in *Stony the Road We Trod*, ed. Cain Hope Felder (Minneapolis: Fortress, 1991), 206–31; Margaret Y. MacDonald, "Beyond Identification of the *Topos* of Household Management: Reading the Household Codes in Light of Recent Methodologies and Theoretical Perspectives in the Study of the New Testament," *NTS* 57 (2011): 65–90.

[21] Compare Aristotle, *Pol.* 1.2.1 to the other NT household codes, such as Eph 5:21–6:9; Col 3:18–4:1; 1 Tim 2:8-15; 6:1-2; Titus 2:1-10.

(*despotēs*). The function of the *oiketēs*, according to NT sources, is the management of household resources and even the administration of meals.[22]

It is striking that 1 Peter does not address the master class at all. It describes them and their arbitrary and unpredictable behavior patterns, but it does not speak *to* them (1 Pet 2:18, 20). Masters are not a part of this particular Christian membership conglomerate, and there is no way for the letter writer to intervene or respond directly to masters who treat Christian servants with kindness or malevolence. Christians are left, in some respects, to the luck of the draw regarding which master they are forced to serve.

The letter does not, however, limit the duties of household servants to passive acceptance of both the good and bad. Rather, 1 Peter goes a step further than Aristotle and assigns household servants agency. Aristotle claims, "the virtue of the servant [of any sort, be they within the actual household or outside of it] is relative to the master."[23] Likewise, Dio Chrysostom, a late first-century Greek orator, in his Fourteenth Oration called "On Slavery and Freedom," juxtaposes *oiketēs* to *despotēs*, reflecting the domestic hierarchy of authority. He says, "But masters (*despotēs*) . . . do not order their servants (*oiketēs*) to do what will benefit *them*, but what they think will be of profit to themselves."[24]

[22] BDAG defines *oiketēs* as "a member of the household" and specifically denotes a house or domestic servant; BDAG, οἰκέτης, 694; H. G. Liddell and Robert Scott, eds., *An Intermediate Greek–English Lexicon* (accordance electronic ed., version 2.1; New Haven, Conn.: Yale University Press, 1996). The lemma *oiketēs* appears only three other times in the NT, in Luke 16:13; Acts 10:7, and Rom 14:4. Within the other NT household codes, the more general term for servant, whether in the actual household space or not, is used (*doulos*). The BDAG defines *doulos* as representing a servant who is an "entity in a socioeconomic context" and who is juxtaposed to a master, a free person, or contrasted to a "fellow Christian." It is a person who is "solely committed to another" as a subject or subordinate; BDAG, δοῦλος, 259–60.

[23] Aristotle, *Pol.* 1.5.9 (Rackham, LCL). Aristotle goes on in this passage to say, "the servant is serviceable for the mere necessaries of life, so that clearly he needs only a small amount of virtue."

[24] Dio Chrysostom, *Oration* 14.9. Other examples in the Greco-Roman literature that place *oiketēs* opposite *despotēs* as master are Philo, *Unchangeable* 64; Josephus, *Ant.* 5.330; 19.12; Josephus, *B.J.* 3.373. Similarly within the Pseudepigrapha there is a discussion about household arrangement and accountability in 4 Ezra 7:103 that lays out the standard Greco-Roman household arrangement of father to children,

First Peter, however, does not determine the moral compass of servants by their masters' behaviors and actions.

The letter maintains a judicious distinction between household servants and masters, portraying them as independent decision makers within the traditional household. Just as the master can be gentle or harsh (1 Pet 2:18), the servant can choose to do good or bad (1 Pet 2:19-20). While the Christian household servant remains in the pagan household under a non-Christian master, 1 Peter insists that they are not powerless. Diaspora Christians' newfound "consciousness of God" (1 Pet 2:19) transforms their daily orientation. Rather than living for their masters, they are now animated by God's righteousness (1 Pet 2:24) and most affected by God's approval or disapproval (1 Pet 2:20, 25). Suffering at the hands of a harsh master, therefore, is not indicative of the servant's failure to offer a proper response to a human authority, nor is it an indicator of their disposition. When Christian servants suffer, it is a reflection of the unethical and warped character of the master's only. This move separates 1 Peter from the conventions of the wider social world because its hierarchical rehearsal is actually an indictment against the master class, who would sanction its arrangement in the first place, not the servants who find themselves subject to it.

Immediately following its description of the power dynamics between human masters and servants (1 Pet 2:18-20a), the letter reasserts the Lord–slave relation (1 Pet 2:20b-24) in a different guise. Verses 20b-24 expand the nature of the Christian–Lord relationship by assigning to Jesus Christ the role of example (1 Pet 2:21). In addition to being the Lord *over* them, 1 Peter portrays Jesus as one *of* them. Before they ever suffered for doing right and carrying the stigma "Christian," Jesus already experienced the pain and shame of such animus without retaliation (1 Pet 2:23). The reference to Jesus' passive acceptance of abuse and suffering without riposte to such attacks, indicates that such responses were logical and legitimate—even anticipated—responses

---

husband to wife, master to servant as well as extended family including kinsmen and friends. All of this 4 Ezra presents as falling within rights and responsibilities of the household (*oikos*). Within the LXX Prov 22:7, the same relationship is reflected: "The borrowers will be household servants (*oiketēs*) to their own masters (*despotēs*)."

to the circumstances. The catch is, the letter does not want its readers to take a combative and conspicuous stance of self-defense. By embedding the discussion about Greco-Roman slavery relations within discourse about the practical meaning and relevance of the confession of Jesus as Christ to readers' domestic circumstances, the letter attempts to assuage feelings of pain, fear, and isolation as well as the community's potential fury at maltreatment. Survival, not reprisal, appears to be the letter writer's priority and he wields creedal formulas like "He committed no sin and no deceit was found in his mouth" (1 Pet 2:22) or "He himself bore our sins in his body on the cross" (1 Pet 2:24) to secure readers' assent.

Consequently, 1 Peter sketches a dual identity for household servants. On the one hand, they are servants (*douloi*) of God with Jesus as their Lord (1 Pet 2:13, 16-17). On the other hand, they are also servants of a human master. The letter closely associates *oiketēs* (household slave) and *doulos* (slave), but it distinguishes them as two separate social roles and functions. In 1 Peter 2:16, *doulos* is reserved as the umbrella term for Christians who are not only subject to human institutions, kings, and governors (v. 13) but also, most importantly, servants of God (*hōs theou douloi*) and subject to Jesus' authority as the "Lord" (1 Pet 1:3; 2:13; 3:15). Before 1 Peter turns specifically to the household power relationships of the *despotēs–oiketēs*, it mentions the *kyrios–doulos* relationship as a separate master-servant relationship and then it revisits the *kyrios–doulos* relationship after discussing the dynamics of the *despotēs–oiketēs* forming an inclusion around the human master–servant relationship. Here, again, one encounters the force of the Lord–slave authority chain. The Lord–slave relation is an alternate reality not just to king–governor relations, but also to master–slave relations to which the addressees find themselves subject.

Marital Relations: Wife–Husband and Husband–Wife

Unlike the other NT household codes, which begin with the institution of marriage and then discuss slavery, 1 Peter relegates marriage to second place. The letter's privileging of the slave status is striking. Only freeborn or freed people have the legal right to marry in the

Greco-Roman context, and typically, they were partnerships of utility not necessarily passion and equality.[25] Similar to other NT household codes, however, 1 Peter addresses the wives before addressing the husbands and proceeds to reconfigure the parameters and inner workings of the marital relationship in some striking ways (cf. Col 3:18-19; Eph 5:22-23). First Peter 3:1 says, "Likewise, wives, be submissive to your own husbands so that if any of them disbelieve the word, they will be gained without word through their wives' conduct." The letter does not remedy the inequity between a husband's free will and a wife's duty. Similar to how it addresses household servants in 1 Peter 2:18-20, it never encourages wives to overstep their social role in the household by verbally challenging their unbelieving husbands or sharing the Christian faith with them. Rather, the letter encourages them to conform to the status quo by sharing Christianity through demonstration only, not speech.

However, 1 Peter entertains the possibility that a wife's actions could lead to her non-Christian husband's conversion. Here, the letter deviates from social ideals championed by Greco-Roman literary and social elites like Plutarch, a late first-century Greek historian, who instruct wives "to worship and adore only those gods which her husband reputes and reverences."[26] Contrary to Plutarch's view, the attitude of 1 Peter may be closer to emerging trends in first-century Roman culture than realized.[27] First Peter assigns a degree of agency and influence to wives in the area of individual and familial religious observance for which elites like Plutarch appear resistant.

Rather than the ideal, 1 Peter embraces the larger development in Roman culture, as opposed to ancient Greek or even Jewish culture, in which women's roles in society are expanding and becoming more encompassing. Women are no longer referred to as property or as inferior but are equal and "friends," with power, influence, and

[25] Mary R. Lefkowitz and Maureen B. Fant, *Women's Life in Greece and Rome: A Sourcebook in Translation* (3rd ed.; Baltimore: Johns Hopkins University Press, 2005), 114–15. See also Shelton, *As the Romans Did*, 37; O. Larry Yarbrough, "Paul, Marriage, and Divorce," in *Paul in the Greco-Roman World: A Handbook*, ed. J. Paul Sampley (Harrisburg, Pa.: Trinity International, 2003), 404–28.

[26] Plutarch, *Advice to Bride and Groom* 19.

[27] Osiek and Balch, *Families in the New Testament World*, 63–64.

decision-making rights. While traditional Judaism maintained that marriage and divorce were private patriarchal decisions, not requiring state ratification or matriarchal consent,[28] by the time of the emergence of the "new woman" in Roman society, affluent women had more autonomy and voice in the outcome of their marriage arrangements and life trajectory.[29] The first-century Stoic philosopher and Roman statesman, Seneca, for example, depicts noble women as equally involved in making decisions about divorce: "illustrious and nobly born women count their age not by adding up consuls but by husbands, and go away [divorce] in order to marry and marry in order to divorce."[30] Although 1 Peter does not address divorce explicitly, it may actually be forbidding it when it directs women to "submit to your own (*idios*) husbands."

The letter recognizes that it is now within the purview of women to separate from their husbands and take another, particularly a "Christian" partner, but it opposes that decision in service to the overall welfare of the diaspora-Christian community. An increase in Christian-wife separations from non-Christian husbands could draw undue attention to the Christian community. Again, the letter is on the defensive. Anything that potentially brings negative attention to the vulnerable community is resisted. Rather than encouraging divorce, 1 Peter outlines a new marital standard. It establishes as

[28] Instances that show the wife (or Israel as subject to God's decisions) receiving a bill of divorce include Deut 24:1, 3; Isa 50:1; Jer 3:8. The same notion of the man giving the wife a bill of divorce is reflected in three synoptic passages: Matt 5:31; 19:7; Mark 10:4. Although Jesus appears to expand this, including women as potential decision-makers on whether divorce should occur or not. Jo-Ann Shelton says, "We have very little information about the prevalence of divorce among the lower class, for whom political advancement was not a concern, but it is suspected that the divorce rate of the lower class was considerably lower than that of the upper class." Shelton, *As the Romans Did*, 50. Cf. Cicero, *Att.* 6.3.8; Pliny, *Ep.* 4.19.

[29] Winter makes a compelling argument that across ancient Roman sources—legal documents, philosophical treatises, orations, and even the Pauline letters—"a new woman" can be identified who is in stark contrast to the "modest wife and widow" image prevalent in other texts such as Greek texts. Bruce W. Winter, *Roman Wives, Roman Widows: The Appearance of New Women and the Pauline Communities* (Grand Rapids: Eerdmans, 2003), xi.

[30] Seneca, *Ben.* 3.16.2; translation from Winter, *Roman Wives, Roman Widows*, 48.

normative that women—Christian women specifically—have their own religious experience, even if it is counter to their husbands'.[31]

Yet the letter's radical position should not be exaggerated. While the letter writer is aware of the social trends in Roman society, he shares Plutarch's nostalgia and expresses traditional Jewish expectations for female modesty and passivity (1 Pet 3:3-6). The letter maintains the marital hierarchy as set out by the Greek philosopher Aristotle and espoused by the Roman system when it encourages wives "to accept the authority" or rule of their husbands who are over them (1 Pet 3:1). Similar to Aristotle's work, 1 Peter also tells wives to be silently obedient (1 Pet 3:4) to their own husbands.[32] In other words, the letter advances standard Greco-Roman household etiquette when it instructs wives to follow its conventions. Christianity does not present an explicit escape, nor does it commend withdrawal from their domestic roles and duties.

Christianity does not erase the social contracts its members are subject to, but it does advance an alternate social arrangement that coexists alongside it. At the same time 1 Peter tells wives they can evangelize their non-Christian husbands through their conduct "without a word" (*aneu logou*, 1 Pet 3:1) in the households, the letter also addresses the communities at large in 1 Peter 3:15 and tells these same women to be prepared to verbally express a public word about their faith (*logon peri tēs hymin elpidos*). This is a provocative example of the letter writer's double vision. On the one hand, 1 Peter projects conventional attitudes regarding the roles and duties of wives within the household to ensure the survival and safety of the larger community. It forbids wives from speaking about their faith to their

[31] Such female autonomy around religious experience and belief is portrayed in Hellenistic Jewish writings such as the story of *Joseph and Aseneth*. For instance, Joseph's initial refusal to marry Aseneth because she is an idol worshipper (8:5-6) suggests that even at their marriage, Aseneth is not required to convert. Her religious experience and autonomy are not automatically forfeited upon marriage. Yet Aseneth shifts between different religious and cultic orientations. For example, whereas in 2:4-5 the narrator describes the nature of idol-worshipping practices, in 6:4 we see her praying to Joseph's God for forgiveness for what she said and then later for worshipping her idols (9:2).

[32] Aristotle, *Pol.* 1.5.8. Here Aristotle quotes Gorgias, who designates silence as a virtue of womanhood.

non-Christian husbands directly and strongly. It relegates them to a performance of silent consent.[33] On the other hand, 1 Peter presents Christianity as an alternate social system with its own communal standards: wives are subject to a new orientation in which they have both voice and agency in both domestic and public spaces. Again, the Christian social system is projected as a separate experience from the Greco-Roman household. As members of the Christian household (1 Pet 4:17) as opposed to the Greco-Roman, wives are considered equal members and siblings of their Christian husbands and fellow Christian brothers and sisters.

As 1 Peter continues to address marriage relations in general, and husbands in particular, the demarcation between conventional Greco-Roman household expectations and the Christian version persists. The letter maintains a conventional understanding of the differences between men and women in heterosexual relationships by adopting Aristotle's natural hierarchy that states men are stronger than women (1 Pet 3:7).[34] Given the authority and power 1 Peter assigns to husbands within the household, it is no wonder it tells wives to evangelize their husbands through deed, not speech (1 Pet 3:1–2). Yet the letter's address to Christian husbands also alludes to the alternate social system of Christianity. While the wives may be the "weaker vessels," they are also fellow Christians. Christian husbands have the responsibility to "show [their wives] honor as coheirs of the grace of life" (1 Pet 3:7).[35]

[33] Plutarch, *Advice to Bride and Groom* 1, 31, 32, 37, 43. Plutarch largely conforms to the conventional notion that the wife is subject to her husband, with her interests being subordinate to the husband's and her life generally arranged in accordance to the needs, interests, and whims of her husband. Likewise, Pliny's letters reflect a similar notion. He consistently applauds specific women, including his wife, for their ability to listen and control their speech. Pliny the Younger, *Ep.* 4.19.2–4; 8.5.1, 2.

[34] Although Aristotle labeled women the "weaker vessel," by the time of the first century, the evidence suggests that Romans did not think women had to act out that so-called defect. A prime example would be Seneca's letter to his mother in the mid-first century CE while he was exiled in Corsica. In the letter, he urges his mother to not "be like a woman" and grieve, but "she is better than that." Seneca, *On Consolation* 16; Maureen Bauman-Martin and Mary Lefkowitz, *Women's Life in Greece and Rome: A Source Book in Translation* (3rd ed.; Baltimore: Johns Hopkins University Press, 2005 [1982]), 192.

[35] Author's translation. The language of joint heirs appears in other NT texts. In those passages, believers are labeled joint heirs with Christ (cf. Rom 8:17) or joint

First Peter establishes a parallel reality for the Christian household. On the one hand, 1 Peter directs Christian husbands to continue to dwell with their wives with an Aristotelian understanding that they are the "weaker vessel." On the other hand, it instructs them to show honor to that same woman as a joint member of the household of God (which Peter literally calls "the gift of Christ").

Consequently, 1 Peter advances the notion of mutuality among the community of believers by also appealing to the Torah. It portrays Abraham and Sarah as exemplars of appropriate social arrangement and interactions that should take place in Christian households (1 Pet 3:4-6). Although it identifies Sarah's habit of referring to Abraham as "Lord," the letter does not tell Christian wives to imitate that specific action. Rather, 1 Peter tells them to be doers of good and to keep fear in the proper perspective as fear of God (1 Pet 2:17) and not fear of their fellow human being (1 Pet 3:14). The effect is that 1 Peter flattens the patriarchal power structure in the Christian household. A woman's devotion to God is measured not by a subordinating posture of submission to her husband, but by the deeds of good and honor she does; her devotion to her Christian husband is the product of the honor and good her husband extends to her. Thus, 1 Peter's characterization of Christian wives as "children of Sarah" echoes its characterization of addressees as "children of obedience" in 1:14.[36] Both husband and wife are accountable to the same authority, God the Father.

Ultimately, 1 Peter presents two social arrangements of the household: the human structure and God's structure. The letter champions conventional notions about the domestic household and its patriarchal structure out of a concern for the real peace and safety of the Christian community. Its apparent extreme conservatism is in fact a means to an end: survival. While it does not challenge conventional marital hierarchies and ideologies, 1 Peter's vision of the marital arrangement is tempered with a new Christian standard of honor. Apart from

sharers with other believers in the promise manifested in Jesus Christ (Eph 3:6; cf. Heb 11:9). Only 1 Pet 3:7 uses the language of "joint sharers" to attenuate the hierarchy of power at work in marriage arrangements.

[36] John Elliott, *1 Peter: A New Translation with Introduction and Commentary* (AB 37B; New York: Doubleday, 2000), 572–73.

1 Peter 3:7, "honor" in 1 Peter is reserved for Jesus Christ and functions as a product of Christian belief (1 Pet 1:7; 2:7). By using "honor" (*timē*, 1 Pet 3:7) as a relational requirement of husbands' responses to wives, 1 Peter increases the status of women within the household from subordinates to equals. The letter further underscores the equality of wives and husbands in God's household (1 Pet 4:17) by identifying both husbands and wives as heavenly coheirs with Christ (1 Pet 1:4), God's possession (1 Pet 2:9), and God's children (1 Pet 1:17; 2:10) with no distinctions based on gender or social roles.

Paternal and Sibling Relations in God's Household

The absence of the parent–child relationship in 1 Peter's household code in 2:18–3:7 is a conspicuous silence in the letter. Other NT household codes address the parental relationship within the immediate context of its structured domestic code (Col 3:18-4:1; Titus 2:1-10), but 1 Peter does not. The letter does actually mention the father and child relationship frequently outside the stylized household code in 1 Peter 2:11–3:7. Instead of being a dimension of the Greco-Roman household, the parental relationship is a significant dimension in the household of God (1 Pet 4:17).

First Peter constructs an alternative Christian household of God by attributing to the believers the position of "children" and God the position of Father (1 Pet 1:14, 17). Birth is a major aspect of this kinship bond because it is through procreation that families are created and sustained. Preservation of family lines through procreation is a major focus in the ancient context of Rome as well as in Judaism. In a letter addressing the death of two sisters, Pliny prays to Fortune to keep the remaining child alive because "he is all that remains of the family."[37] First Peter makes a stark distinction between the natural births within the conventional household and the birth of new believers. Natural birth is the result of sexual encounters, while Christian birth is the result of missionary encounters (1 Pet 1:12, 25). Birth into the house of God is the result of God's initiative and God's seed (1 Pet 1:3, 23). Moreover, 1 Peter's image of birth and descriptions of God's role

[37] Lefkowitz and Fant, *Women's Life*, 193; Pliny, *Ep.* 4.21.

transform normative Jewish understandings of God's role in the diaspora condition. Rather than God initiating the diaspora to alienate people, the letter envisions that God initiates birth to unite formerly dispersed and unaffiliated bodies and to extend the heavenly family.

Central to birth into the household of God is a christological claim that Jesus Christ is the firstborn of the family, though not the only (1 Pet 1:3; 4:17). The letter depicts Jesus as the first and closest to the Father, and this becomes the common denominator for all believers. It is because of the work God accomplished through Jesus that Christians have not only a relationship to God the Father, but a transformed relationship to each other. As children of God tied to the same household, Christians are also members of a divinely orchestrated fraternal and sororal relationship. Christians are siblings to each other and Jesus is the "big brother." Even though they may not be members of the same Greco-Roman household nor occupy the same household and marital roles, Christians are members of the same household of God who are expected to love one another (1 Pet 2:17, *tēn adelphotēta agapate*). Within their immediate congregations, 1 Peter directs readers to be of one mind (3:8, *omophrones*) and act as a loving brotherhood and sisterhood (*philadelphoi*). The letter's construction of the sibling relationship is not just local but global. It informs the addressees they have a global kinship with the other Christian brotherhoods and sisterhoods (*adelphotēs*) "in the world" (1 Pet 5:9) and it reminds readers that they are not orphans or homeless. They are descendants of the Creator (1 Pet 4:19) and heirs of a divinely orchestrated ancestry (1 Pet 3:7; 1:4). First Peter assigns Christians a clear kinship network by naming God their Father and Jesus their Lord and thus invites readers to envision themselves as a familial band of children and joint heirs in God's household.

Elder–Youth Relations in the Household of God

First Peter transforms the elder–youth relationship as manifested in the traditional Greco-Roman household, like the paternal and sibling relationship, into an essential relation active in God's household. The letter presents the relationship between elders and youth in 5:1-5 stylized in a manner similar to the household code in 2:11–3:7. Whereas other NT passages depict this connection as a component of standard household relationships that Christians adopt and observe (1 Tim 5:1, 17, 19), 1 Peter depicts elder–youth relations as reflective of the Christian household arrangement strictly.

First Peter designs the connection between elder and youth into the second basic relationship in the Christian household kinship. It separates the elder–youth attachment from the standard household form and Aristotelian-type hierarchy captured in 2:18–3:7. The other NT household codes, typically shift from marital relations to slave relations and then to paternal relations, but 1 Peter deviates. This structural arrangement makes a distinction between Christian action and duties within normative domestic spaces and Christian behavior and responsibility within the Christian body. The elder–youth relation is a model for Christian household structure. It is a reciprocal relationship, and while elders may have more responsibilities to the community than the young, youth are not free of obligation. In fact, the letter diminishes the power differential between elders and youths by reminding both groups that God outranks all (1 Pet 5:2, 5).

A key metaphor in 1 Peter's construction of the elder–youth relation is that of a shepherd and his flock. Although this is a pastoral image, it is still tied, albeit indirectly, to domestic space. When 1 Peter instructs elders to "shepherd the flock of God among you," it is not using formal language of installation and institutionalization. The letter does not use the term "church" (*ekklēsia*) when delineating the ethics generated from Christian association within God's household. The quality of Christian association, particularly as conveyed in elder–youth terms, is determined by Christian interaction and its ethical positions toward domestic as well as civil authorities. Through the lens of 1 Peter, the ethics of Christianity derive from and shape two contexts: the city and the household, leaving organized institutional religion outside the scope of 1 Peter's vision.[38]

[38] See R. Alastair Campbell, *The Elders: Seniority within Earliest Christianity* (SNTW; London: T&T Clark, 1994), 238. For other studies on elders in 1 Peter, see Travis B. Williams, *Persecution in 1 Peter: Differentiating and Contextualizing Early Christian Suffering* (NovTSup 145; Leiden: Brill, 2012), 123–26; John H. Elliott, "Elders as Leaders in 1 Peter and the Early Church," *CurTM* 28 (2001): 549–59.

Conclusion

In sum, the First Letter of Peter envisions that its readers manage multiple power relations. Its discourse around diaspora Christianity is related to both internal cultic practices as well as external social relations. First Peter constructs and defines the contours of diaspora Christianity by its relational ethics as well as its theological propositions. As much as diaspora Christianity is defined by its conceptual and cosmological viewpoint, it is also characterized by the mixed interactions between slaves and masters, wives and husbands, Christians and non-Christians, and Christians and God. The letter envisions that with the right strategy, Christians can navigate two realities: the sociopolitical world governed by humans and the cosmos governed by God.

Ultimately, 1 Peter's conceptual map of diaspora depicts its readers as members of a global body. The letter never suggests that Christian kinship replaces familial kinships or domestic networks in society. Rather, the Christian diaspora is made up of two competing kinship networks that, for the present, coexist. It encompasses a range of interactions, all of which display two sets of behaviors, attitudes, and locations.[39] At times, they complement each other, as in the case of citizenship and kinship. At other times, as in cultic practice, they remain irreconcilable alternatives that demand Christian decisiveness and commitment. Within the community, the Christian orientation around kinship, citizenship, and cult nurtures collective mutuality and commitment to God. It accentuates their essential convictions. To non-Christian onlookers, however, Christian cultural orientations and religious practice can either attract or repel. Christian social interactions, therefore, include not only ritual practices and moral behavior but also civil and domestic performance and perception.[40]

[39] Reinhard Feldmeier, *Die Christen als Fremde: Die Metapher der Fremde in der antiken Welt, im Urchristentum und im ersten Petrusbrief* (WUNT 64; Tübingen: Mohr Siebeck, 1992); Miroslav Volf, "Soft Difference: Theological Reflections on the Relation between Church and Culture in 1 Peter," *ExAud* 10 (1994): 15–30.

[40] Wayne A. Meeks, *The First Urban Christians: The Social World of the Apostle Paul* (2nd ed.; New Haven, Conn.: Yale University Press, 2003), 141.

Part II

Diaspora the Way Others Imagine

The next three chapters present a selection of literary moments of diaspora construction extant among Hellenistic Jewish writings that imagine diaspora in terms both similar to and distinct from notions put forward in the New Testament First Letter of Peter. Unlike 1 Peter, which deploys the actual Greek word "diaspora" in its prose, these writings do not. Instead of naming their contexts "diaspora," they forgo the label altogether, opting instead to tell the story of diaspora by *narrating* the conditions, circumstances, conceptions, and challenges of dispersion, leaving to the readers the task of labeling the experiences appropriately. No argument is advanced here about whether the discernible symmetry or correlation that exists among these writings is the result of literary dependence or literary parallel. Rather, the conceptual affinity (as well as distance) that exists between 1 Peter and other Hellenistic Jewish writings is indicative of versatile, flexible, and brilliant diaspora thinking.

Diaspora conception, even as an inchoate descriptor of Hellenistic Jewish ways of life, engages a basic set of concerns that are responded to and shaped in different ways from one ancient text or context to another. These three sources—the Daniel court tales, the Letter of Aristeas, and a selection of Philo's writings—are just a sampling of diaspora imaginings that resonate in Hellenistic Jewish writings. Indeed, there are many other biblical and extrabiblical primary sources meriting acknowledgment and review, such as Esther and Tobit, but the focus here is to add 1 Peter to the list of literary construals of diaspora conception and lifestyle, not to provide an exhaustive list.[1]

With diaspora as the focus, each source under investigation in part II appears to be engaged in the same constructive social program as 1 Peter, albeit in its own respective way. Each engages the context of dispersion by addressing topics particularly pertinent to that experience. As stated in the introduction, these topics include notions of homeland departure, collective memory and myth, allegiance and attachment, return and restoration, collective ethnic identity, local and global kinships, host environments, trauma and alienation, resettlement, tolerance, and plurality. Ultimately, readers will see that 1 Peter can be engaged in another kind of literary conversation that is not strictly doctrinal, historical, or canonical but is a conversation around its constructive force as a diaspora-focused writing among a catalog of others.

[1] Increasingly, new studies on the diaspora and related ideas such as sojourners and exiles continue to appear in biblical studies. Some particularly helpful studies worth noting are Benjamin Harrison Dunning, *Aliens and Sojourners: Self as Other in Early Christianity* (Philadelphia: University of Pennsylvania Press, 2009); Daniel Smith-Christopher, *A Biblical Theology of Exile* (Minneapolis: Fortress, 2002); John M. G. Barclay, *Negotiating Diaspora: Jewish Strategies in the Roman Empire* (LSTS 45; New York: T&T Clark, 2004), 2–3; Erich Gruen, *Diaspora: Jews amidst Greeks and Romans* (Cambridge, Mass.: Harvard University Press, 2002), 122–23; "Diaspora and Homeland," in *Diasporas and Exiles: Varieties of Jewish Identity*, ed. Howard Wettstein and Catherine Soussloff (Berkeley: University of California Press, 2002), 18–25; Margaret Williams, *The Jews among the Greeks and Romans: A Diasporan Sourcebook* (London: Duckworth Press, 1998); John M. G. Barclay, *Jews in the Mediterranean Diaspora: From Alexander to Trajan (323 BCE–117 CE)* (Edinburgh: T&T Clark, 1996); Peter Schäfer, *The History of the Jews in the Greco-Roman World* (New York: Routledge, 2003).

4

DIASPORA LIFE IN BABYLON

The Court Tales of Daniel

Up to this point, 1 Peter has been interpreted as a diaspora-focused source that constructs a strategy for existing as the Christian kinship scattered across the Roman world. The letter's social approach divided diaspora life into two realities and addressed issues related to cult, citizenship, and kinship. Yet 1 Peter is not the only ancient writing to deploy and configure diaspora as a livable situation. The Daniel court tales (LXX Dan 1–6) represent another stream of diaspora discourse and imagining comparable to 1 Peter.[1] In both writings, the minority community is provided a template for living a double-conscious life in the land of foreign power holders. The court tales' vision of how to navigate the "two realities" of diaspora life and issues related to cult, citizenship, and kinship provides a useful frame for further analysis of 1 Peter's diaspora strategy as well as advancing contemporary thinking around the spectrum of ancient diaspora constructions available.

While the First Letter of Peter and the first six chapters of Daniel view diaspora as a viable identity and actual context for its readers, their literary differences are striking. Rather than a single, coherent

[1] The court tale, also referred to as the "wisdom court legend," is defined by Lawrence Wills as "a legend of a revered figure set in the royal court, which has the wisdom of the protagonist as a principal motif." See Wills, *The Jew in the Court of the Foreign King: Ancient Jewish Court Legends* (Harvard Dissertations in Religion 26; Minneapolis: Fortress, 1990), 37; Susan Niditch and Robert Doran, "Success Story of the Wise Courtier: A Formal Approach," *JBL* 96 (1977): 179–93.

epistle addressed to disparate groups living throughout a particular region, Daniel is a set of six contiguous and fictive narratives about four Jews living abroad in a single location, Babylon.[2] Although the court tales likely emerged in the sixth and fifth centuries BCE outside Palestine "in the eastern Jewish Diaspora" and were developed gradually over multiple stages, they received their final shape and attachment to their apocalyptic section (Dan 7–12) in the second century BCE among Jews living in Palestine.[3] Thus, the tales circulated among a variety of Jewish audiences, outside and inside Judea after the Babylonian exile, spanning centuries of time before their final form. As such, the Jewish readership and redactors of the tales were a diverse and changing population in terms of chronology, context, and intention.[4]

In 1 Peter, the readers appear to exist as a voluntary diaspora community living in familiar surroundings. Their geographic location has not changed, although their ideological orientation has shifted and their kinship networks and epistemological sensibilities have expanded. Daniel, in contrast, depicts a forced mode of diaspora living. The four Jewish friends, as spoils of war, are compelled to live and

[2] The tales reflect an inventive and often historically inaccurate account of events in the Babylonian and Median courts that is central to Jewish history and imagination. Carol Newsom puts the composition history in these terms: "It has long been recognized that these narratives are fictional: short stories with historical settings. They are carefully plotted but full of historical errors. They also incorporate common folkloristic elements, and recycle and adapt earlier narratives and traditions originally about other characters. To acknowledge their fictional nature is not to diminish their theological significance, however, for narrative is a powerful instrument for theological reflection." Newsom's suggestion that the narrative portion of the book of Daniel has value and makes important theological claims in its own right informs my approach to the court tales. I am not interested in verifying or exploring the historical reliability and origins of the tales, although their developmental origins in the sixth-century Babylonian diaspora are significant. Like 1 Peter, the Daniel tales are as much literary creations *from* a specific diaspora context as they are creations *about* diaspora contexts. Newsom, "Daniel," in *Women's Bible Commentary*, 3rd ed., ed. Carol A. Newsom, Sharon H. Ringe, and Jacqueline E. Lapsley (Louisville, Ky.: Westminster John Knox, 2012), 293.

[3] Newsom, "Daniel," 293–94.

[4] Ran Zadok, *The Earliest Diaspora: Israelites and Judeans in Pre-Hellenistic Mesopotamia* (Tel Aviv: Diaspora Research Institute, 2002), 55–56; Carol Newsom, *Daniel: A Commentary* (OTL; Louisville, Ky.: Westminster John Knox, 2014), 22.

survive within foreign imperial structures under the surveillance of foreign administrators. The text depicts their efforts to maintain their Jewish identity, practices, and beliefs in foreign environments. Yet there is a striking and persistent silence regarding the maintenance of interregional kinship bonds, especially between the Jewish captives in Babylon and the Jews remaining in Judea. Only the prayer toward Jerusalem in LXX Daniel 6 suggests the relation between those residing outside the land and those remaining in Judea. The absence of attention to the wider Jewish community remaining in Judea as well as present in Babylon with the four Jewish friends is uncharacteristic of diaspora discourse and perhaps even the genre known as the Jewish court tales.[5]

Moreover, while 1 Peter speaks directly to its audience, the direct speech of LXX Daniel 1–6 occurs within the narrative itself. Nevertheless, its readers are privy to those conversations. The tales thus function pedagogically similarly to the letter's paraenetic discourse.[6] Each tale presents its own independent, though often overlapping, view of the social and cultural scripts diaspora Jews navigate. Such scripts evince a double-conscious understanding, or a hidden transcript, including aspects of both difference and acculturation.[7] Each tale depicts its protagonists managing public expectations and foreign social conventions at the same time as they are crafting their peculiar religious identity and culture in that new context. At each moment, at least one of the three social institutions addressed in 1 Peter—kinship, citizenship, and cult—is on display as an issue the protagonists are negotiating. Each of those institutions takes one of two forms in the tales: either the structure for living under human authority or the structure for living under God's sovereignty.

[5] For example, the book of Esther shows an unwavering interest and concern in the wider Jewish community living under Persian rule.

[6] Smith-Christopher, *A Biblical Theology of Exile* (Minneapolis: Fortress, 2002), 9, 163–88; Smith-Christopher, "The Book of Daniel: Introduction, Commentary, and Reflections," in *The New Interpreter's Bible*, ed. Leander Keck (vol. 7; Nashville: Abingdon, 1996), 7, 17–194; Smith-Christopher, *The Religion of the Landless: The Social Context of the Babylonian Exile* (Bloomington: Meyer-Stone, 1989).

[7] James C. Scott, *Domination and the Arts of Resistance: Hidden Transcripts* (New Haven, Conn.: Yale University Press, 1990), 4–5, 18.

This chapter outlines the specific shape of diaspora existence exhibited in the final form of the Greek version of the first two court tales, Daniel 1 and 2. Although all six court tales are creditable candidates for such a study, the limited space devoted to Daniel demands a limited investigation.[8] Yet we will consider the other tales along with other important diaspora-type voices from the LXX such as Joseph, Esther, and Tobit to produce a robust sampling of diaspora thinking occurring in the Daniel tales and beyond. This chapter intends not to be exhaustive but suggestive of other diaspora constructions contemporary to 1 Peter. The first two Daniel tales are treated as a progressive characterization of the diaspora context and the characters' responses to their situation in terms of their identities, attitudes, and practices. Given the focus on Hellenistic and Roman iterations of diaspora discourse and lifestyles, and specifically the correspondences between the Daniel story cycle and the NT First Letter of Peter, the Greek translations of Daniel, specifically the Old Greek (OG) and the Theodotian (Th) versions, are primary and create consistency in the text types used.[9]

[8] Moreover, focusing on the first two court tales does not require the in-depth discussion about the complex composition and textual history between the LXX and Masoretic text versions. The Masoretic text is not always considered the original or earlier text of the Daniel tales. Like the Greek textual versions, the MT also includes secondary additions and expansions not present in Greek versions of Daniel. In other words, in both the MT and Greek versions of Daniel, redactional additions exist, which at different points in the text types make them secondary. Ultimately, "two divergent texts" exist, especially in Dan 4–6, which remain an unresolved puzzle for scholars. For in-depth discussion of this complex issue, see John J. Collins, *Daniel: A Commentary on the Book of Daniel* (Hermeneia 27; Minneapolis: Fortress, 1993), 4, 3–11.

[9] When I utilize the LXX designation, I am referring to the OG version. When the Th offers a significant variant version of the tale, I will clarify that it is the Th I am referring to and not the standard LXX version in Ralf's. Both the LXX and Th versions are attested in the NT, particularly in Revelation and Matthew. The translation and interpretation of both versions are based on Joseph Ziegler's critical edition and John J. Collins' Hermeneia commentary on Daniel. Collins, *Daniel*, 9, 11; G. K. Beale, "A Reconsideration of the Text of Daniel in the Apocalypse," *Bib* 67 (1986): 539–43; Adela Yarbro Collins, "The Son of Man Tradition and the Book of Revelation," in *The Messiah: The First Princeton Symposium on Judaism and Christian Origins*, ed. James H. Charlesworth (Minneapolis: Fortress, 1992), 536–68; Joseph Ziegler, *Susanna; Daniel; Bel et Draco Bible*, Old Testament (2nd

LXX Daniel 1:1–21: Challenges Facing Diaspora Lifestyles

Daniel 1 captures the traditional understanding of the Jewish diaspora. It briefly describes the Babylonian sacking of Jerusalem and the removal of some Jews and sacred temple vessels from their homeland in the sixth century BCE (LXX Dan 1:1–2). The tale also recasts diaspora to mean something other than just a punitive measure taken by God against his people. Here, diaspora connotes the reconstitution of a people's identity outside their ancestral homeland but where the divine presence remains active. Consequently, Daniel 1 captures the tensions and conflicts Jewish captives faced in their new environments as subjects of foreign authorities and forced residents of pagan societies.

God Initiates Displacement

Daniel 1 establishes diaspora as the context for the entire narrative series. The conventional Jewish understanding of diaspora is that it signifies God's act of scattering the Israelites among foreign powers because of their failures to obey.[10] Although the term "diaspora" does not appear in the Daniel tales (it does occur in the apocalyptic visions section in LXX Dan 12:2), Daniel 1 conforms to standard Jewish understanding. It portrays capture and dispersal as foremost an act of God, not humans. It says "the Lord delivered" Jerusalem into Nebuchadnezzar's hands, which implicates God in the mass dissemination of Jews. Within the first two verses, the author narrates a forced geographic shift from Jerusalem to Babylon. The tale, however, does not elaborate on the reason for such a divine act. On the surface, it appears the Judeans in general, and the four Jewish friends in particular, are victims of Nebuchadnezzar's militaristic conquest and God's unjustified maneuvering.

ed.; rev. Olivier Munnich; Septuaginta 16:2; Göttingen: Vandenhoeck & Ruprecht, 1999); Tim McLay, *The OG and Th Versions of Daniel* (Atlanta: Scholars Press, 1996); Johan Lust, "Daniel 7:13 and the Septuagint," *Ephemerides Theologicae Lovanienses* 54 (1978): 62–69.

[10] Stephane Dufoix, *Diasporas* (Berkeley: University of California Press, 2008), 4.

Although Daniel 1 does not make an explicit statement about Israel's culpability in their Babylonian defeat, its reference to Jehoiakim recalls the tradition found in LXX 2 Chronicles 36:6-7 that recounts his reign and captivity.[11] Daniel 1 states that Nebuchadnezzar attacked Jerusalem during the third year of Jehoiakim's reign. This chronology is unlikely, given that a more reliable biblical reference reports that Nebuchadnezzar was campaigning in Syria, not Judea, at that time (LXX 2 Kgs 23:34). It was under the reign of Jehoiachin, Jehoiakim's son, that Jerusalem was ransacked (LXX 2 Chr 36:9-10). However, the historical inaccuracy in LXX Daniel 1:1 is not negligible. It signals that the tales are historical fiction that draw upon, but do not always accurately report, the events from a well-known past. The value of Daniel 1 and texts like it is not in their proficiency in accurately reporting past events, but in the glimpse they provide contemporary readers regarding the diaspora thinking at work at the time they were written.[12]

Daniel's opening Jehoiakim reference serves a larger literary function and shapes a particular Jewish diaspora consciousness. Reference to Jehoiakim provides more than just a historical point from which to read the tales. It also carries a stigma of wrongdoing and disobedience. In LXX 2 Kings 23:37, Jehoiakim is described as "having done evil in the eyes of the Lord according to all that his ancestors did before him."[13] Within the immediate context of LXX 2 Kings, the same phrase, *ponēron en ophthalmois kyriou*, is used repeatedly as a

[11] Two passages from the LXX recount the story of Jehoiakim. While LXX 2 Chr 36:5-8 tells of his reign and exile, LXX 2 Kgs 23:36–24:7 recounts his death. Both passages describe Jehoiakim as one who "did evil before the Lord" (*poiēsen to ponēron enantion kyriou*).

[12] Erich Gruen makes a similar statement: "Most of the surviving texts constitute inventive retelling of biblical tales or the creation of fanciful narratives, not contemplation of the Jewish plight. But the effort still pays dividends. Analysis of certain works can afford a glimpse, however tentative and indirect, into diaspora mentality and into the manner whereby Jews conceived their own place in diaspora society." Gruen, *Diaspora: Jews amidst Greeks and Romans* (Cambridge, Mass.: Harvard University Press, 2002), 135.

[13] LXX 2 Chr 36:5 makes a similar point about Jehoiakim. It is striking that the language of "in the eyes of" is missing from the text. Instead of *ophthalmos*, the author uses the preposition *enantion*, meaning "before."

descriptor for the disobedience of rulers from both Israel and Judah.[14] In particular, the phrase describes Manasseh as "doing evil in the sight of the Lord" (LXX 2 Kgs 21:16). No fewer than four occurrences of the Greek phraseology appear in LXX 2 Kings 21 as a depiction of Manasseh's unlawful activities.[15] Jehoiakim's father and son are also described as engaging in evil acts in the eyes of the Lord (LXX 2 Kgs 23:22; 24:9).

In turn, Daniel 1:1 sets the reader up to anticipate God's punishing response. Just as LXX Daniel 1:2 says the Lord "delivered over" (*paradidōmi*) Jerusalem to Nebuchadnezzar, the prophets had already declared that because of the evil deeds of Judah's rulers like Manasseh and Jehoiakim, God will "deliver over" (*paradidōmi*, LXX 2 Kgs 21:14) Jerusalem and Judea to their enemies. The rhetoric in LXX Daniel 1:1-2 that "the Lord delivered Jerusalem and Jehoiakim into Nebuchadnezzar's hands" signals the background discourse on Judea's repeated indiscretions against God (cf., LXX 2 Kgs 24:3-4). The primary literary function of the Jehoiakim reference is to rouse diaspora consciousness and jar historical recollection, not to provide accurate historical reporting. It suggest the authors are aware of and at least grappling with the conventional understanding of diaspora as a punitive measure enacted by God, which, in contrast to 1 Peter, is a distinct conceptual struggle.

The disobedience that brought on God's act to destroy Jerusalem and disperse the Jews that Daniel 1 implies with its reference to Jehoiakim, subsequent tales like the LXX Daniel 3 Addition, known as "The Prayer of Azariah," make explicit. Like LXX Daniel 1:2 with its use of *paradidōmi*, LXX Daniel 3:32 reiterates the point that God "handed over the Judeans to their enemies," but then elaborates

[14] Again, 2 Chronicles' accounting of Jehoiakim's son, Jehoiachin, reports that the latter also did evil before the Lord, but again the specific term *ophthalmos* is absent. In terms of Israel's rulers, the phrase "doing evil in the sight of the Lord" describes the acts of rulers such as Jehoram (LXX 2 Kgs 3:2), Jehoahaz (LXX 2 Kgs 13:2, 11), Zechariah (LXX 2 Kgs 15:8-9), and Pekahiah (LXX 2 Kgs 15:28). Among the rulers of Judah mentioned, the phrase describes Ahaz (LXX 2 Kgs 16:2) and especially Manasseh (LXX 2 Kgs 21:16).

[15] Josiah is the one Judean king who receives the approbation of doing "what was right in the eyes of the Lord" (LXX 2 Kgs 22:2).

further by explicitly stating why God acted this way: "And you have executed judgments in all you have brought upon us and upon Jerusalem, your holy city of our ancestors because in truth and judgment you have done all these things because of our sins. For we have sinned in everything" (LXX Dan 3:28-31, NETS). Although the Greek addition in Daniel 3 underscores the traditional understanding of diaspora as a punitive measure exacted by God, it is nonetheless a superficial issue for the first Daniel tale. Rather than focusing on the reason why diaspora happened, the primary concern of Daniel 1 is the relationship between the Gentile kings and the God of Israel and how the diaspora Jews live in the gray areas of that relationship. In other words, this Daniel story takes the diaspora motif and shifts the focus from "why" it happened to "how" diaspora Jews survive and even thrive in its wake. How do they negotiate the power of finite human rulers and the infinite reign of God? How is it possible for diaspora to become a "home" for them?

The Double Duty of Resident-Citizenship

Daniel 1 depicts a diaspora strategy calibrated for those Jews forced to live a double life as "outsider" and then "imperial asset."[16] Instead of diaspora being about human disobedience and divine retribution, Daniel 1 conceives diaspora as a double-conscious praxis. One indicator that such consciousness is at work is the way the Jewish captives operate within and alternate between two bodies of knowledge and two sets of cultural convention.

The Judeans' first knowledge base is grounded in the erudition and conventional wisdom germinated in their Judean homeland. In LXX Daniel 1:4, the royal Jewish captives are described as already being knowledgeable in all wisdom and educated (*grammatikos*). Indeed, their educational background is a prerequisite for their relocation in the king's household (*en tō oikō tou basileōs*) and a skill that the Babylonians plan to leverage in service to their own colonial ends (LXX Dan 1:3, 20). The second body of knowledge grows from the erudition

[16] Wills, *Not God's People: Insiders and Outsiders in the Bible World* (Religion in the Modern World; Plymouth: Rowman & Littlefield, 2008).

and language of the Babylonians. The text suggests they received a second education in the form of Chaldean language and literature, not a reeducation. There is no indication in the text that the Babylonians attempted to undo or usurp the Judeans' first knowledge. Rather, the understanding they carried from their homeland remains intact and is simply augmented with the specific knowledge of the people among whom they are forced to resettle.

It is the colonizing Babylonians who initiate the construction of a double-conscious Jewry living and working outside of their homeland, not the Jewish captives themselves. They are forced into a captive diaspora situation in which the Babylonians deem their indigenous Jewish knowledge beneficial and exploitable. While the dominant Babylonians expect their Jewish captives to be bilingual both culturally and socially, the text never indicates whether the Babylonians' attempted to duplicate the process for themselves. They appear to make no strides toward becoming bicultural, or at least not in the same sense. That challenge is unfairly left to the group that is already disenfranchised and burdened with the task of adapting to new, hostile surroundings.

The claim that the four Jews received an education specifically in Chaldean literature (*grammata*, LXX Dan 1:4) reinforces the notion that their newly acquired dual knowledge forms serve Babylonian political aims. Within the LXX, *grammata* are the political documents and propagandistic communications that serve the hegemonic strategies and aims of foreign courts and its agents. For instance, 1 Esdras 3 recounts the contest of Darius Hystapsis' (522–485 BCE) three bodyguards. Here, three bodyguards all propose the one thing that is strongest of all. The text calls these proposals *grammata*. Likewise, the public proclamation of the Persian King Artaxerxes' intention to destroy the Jewish race and to seize their possessions in one day is called *grammata* in LXX Esther 4:3 (e.g., LXX Esth 8:10; 9:1). Also, the royal records or archives read by King Artaxerxes are called *grammata* (LXX Esth 6:1, 2; cf. 2:23). Thus, one of the functions of *grammata* was to serve as communication about the militaristic and hegemonic aims of foreign powers. They were literary tools of war and conquest used to secure, assess, and prepare for the domination of others. Within the LXX, that almost always amounted to the domination of Israelites by a foreign power.[17] However, unlike the other biblical texts, the Judeans in Daniel are both the bearers of foreign political correspondences and agendas as well as victims of it. In the diaspora, the Judeans live in both worlds. They are vulnerable targets of foreign manipulation and conquest and are trained agents and assets serving foreign imperatives.

Throughout the biblical record, there are numerous examples of marginal foreigners serving as mediating voices between the disenfranchised and enfranchised segments of a population, especially within the setting of a foreign court.[18] Classic examples such as Joseph's service in the Egyptian courts (LXX Gen 45; 47:1-12; 50:1-14, 21-22) and Esther's endeavors as queen in the Persian courts (LXX Esth 4:3; 6:1-2; 8:5, 10; 16:17; 9:1) recount the ways protagonists from the "underdog" group leveraged multiple bodies of knowledge to secure their well-being and the well-being of the Jewish people.[19]

In Daniel 1, however, there are no references to the Jewish body who indirectly or directly benefit from the biculturalism of the four friends. It seems the ones who most benefit from the bilingual capacities and gifts of the Jewish captives are the Babylonians themselves. While the Babylonians encourage the bilingual capabilities of the Judeans, the unintended by-product of their colonizing strategy is that the Jews are imbued with a double consciousness that allows them to think and maneuver between two opposed cultures, epistemologies,

[17] The 1 Macc 5:10 reference to *grammata* actually designates the Jewish correspondence to Judas and his brothers about the Gentile attacks against them in Gilead. Even though the letter (*grammata*) is an insider correspondence of the Jews, it is still an indication of its meaning as an insider political communication.

[18] The Jewish court narrative is an established and well-attested form in the MT. For studies on the form, see Lawrence M. Wills, *The Jewish Novel in the Ancient World* (Ithaca, N.Y.: Cornell University Press, 1995); Wills, *Ancient Jewish Novels: An Anthology* (Oxford: Oxford University Press, 2002); Sara Raup Johnson, *Historical Fiction and Hellenistic Jewish Identity: Third Maccabees in Its Cultural Context* (Berkeley: University of California Press, 2004), 9–12.

[19] Susan Niditch, *A Prelude to Biblical Folklore: Underdogs and Tricksters* (2nd ed.; San Francisco: Harper & Row 2000 [1987]), 44–50; Niditch, *Folklore and the Hebrew Bible* (Eugene, Ore.: Wipf & Stock, 2004), 21; Noah Hacham, "3 Maccabees and Esther: Parallels, Intertextuality, and Diaspora Identity," *JBL* 126 (2007): 765–85; Elsie R. Stern, "Esther and the Politics of Diaspora," *Jewish Quarterly Review* 100 (2010): 25–53.

and beliefs in service to ensuring their own survival and maintenance of, at least, some of their cultural identity markers and beliefs.

Daniel's notions of forced colonial bilingualism and the double-conscious praxis of the minority (or underdog) group, especially in the area of education, are not peculiar. The pattern of education the tale depicts mirrors other Mediterranean educational processes in which a language teacher is able to leverage his training in order to secure a stable situation during precarious times.[20] For example, Jewish historian Josephus describes his dual knowledge base as an important aspect of his professional profile and an instrument for securing a place in his broader environment. "For those of my own nation freely acknowledge that I far exceed them in the learning belonging to the Jews. I have also taken a great deal of pains to obtain the learning of the Greeks, and understand the elements of the Greek language."[21] Josephus juxtaposes his native Jewish education (*kata tēn epichōrion paideian*) to Greek education (*tōn Hellēnikōn de grammatōn*). For him, the value of this double knowledge is that he can operate in both strictly Jewish as well as Roman contexts. His bilingualism serves as a vehicle to move between two worlds. Likewise, Daniel and his friends use their double knowledge to carve out what their Jewish identity looks like in Babylon. Daniel 1:17 makes a glowing appraisal of Daniel's fluency in both Judean and Babylonian epistemological frameworks, stating, "And the Lord gave the young men knowledge and clever insight in every literary art. And to Daniel he gave insight into every vision and dreams and in all wisdom."

[20] In describing the early pattern of Greek education evinced in Homer, particularly the role of the *grammatistēs* in a foreign court, one scholar says, "In some respects, Phoenix, the tutor of Achilles, foreshadows the career of the tutor (*paidagōgos*) and the teacher of letters (*grammatistēs*) of the classical period. A man of good breeding encounters misfortune and must seek employment. He becomes a dependent in another noble household and because of his personal excellence becomes the young master's companion." Carolyn Dewald, "Greek Education and Rhetoric," in *Civilization of the Ancient Mediterranean: Greece and Rome*, ed. Michael Grant and Rachel Kitzinger (vol. 2; New York: Charles Scribner's Sons, 1988), 1078.

[21] Josephus, *Ant.* 20:263 (Rackham, LCL).

Double-Conscious Cultic Practices

Securing education in a foreign *grammata* and dialect was not only a tool of foreign domination but also an instrument for surviving it. Daniel uses information from Babylonian culture and political processes to serve his own religious and cultural sensibilities. It provided access to foreign authorities and decision makers who had the power and means to adjust protocols inhibiting a devoted Jewish life abroad. Can indigenous Judeans remain devoted Jews when forced to live outside of their homeland and to serve foreign powers? Daniel 1 answers this question in the affirmative. Diaspora people can survive, even thrive, abroad as an "underdog" group if they have access to the right resources and power brokers. However, the specific problems they face are clear. Their cultic practices, especially in terms of diet, pose a problem.

In terms of cultic practice, the first tale explicitly references diet as a challenge facing Jews living abroad. When the issue of diet appears in LXX Daniel 1:5, it is initially presented as an element designating the Babylonian social location and not a tenet of cultic practice. Since the Jews are now located within the imperial household, they are subject to that cultural environment. The cultural significance of food cannot be overstated. It is an important marker of cultural identity and represents an approach to understanding the social values, beliefs, and practices that contribute to forming a cohesive and stable community.[22] The mention of the "king's table" and wine underscores the complex reality that the Judean royals are now subjects to and beneficiaries of foreign cultural power. The circumstances surrounding the Judeans' daily allotment of food and wine from a foreign royal table (*trapeza*, LXX Dan 1:5) recalls the encounter between the conquering Babylonian king, Evil-Merodach, and the overthrown Judean king, Jehoiachin (LXX 2 Kgs 25:29–30). The image of royal provisions for

[22] Carole Counihan and Penny Van Esterik, "Why Food? Why Culture? Why Now? Introduction to the Third Edition," in *Food and Culture: A Reader*, ed. Counihan and Van Esterik (2nd ed.; New York: Routledge, 2013), 1, 4; Claude Lévi-Strauss, *The Origin of Table Manners* (Chicago: University of Chicago Press, 1968).

the Judean exiles signals that the foreign king's table is the seat of political power and abundance.[23]

Within ancient Greek literature and biblical literature, the image of luxurious royal banquets and the king's table were often accompanied by descriptions of who was able to participate in the events or partake in the food.[24] According to Herodotus, on special days like birthdays, the Persian kings' tables included "an ox or a horse or a camel or a donkey baked whole in the oven."[25] Other sources, such as Ctesias, estimated the king's table would feed upward of fifteen thousand people daily. Such large numbers suggest that although many people could have partaken of the king's table and its provisions, not all were necessarily in the direct presence of the king.[26]

Biblical witnesses indicate that there are real consequences for not consuming the royal provisions and partaking in festivities associated with the royal table. Case in point is Vashti's dismissal from the royal court and loss of royal rank (LXX Esth 1:19) for refusing to attend the royal banquet at the command of the king (LXX Esth 1:15). In contrast to her predecessor, Esther embodies the opportunities that await those who comply with conventional expectations and royal commands. She throws a royal banquet for the king, who in turn offers to fulfill her personal request before even hearing the details (LXX Esth 5:1-8). The book of Esther depicts the royal table and indirectly foreign royal power, as a volatile space. Although the situation is slightly

[23] According to Carol Newsom, "Eating at the same table (1 Sam 20:30-34; 2 Sam 9:9-13) or providing food from one's own portion (Gen 43:34) signifies both an honor conferred and an expectation of loyalty." Newsom goes on to note that the practice of the king supplying his own food and wine to royal captives is more likely Persian than Babylonian. Newsom, *Daniel*, 45.

[24] Pierre Briant asserts Greeks like Xenophon were fascinated with the symbolic function of Persian kings' tables (cf. Xenophon's portrait of the Great King in the *Agesilaus*: "The Persian king has vintners scouring every land to find some drink that will tickle his palate; an army of cooks contrive dishes for his delight" (*Agesilaus* 9.3). Pierre Briant, *From Cyrus to Alexander: A History of the Persian Empire* (Paris: Eisenbrauns, 2002), 200, 286–92.

[25] Herodotus, 1.133, cited in Briant, *From Cyrus to Alexander*, 200, and also in Lloyd Llewellyn-Jones, *King and Court in Ancient Persia 559 to 331 BCE* (Edinburgh: Edinburg University Press, 2013), 129.

[26] Briant, *From Cyrus to Alexander*, 286–87.

different in Daniel, in which the Judeans are not in the actual presence of the king, the significance and implications of being those who benefit from the provisions of the king's table remain. If challenged in any way, either by direct address or by refusal to consume its provisions, the king's table can be a place of dismissal, condemnation, and even execution. If the royal commands stemming from the king's table are observed, however, it offers access to royal authorities, resources, and decisions that would otherwise be unavailable.

In Daniel 1, royal power is embodied in the decisions and actions of the eunuchs. What the king commands, the chief eunuchs execute (LXX Dan 1:3, 7, 10). It is through the exchange between Daniel and the chief eunuch, Abiesdri, that the consequences of disobeying the king are made clear. Abiesdri says his very life is in danger if the food and drink the king has appointed are not consumed and their effects apparent in the Jews' physical appearance. Like Esther, there are consequences for not following the king's command and partaking of the royal apportioned diet. Yet it is not Daniel and his friends who become the objects and victims of the king's disapproval but the eunuch serving as the executor of the king's desires.

Moreover, the discussion between Daniel and Abiesdri brings into focus the second table, which lies just below the surface of the narrative. Although Daniel is instructed to partake in the Babylonian diet provided at the foreign table, Daniel clings to the menu and customs of the Jewish table: "And Daniel was determined in his heart that he not [defile himself with the royal rations]" (LXX Dan 1:10). Daniel's interiority is brought into focus here. When presented with the foreign table, Daniel chooses to remain devoted to his Jewish table and "not be contaminated" by the former (*alisgēthē*). Just as the foreign ruler extends a reward and even protection for dining at his table, the Judean God offers a reward to Daniel for maintaining fidelity to distinctively Jewish practices by giving "Daniel honor and favor before the chief eunuch" (LXX Dan 1:9).

At this point in the Daniel tale, another form of diaspora double consciousness emerges. Daniel knows and understands the conventions of two different cultural tables as well as the expectations of its visible effects on partakers' physicality. The idea that there are two tables that Daniel is maneuvering and balancing is why Daniel says to the chief eunuch, "Test your servants over a period of 10 days . . . and if our appearance seems more pale than the other young men who are eating of the royal dinner, as you observe so deal with your servants" (1:12-13).[27] The story reflects a common sentiment within Hellenistic Judaism to remain loyal to Jewish food laws. For example, 1 Maccabees 1:62-63 says, "Many in Israel were fully resolved and confirmed in themselves not to eat unclean things. And they chose to die, that they might not be defiled with the meats and that they might not profane the holy covenant: and they died."[28] Similarly, the book of Tobit documents an awareness of two tables and diets. While some Jews partook of the foreign Gentiles' table and diet, Tobit says he resisted: "When I was carried away captive to Nineveh, all my brethren and those that were my kindred did eat the bread of Gentiles; but I kept myself from eating because I remembered God with all my soul" (LXX Tob 1:10-12). In contrast, Esther does not observe Jewish dietary laws and partakes in apportioned royal foods (LXX Esth 2:9).[29] In Daniel, however, the Jews reject the foreign table in favor of a peculiar vegetarian diet (LXX Dan 1:12, 16).

Although the text is silent about why Daniel thought the king's food would be defiling, two cultural tables are juxtaposed in the story.[30] By itself, diet is not necessarily a marker of cult. However, as a diaspora people, the Judeans are forced to rethink the intricacies of

[27] In addition to the table issue, another issue at work in this text is the dynamic relation between Daniel and the chief eunuch. The notion of the "hospitable Gentile" or "helpful stranger" appears in the Daniel story cycle (see also LXX Dan 2:14, 15, 24, 25) and brings to mind the ethic of hospitality at work in 1 Peter's notion of diaspora. The idea that within the diaspora the minority group can find help and support from the "helpful Gentile" or "helpful other" is certainly at work. In particular, I am thinking of Paul's encounter with Lydia in Acts 16:15 or 1 Peter's directive to the diaspora Christians to "be hospitable to one another without complaining" (1 Pet 4:9). I am indebted to Carol Newsom for this insight.

[28] Norman W. Porteous, *Daniel: A Commentary* (OTL; Philadelphia: Westminster Press, 1965), 29.

[29] Other examples of an awareness of two diets and the various choices made are extant in Jdt 12:1-4; *Jub.* 22:16; Josephus, *Life* 3.14.

[30] Two streams of thought dominate regarding the reasons why Daniel would have been concerned about defiling himself. One view is that the issue involves pentateuchal laws. The second view suggests the issue was the moral integrity of the Jews. See Collins, *Daniel*, 141–42 and Newsom, *Daniel*, 48.

their diet within the context of their foreign captors. In this case, diet is an issue of cultic belief, identity, and practice as well as social place and acceptance.

Double Names and Two Kinships

Inserted between verses 5 and 16 of LXX Daniel 1 is perhaps one of the most obvious displays of diaspora double consciousness. In verses 6 and 7, the friends are forced to change their names from Judean to Chaldean. Two points are worth noting here. First, Daniel does not object to the name change, although he objected to the dietary requirements. Indeed, within the Jewish literature, there are several examples of other Jews taking on Gentile names once they are positioned in foreign courts (e.g., Joseph and Esther).[31] Daniel's silence on the issue seems to bespeak consent. Despite the characters' apparent acceptance of Chaldean names, the omniscient narrator retains the use of their Judean names (LXX Dan 1:11, 19) using their Babylonian names only occasionally (LXX Dan 2:49; 3:12, 13, 16, 20, 93, 95).[32] As such, the tale sets up a rhetorical double consciousness. On the one hand, they are indigenous Judean royals; but on the other hand, in the diaspora, they are now members of a Babylonian royal world.

Consequently, at the outset of the Daniel story cycle, the stage is set for the Jewish protagonists to experience a broader social and cultural dilemma stemming from religious devotion and acumen.[33] Their collective commitment to both their religious heritage as well as their specialized education reflects an awareness and mastery of two worlds: the world of the Judeans and the world of the Babylonians. Similar to 1 Peter, the book of Daniel reinvents the diaspora motif by shifting its primary concern from issues of faithlessness to issues of faithfulness to one sovereign God in the land of human Gentile rulers, who do not recognize the God of Israel but demand loyalty to their political rule and social practices.

[31] LXX Gen 41:45; LXX Esth 2:7.

[32] Collins, *Daniel*, 141.

[33] W. Lee Humphreys, "Life-Style for Diaspora: A Study of the tales of Esther and Daniel," *JBL* 92 (1973): 219.

As such, contemporary readers of Daniel encounter stories that are negotiating and navigating issues related to sovereignty, just as in 1 Peter. Like the NT letter, the tale depicts the dual realities of living as resident-strangers and kinsfolk under both human authorities and God's authority. The Jews possess knowledge of two cultural and political systems, and their double names indicate they move between two kinship groups. Yet similar to 1 Peter, Daniel asserts there are aspects of Jewish religious life and belief that are irreconcilable to their new foreign setting. Whereas in 1 Peter the issue was polytheistic practice, in LXX Daniel 1 the issue is food. Nevertheless, in both writings, diaspora functions as a mechanism that re-creates community and identity and re-envisions relations between strangers—particularly, foreign imperial powers and subjugated minorities.

Daniel 2:1-49: Extending the Theological Narrative of Diaspora Double Consciousness

The second narrative picks up where the first concluded in terms of the social context and some of the cultural decisions the Jews had to make by stating that Daniel and his three friends are stationed "before the king" (LXX Dan 1:19; 2:2). In this tale, the king has a dream he cannot interpret. After soliciting the interpretive assistance of his court "magicians, enchanters, sorcerers, and Chaldeans" who fail to provide adequate insight, Daniel and his friends beseech their Judean God for answers, saving themselves and their colleagues from imminent death and quenching the king's violent frustration and perplexity. Like Daniel 1, the second tale continues to redefine diaspora as an idea about the relations of different peoples outside the Jewish homeland and develops specific responses to challenges it deems characteristic of life abroad. In Daniel 2, however, the meaning is further developed into being about the tension between human and divine sovereign powers.

Two Names for Two Spaces

Daniel 2 continues the theme of two names, Judean and Chaldean, from chapter 1 and extends it (LXX Dan 1:17; 2:17, 26).[34] The function of the double names serves an added literary purpose here in contrast to the first tale. This tale shifts between the two different names based on the space the Jews occupy. The movement between Jewish and Chaldean names mirrors the social movement occurring in the story's designation of Jewish space and Babylonian space.[35]

After learning about the life-and-death predicament facing all the king's courtiers (including the three friends), the tale says Daniel departed to his home and described everything "to Hananias, and Misael, and Azarias, his companions" (LXX Dan 2:17). The explicit reference to Daniel's own home (*Daniēl eis ton oikon autou*) and the use of the Jewish names upon his entrance indicate the possibility that "Jewish space" can exist abroad. Although Daniel's household is still fundamentally located in the diaspora, the use of their Jewish names suggests they were able to safely carve out a distinctly Jewish space for themselves. In contrast, when Daniel is within the space of the king's court, the names used are Chaldean. In LXX Daniel 2:26, the narrator states Daniel's Chaldean name as a clarifying aside before the king actually addresses him: "and the king said to Daniel, but called Baltasar in Chaldean." Likewise, when the narrator tells the readers that Daniel petitioned the king on behalf of his three Jewish companions later in the story (LXX Dan 2:49), the narrator once again uses their Chaldean names, not their Jewish names.

The subtle transitions between two different sets of names and two different social settings are another instance of diaspora double consciousness. The protagonists are adjusting to the realities of two

[34] Collins, *Daniel*, 140–41.

[35] The examination of how biblical texts portray social spaces has been a recent and ongoing subject of exploration in biblical studies. Some of the research marking the significance of this work is as follows: J. L. Berquist and Claudia V. Camp, *Constructions of Space I. Theory, Geography, and Narrative* (New York: T&T Clark, 2007); J. L. Berquist and Claudia V. Camp, *Constructions of Space II: The Biblical City and Other Imagined Spaces* (New York: T&T Clark, 2008); D. M. Gunn and P. M. McNutt, *Imagining Biblical Worlds: Studies in Spatial, Social and Historical Constructs in Honor of James W. Flanagan* (New York: Sheffield Academic Press, 2002).

different types of spaces and managing two different sorts of identities and expectations. Their reality exhibits a pervasive conundrum of dual identities and practices the stories themselves preserve, rather than remedy.

Wielding Dual Epistemologies and the Awareness of Two Ruling Powers

Moreover, the second tale portrays the four Jewish friends possessing and utilizing two different epistemological frameworks. After King Nebuchadnezzar has his dream, he calls for only the "magicians, enchanters, sorcerers, and Chaldeans" (LXX Dan 2:2, 10). In this initial consultation over the dream, the Judeans are not included. Their absence from that first meeting moves the story forward in productive ways, however. After all, because they are absent, readers hear the exchange between Daniel and Arioch (LXX Dan 2:14, 15) and are provided a glimpse into the conversations and practices that take place in Daniel's personal home (LXX Dan 2:17-19). Still, their absence from the meeting highlights the Judeans' difference from the rest of the group, even though they too face the same demise if Nebuchadnezzar's initial request is not fulfilled successfully (LXX Dan 2:3, 8-10, 18).

One interesting development in Daniel 2 that is unclear in Daniel 1 is the belief in the unfolding of two different story lines in the form of two different sovereign authorities at work. In Daniel 1:2, God hands Judah over to Nebuchadnezzar, rather than Nebuchadnezzar just taking Judah of his own accord. At the outset, the court tales present the idea that there are divine forces at work, even in the most violent and mundane human events and affairs. In Daniel 2, the notion that there are two worlds and two types of power operating simultaneously is underscored. Nebuchadnezzar is not a puppet of God in the second story, but an independent agent acting of his own accord. Here, the text juxtaposes earthly actors and heavenly actors. In terms of the earthly situation, the author depicts the diaspora world as including a pagan king; foreign imperial administrators and enforcers (LXX Dan 2:17); pagan enchanters, magicians, and sorcerers; and Judean captives and subordinates. It is a world of various human kingdoms and militaristic regimes (LXX Dan 2:39-40). It is also a created world full of animals, birds, air, fish, and water (LXX Dan 2:38). In this material world full of human rulers and subordinates, it appears kings and kingdoms decide the fate of the cosmos.

However, with Daniel's blessing that commences in Daniel 2:20, another cosmological drama comes into view. He names the Lord Most High who is "blessed forever" (LXX Dan 2:20) as the one who possesses all wisdom and knowledge, controls the natural elements of the world, and even operates as the animating or destructive force of human empires (LXX Dan 2:21). When Daniel declares, out of imperial protocol, to Nebuchadnezzar, "Oh King! You will live forever," one cannot help but laugh because the logic of the tale is that even Nebuchadnezzar is at the mercy of the "Lord in heaven" (LXX Dan 2:28).[36]

Exercising Distinctly Jewish Practices

Though Daniel 1 portrayed the dietary practices of the Jews abroad, Daniel 2 puts on display several other religious practices specific to the Judean friends (LXX Daniel 2:17-19). One practice includes a combined effort of fasting (*nēsteia*) and entreating (*deēsis*) God out of need for a divine response (LXX Dan 2:18). Textually speaking, this combination is striking in that no other LXX passage, particularly no diaspora-focused text, so closely relates fasting (*nēsteia*) to entreating (*deēsis*) using the coordinating conjunction *kai* (and).[37] When *nēsteia* and *deēsis* appear in diaspora-centered texts, they often have separate and distinct cultic functions. Broadly speaking, fasting in a cultic context was associated with liturgical rites, such as the Day of Atonement (Lev 16:29, 31; 23:27, 32; Num 29:7),[38] or it was the precursor to liturgi-

[36] Hector Avalos, "The Comedic Function of the Enumerations of Officials and Instruments in Daniel 3," *CBQ* 53 (1991): 580–88; E. M. Good, "Apocalyptic Comedy: The Book of Daniel," *Semeia* 32 (1984): 41–70.

[37] Moreover, the phrase "he urged fasting and supplication" is an expansion of the HB and is found in P967, MS88, and Syh. Collins, *Daniel*, 149n49.

[38] It is debated whether these texts referenced from Leviticus and Numbers are postexilic, but they prove useful for getting a general sense and meaning of *nēsteia* in the LXX.

cal ceremonies of corporate confession, penitence, and the recitation of Israel's history (LXX Neh 9:1-37). Other times, it involved a small group and reinforced supplicatory prayer.[39] In postexilic contexts, such as those that contributed to the development and transmission of the Daniel story cycle, fasting is a communal ritual.[40] For instance, in LXX Ezra 8:21 or 2 Maccabees 13:10, fasting is a practice Jews perform in response to a specific fear or need related to battle or (re)settlement.[41] Like the context described in Daniel 2, fasting occurs when Jews are navigating mixed cultural terrains as they are in constant contact with ethnic foreigners (*allotrios*, LXX Neh 9:2) as well as anticipating battle and conflict with Gentile attackers (1 Macc 3:44-48).[42]

In addition to fasting, Daniel 2 speaks of two kinds of Jewish prayer—the prayer of supplication (*deēsis*, LXX Dan 2:18, cf. 4:33)[43] and the prayer of blessing (*eulogeō*, 2:19). *Deēsis* is a type of Jewish prayer born out of an "urgent request to meet a need" and "exclusively addressed to God" (1 Kgs 8:38; Sir 35:16).[44] In Daniel 2, supplicatory prayer functions as a direct and intentional avenue, on the part of the Jewish exiles, to access and seek the help of "the Lord Most High." In addition to being a prescribed cultic practice in which Daniel commanded his Jewish cohort to observe, it was a tool for securing their safety in a foreign and hostile environment. LXX Job 8:6 offers further insight into the literary and cultic function of supplicatory prayer.

[39] *ABD* 2:773–74.

[40] Daniel Smith-Christopher, "Excursus: On Fasting, Communal Prayer, and Heavenly Warfare" (*NIB* 7:124).

[41] In Ezra 8:21, the prophet has gathered a group of leaders, numbering a little over fifteen hundred men, to accompany him to Jerusalem (cf. Ezra 7:28–8:20). In contrast, in 2 Macc 13:9-17, the Jews corporately fast and petition the Lord, prior to Judas engaging their Gentile opponents (2 Macc 13:13-17).

[42] The language of fasting in the form of *nēsteuō* or *nēsteia*, appears to have gained significance in postexilic literature as a form of corporate cultic practice. Some examples are Isa 58:3-14; Esth 4.1-3; Jdt 4:13; 8:6; Matt 6:16-18.

[43] In the intertestamental or postexilic literature, fasting is often related directly to prayer and even almsgiving. The issue, however, is that in most of these direct correspondences, the term for prayer at use is the more general and common word *proseuchē* (Tob 12:8, Acts 13:2-3, 14:23), rather than *deēsis* found in Dan 2. The *ABD* notes that within the Jewish milieu at the emergence of early Christian groups, fasting functioned as the "natural adjunct to fervent prayer." *ABD* 2:774.

[44] BDAG, δέησις, 213.

It suggests that supplication (*deēsis*) from a pure and genuine person of God, such as Job, can result in God not only hearing the request but responding in a way that restores those individuals to right standing in life (see also Jdt 8:31). In LXX Daniel 2, that righteous standing or restoration is about one being destined to live in the diaspora, and not being executed within it (LXX Dan 2:18).

Although fasting and supplicatory prayer are significant indicators that Daniel 2 is concerned with the issue of how faithful Jews access the divine in the diaspora, the ubiquity of visions and dreams as authentic religious experiences in the diaspora is more significant. Indeed the religious experience of visions (e.g., LXX Dan 7:1, 7; 8:2, 17; 10:1) and dreams (e.g., LXX Dan 4:5, 18–19, 33) is a major theme running throughout the entire book of Daniel. The reference to Nebuchadnezzar's unexpected experience of visions and dreams (*horamata kai enypnia*) recalls Daniel 1:17, where readers are told that Daniel has insight into every vision and dream (*panti horamati kai enupniois*).[45]

The text is clear, however, that readers should not correlate too closely Nebuchadnezzar's experience with visions and dreams with Daniel's experience. In fact, the text distinguishes the capacity to have a vision from the ability to comprehend it. Whereas Nebuchadnezzar receives visions and dreams (LXX Dan 2:1), he is unable to remember and interpret them. In the initial exchange between the king and his Chaldean advisors (enchanters, magicians, and sorcerers), the question of who can report the king's dream and provide the correct interpretation is repeatedly asked (Dan 2:2–6).[46] The repetition of words meaning "to announce" (*anaggellō*, LXX Dan 2:2, 4, 6) and "to judge" (*krinō*, LXX Dan 2:6, 7) in the opening verses of the story express the focal concern, which is proper recognition of not only the contents of

[45] Whereas MT has "dreamed dreams," Th has "dreamed a dream."

[46] Moreover, the literary shape of the tale into a contest makes the question more pronounced. Wills describes the shape and function of chapter 2: It is "a court contest in which Daniel surpasses all the other courtiers in dream interpretation. When the king has a troubling dream, he demands that his wise men must not only interpret it, but must first tell him the content of the dream. This unusual requirement serves to increase the task to a super human level, for as verses 10–11 state, this lies beyond the abilities of even the wisest Babylonian sage." Wills, *Jew in the Court*, 81–82.

the dream and its meaning but also its source.[47] Whereas Nebuchadnezzar has received a series of visions and dreams and is at a loss as to whom he can consult for clarity (LXX Dan 2:2-12), Daniel's search for insight into the vision is directed to a single source, "the Lord Most High" (LXX Dan 2:18-19).

Daniel's prayer of blessing to the Lord in 2:19-23 (*eulogeō*) is an important indicator of the difference between Nebuchadnezzar's and Daniel's vision experiences. The blessing claims that Israel's God is the one in control of seasons and time (*kairos kai chronos*),[48] the rise and fall of human kings,[49] and the wisdom, knowledge, and insight available to sages (*sophos*).[50] In the LXX, blessings, particularly the formulaic "Blessed be God," are common forms of public liturgical prayers (cf. Tob 13:1-2), which offer thanksgiving and commendation to God. Daniel's blessing in Daniel 2:20 begins with the proclamation "Let

[47] The repetition of the word *anaggellō* (LXX Dan 2:2, 4, 6), with the word for "messenger" or "angel" at its root (*aggelos*), foreshadows a point made later in the story that the one who can tell the king the dream and its meaning is the one who represents the true sovereign power, God, to whom even Nebuchadnezzar is subject.

[48] The reference to seasons and time, or *kairos* and *chronos*, and the concern with periodization parallel another theme in 1 Peter's conceptualization of diaspora. Time, as that which is controlled by God, is a significant motif in 1 Peter's theological viewpoint and appears to be important in Daniel 2 as well (1 Pet 1:5, 11, 17, 20; 4:2, 3, 17; 5:6). Daniel and 1 Peter have some clear parallels in the logic of diaspora being framed in their respective writings.

[49] Notice the interplay of two compound verbs (*methistēmi*, *kathistēmi*), both with *istēmi*, meaning "to set up," at their root. The literary structure and play on words that occur in this part of the verse are rooted in the poetic and hymnic genre of postexilic Judaism. For our purposes, it is important to note that such wordplay appears to be answering a core question of Daniel 2: who is the source? This part of the blessing, specifically, asserts that the source of human kings is not of their own making but is in fact based on the making and choosing of Daniel's God. Moreover, earlier in the story all the advisors of Nebuchadnezzar are described as "wise ones of Babylon" (LXX Dan 2:12; see also 2:10), but Daniel's blessing as well as his address to the king identify wise ones as those who receive insight from Israel's God (LXX Dan 2:21; 2:27-28). We see this in Daniel's public confession that the king's vision "was shown to me" (LXX Dan 2:30).

[50] While in LXX Dan 2:21 Daniel blesses God for giving wisdom and understanding to wise people (talking of them in the third person), in LXX Dan 2:25 Arioch presents Daniel to the king as a wise person: "I have found a wise person among the captives of the sons of Judea who will disclose everything in detail to the king."

the name of the Lord be blessed forever" (*eulogēmenon eis ton aiōna*). Tobit 12:17 contains a comparable blessing: "bless God forever" (*eulogeite eis ton aiōna*). Tobit's blessing is instructive in that it is the angelic agent of God Raphael who offers the blessing in the presence of two devoted diaspora Jews, Tobit and Tobias. The function of the blessing, in this case, is to inform the characters within the narrative that Israel's God is the source of the message and the authority behind the messenger, Raphael, as much as it is to praise God. Likewise, Daniel's blessing is a marker of the Judeans' distinct identity and religious orientation, even in the Babylonian world, because it establishes the source of their birthright, interpretative insight, and authority. Thus, Daniel proclaims, "You, Lord of my ancestors, I acknowledge and praise" (LXX Dan 2:23).

In sum, the literary references to "visions and dreams" in Daniel 2 introduce mantic encounter as a tool for negotiating the cognitive dissonance in the diaspora.[51] Like fasting and prayer, visions and dreams are another vehicle through which the heavenly and divine realm is seen interacting with the human world in the diaspora. The interpretation of dreams, more so than just the reception of them, indicates a "divinely authorized" person.[52] The function of this divinely authorized person is to point out to the Gentile ruler that Israel's God is the real sovereign power. Furthermore, Daniel's ability to interpret visions and dreams indicates that in the diaspora, the Jewish captives are neither abandoned nor punished. Indeed, the conventional punitive character of diaspora conceptualization in diaspora-focused texts seems to fade into the background. In Daniel 2 diaspora life under foreign hegemony is not a place where God is more distant. Rather, God draws most near and God's sovereignty is most on display not

[51] Newsom talks about the cognitive dissonance felt by diaspora Jews who live at the juncture between "the sovereignty of the God of Israel and the reality of Gentile sovereignty on earth." Newsom, *Daniel*, 74; Newsom, "God's Other: The Intractable Problem of the Gentile King in Judean and Early Jewish Literature," in *The "Other" in Second Temple Judaism: Essays in Honor of John J. Collins*, ed. Daniel C. Harlow, Karina Martin Hogan, Matthew Goff, and Joel S. Kaminsky (Grand Rapids: Eerdmans, 2011), 31–48. Collins, *Daniel*, 49.

[52] Klaus Baltzer, *Deutero-Isaiah: A Commentary on Isaiah 40–55*, ed. Peter Machinist, trans. Margaret Kohl (Hermeneia 23C; Minneapolis: Fortress, 2001), 118.

just for the faithful Jews but also for the hostile Gentile ruler who claims supremacy.[53]

Eschatological Hope and False Sovereign Consciousness

In addition to referencing and narrating the religious experience of visions and dreams, the text delineates the content of Nebuchadnezzar's dream and Daniel's interpretation of it. The content of Nebuchadnezzar's dream is also important for understanding how the diaspora community navigates its foreign context. According to Daniel's rehearsal, Nebuchadnezzar stands before an image in humanoid form, although it consists of a mix of metals: a head of gold, chest and arms of silver, belly and thighs of bronze, legs of iron (LXX Dan 2:33), and feet of both iron and clay (LXX Dan 2:33). As the king observes the details of the likeness, another image appears in the dream, stone cut from the mountain, "without hands," which struck and destroyed first the image and then "the whole earth" (LXX Dan 2:35).

By itself, the dream juxtaposes, in different ways, human and divine authority. First, the detailing of the single humanoid image begins from the top, with the head, and concludes at the bottom, with the feet. The directional shift downward, in which different body parts consist of different metals, suggests the temporal change and sequence of human entities.[54] Moreover, the image's arms, legs, and feet are mentioned, but its hands are not. However, the text does mention hands and that Nebuchadnezzar observes the stone being cut from the mountain without visible hands. The irony is that Nebuchadnezzar's dream portrays a humanoid image without hands that is eventually destroyed by an invisible force that needs no hands (and in turn no physical body) to accomplish its task.

Daniel's interpretation of the vision clarifies its meaning and introduces what is known as the "four-kingdom schema." The four-kingdom schema appears to be originally a Persian invention that

[53] Wills, *Jew in the Court*, 82n22.
[54] Newsom, *Daniel*, 76.

asserted Persian sovereignty.[55] The earliest evidence of the schema is extant in two Greek authors, Herodotus (fifth century BCE) and Ctesias (fourth century BCE; preserved in Diodorus Siculus 2.1-34).[56] It denotes the ancient imperial fascination with "the transfer of kingship and sovereign power from one nation to another" with the sequence moving from Assyrians to Medes to Persians.[57] In Daniel 2, however, the sequence is adapted to Jewish history and experience as a subjugated diaspora minority. In other words, the proposed schema comes from the bottom up and is not propaganda from the top down. Daniel 2 sets forth the sequence of Babylon, Media, and Persia, which is ahistorical in that Media did not rule after Babylon.[58] It does not appear that historical accuracy is the focus but rather the message of who ultimately controls power and history in the diaspora.[59]

Like 1 Peter, Daniel 2 relates diaspora consciousness to eschatological expectation and the end of human hegemony and time. For readers of Daniel 2, the riddle of the vision and its interpretation is solved before it is told. Prior to Daniel's disclosure to the king, his blessing (LXX Dan 2:20-23) named God as the source of imperial shifts of power on earth and points readers toward issues related to the beginning and ending of time and the rise and fall of empires. Within the story, however, one awaits Nebuchadnezzar's recognition and acknowledgment of the power of Israel's God. The repeated

[55] David Flusser, "The Four Empires in the Fourth Sibyl and in the Book of Daniel," *Israel Oriental Studies* 2 (1972): 148–75; D. Mendels, "The Five Empires: A Note on a Propagandistic Topos," *American Journal of Philology* 102 (1981): 330–37; Joseph W. Swain, "The Theory of the Four Monarchies: Opposition History under the Roman Empire," *Classical Philology* 35 (1940): 1–21; John J. Collins, *The Apocalyptic Imagination: An Introduction to Jewish Apocalyptic Literature* (2nd ed.; Grand Rapids: Eerdmans, 1998).

[56] Newsom, *Daniel*, 80; Collins, *Apocalyptic Imagination*, 93.

[57] Newsom, *Daniel*, 80. See also the schema as it appears in Tob 14:4.

[58] Collins limits what can be concluded about the revised schema in Dan 2: "while the schema Assyria-Media-Persia was not universal, it was widespread; and it can explain the inclusion of Media in Daniel, whereas the Babylonian prophecy cannot." Collins, *Apocalyptic Imagination*, 96n43; cf. 94. See also Newsom, *Daniel*, 81; Collins, *Daniel*, 166.

[59] Daniel Smith-Christopher, "The Book of Daniel: Introduction, Commentary, and Reflections," in *The New Interpreter's Bible*, ed. Leander Keck (vol. 7; Nashville: Abingdon, 1996), 55.

references to the "end of days" (*eschatōn tōn hēmerōn*, 2:28, 29, 45) signal a future "change of guard," albeit a distant one.

Consequently, the deployment of the four-kingdom schema shows that God's will is actually the real animating force of history. While Nebuchadnezzar appears confident in his ultimate authority to give gifts, offer social glorification, and even prolong life (LXX Dan 2:9, 12-13, 16), Daniel 2 depicts it as a false consciousness. The dream raises an essential question of diaspora life: If the Jewish God is all-powerful, why is Nebuchadnezzar the supreme king over them? Put another way, why are the Jews subject to human sovereignty if God is in fact with them? Again, where one expects the Deuteronomistic explanation of punishment (LXX Deut 28:15, 25), Daniel 2 posits another notion entirely—namely, that God's sovereignty supersedes the perceived scale of Nebuchadnezzar's sovereignty and that God's sovereign rule is fated to outlast Nebuchadnezzar and subsequent rulers. Although Gentile empires exercise sovereign rule, their rule is temporal and limited according to divine will. Why God chooses to delegate sovereignty is never explained, but the dream does indicate that at some time in the not too distant future, the Gentile system of foreign rule will come to an end.

Earlier in the chapter, the literary and conceptual differences between 1 Peter and the Daniel narratives were identified. Daniel 2 offers further insight into this difference. Whereas 1 Peter is a direct correspondence between two parties, the Daniel tales have at least two audiences in view. In one sense, the message about the sequence of kingdoms and the eschatological hope it inspires is intended for the immediate hearers of the tales. The tale speaks to those who are outside the narrative about the larger implications of their disenfranchisement and domination.[60] The four-kingdom schema informs them that their dispersion is neither a punishment nor interminable. The other message of Daniel 2 occurs within the narrative world of the tale. Here, the purpose of the schema and vision is to inform Nebuchadnezzar of the sovereignty of God and the rule of God's will. The tales seek the recognition that God is sovereign of all from two audiences:

[60] This represents another aspect of the sixth-century BCE origins of the tales.

the hearers outside the narrative and the Gentile ruler inside the narrative. As a result, the religious dilemma diaspora Jews face in a foreign land—serving the one God and human rulers—is diminished. If Nebuchadnezzar acknowledges the sovereignty of Israel's God as all supreme, then the distance between Gentile rulership and divine rulership is reduced and diaspora people no longer have to navigate between two opposing powers because to serve the human ruler is to serve their God who determines the scale and scope of that reign.

Daniel 2 exhibits both new and old elements of diaspora double consciousness. Daniel and his friends still find themselves captives in the diaspora. They live as wise and knowledgeable ones in the Babylonian kingdom just like the non-Jewish wise men, but they are repeatedly singled out as different from that group (LXX Dan 2:24, 25, 27). Equally dual is their identity. They have a dual life in which they exist as devout, practicing Jews in their private home space, while posing as skilled and assimilated advisors in the public foreign courts of Nebuchadnezzar. The Jews' current location within the diaspora, whether private or public space, determines the persona they embody at the moment. They are constantly in a period of temporality and transition.

Conclusion

The first two tales provide a sampling of the kind of diaspora thinking at work across the Daniel story cycle. Similar to 1 Peter, the Daniel court tales make decisions about social and religious life for dominated peoples in dispersion. Several commonalities warrant further definition. First, both writings exhibit an awareness of the traditional meaning of diaspora, but choose to reinvent its message. For both Daniel and 1 Peter, the significance of diaspora is that its location demands the reconstitution of a people. Neither text exhibits nostalgia for an ancestral homeland nor crafts a theology of return. At most, there are elements of eschatology in them, but no developed theology around a physical and geographic homecoming. As such, the texts do not configure "home" as a place from which its audience is absent. "Home" is conceived as the place (or places) of which the group resides currently.

This diaspora place, however, is not without its challenges, but is a place in which both accommodating and deviant behavior occur. In both the Daniel story cycle and 1 Peter, practices are configured and reconfigured with some being compatible in the diaspora and others incompatible. Perhaps the most significant re-visioning of religious practice and sensibility is idolatry. For both writings, the worship of other gods is a hard boundary of Jewish Christian conviction. Diaspora people of God cannot participate in the social life of Gentile cult and worship (e.g., LXX Dan 3:18, in particular). At the same time, both texts keep Gentile cult intact. Neither text requires the transformation of Gentile polytheism into monotheism. At the most, Daniel plays with the notion that Gentile worship can be emended to include explicit recognition of Israel's God (e.g., LXX Daniel 6:26-27), but even that is a perspective that 1 Peter does not take up.

Both sources identify three essential dimensions of diaspora life. They define clearly a kinship group abroad. Despite the necessity of having to traverse and interact in the household system of the dominant society, both craft an alternate household configuration for the diaspora community to live within. They envision diaspora as the (re)constitution of a distinct people with their own social organization and space. The second essential aspect of diaspora identity is the maintenance of that distinct identity through a corporate ritual life of prayer, confession, and proclamation. Most important, both Daniel and 1 Peter assert that in the diaspora, divine presence is available, although it may be silent. They anticipate that diaspora people will face threatening circumstances, persecution, attack, and even death and that God's intervention may not always manifest. Yet the reality of God's existence and the certainty of God's sovereignty remain. According to the diaspora thinking evident in both writings, God's sovereignty is real and active whether or not God rescues diaspora people from their opponents, delivers them from Gentile rulers, or favors and elevates them in the land of another.

Strikingly, one common theme of diaspora discourse that is evident in 1 Peter but absent from Daniel's six tales is attachments to other diaspora communities. The Daniel narrative cycle provides no references to other diaspora communities, nor does it portray the relationship between the Babylonian exiles and the people who remained in Jerusalem. From the vantage point of Daniel, diaspora appears to produce complete detachment from one's original territorial homeland and people. The tales envision diaspora Jews, while subjects of foreign powers, as participating in the civil and social life of their foreign environments successfully. They are expected to seek the welfare of the society and rulers they live among now, with little consideration of their former home (cf. LXX Jer 36:1-9). The tales envision Jews abroad remaining devoted to their faith in a quiet and discrete manner but also anticipate the conflict and contests awaiting them in various civil spaces. Ultimately, the Daniel tales bear the markings of diaspora discourse evident in other Hellenistic Jewish texts, and their challenges resemble the diaspora condition envisioned in 1 Peter.

5

Diaspora in Egypt

The Letter of Aristeas

The Letter of Aristeas represents another extant formulation of diaspora experience and thought that has come down to contemporary readers. It is an instance of diaspora imaginings that reflects similar ideas, attitudes, and foci to what is found in 1 Peter. Unlike 1 Peter and the Daniel tales, however, the Letter of Aristeas is located outside the standard canons of Judaism and Christianity. It is neither a Hebrew, Septuagint, or New Testament text. Rather, it is a writing that belongs to the collection known as the Pseudepigrapha. Most texts in the Pseudepigrapha originated between the mid–Second Temple period of Judaism and the origins of Christianity (ca. 250 BCE–200 CE).[1] Investigating the Letter's impression of diaspora serves as a reminder that the beginnings of diaspora conception and construction are not confined strictly to early Jewish and Christian Scriptures. First Peter can be located among numerous diaspora-type renderings circulating within Hellenistic Judaism at the time 1 Peter was written that are similar and distinct in varying ways. As with Daniel, one must not take these diaspora-focused parallels to mean the Letter of Aristeas is a source of 1 Peter's construction (and certainly not vice versa as 1 Peter most definitely postdates the Letter of Aristeas). Such an argument is irrelevant and unnecessary because what is most valuable is recognizing and appreciating the diverse constructs of diaspora present among biblical and extrabiblical texts.

[1] James H. Charlesworth, "Pseudepigrapha," *ABD* 5:537.

On one level, diaspora is self-evident in the Letter because it assigns Ptolemaic Egypt as its provenance, but its theological content and social concerns also meet the criteria for diaspora discourse. Like the Daniel court tales, the actual Greek neologism, *diaspora*, does not appear in Aristeas; yet similar to 1 Peter, Aristeas addresses concerns regarding cultic practice, kinship, and citizenship. It also boasts its own configuration of diaspora themes and concerns, which constitute its particular conception of diaspora life that, like 1 Peter, is characterized by sets of social dualities and cultural negotiations taking place at the local and global levels.

Although the Letter claims to be a firsthand account from an informed Greek admirer of Judaism, historical details within the writing make that claim highly unlikely (§295).[2] First, there is no independent evidence that the letter writer, Aristeas, nor his brother Philocrates, the letter recipient, ever existed.[3] Moreover, the letter presents as factual a glaringly ahistorical detail when it names Demetrius of Phalerum, the founder of the Alexandrian library, the immediate supervisor of the translation project. This is historically impossible given that Demetrius was immediately exiled after Philadelphus, the Ptolemaic king featured in the Letter, assumed the throne.[4] Whereas the Letter purports to be produced by a third-century BCE Greek courtier, its inaccurate knowledge of Ptolemaic chronological history coupled with its detailed knowledge of Jewish customs make it

[2] For thorough rehearsals and in-depth surveys of the historical inaccuracies in the letter, see Ronald Charles, "Hybridity and the Letter of Aristeas," *Journal for the Study of Judaism* 40 (2009): 243; Terence L. Donaldson, *Judaism and the Gentiles: Jewish Patterns of Universalism (to 135 CE)* (Waco, Tex.: Baylor University Press, 2007), 109.

[3] The absence of proof does not mean Aristeas and his brother did not exist. But for the suspicious historian, evidence of some sort is still desired. Emil Schürer, *The History of the Jewish People in the Age of Jesus Christ (175 BCE–AD 135)*, trans. Geza Vermes and Fergus Miller (3 vols.; Edinburgh: T&T Clark, 1986), 3:677; Henry G. Meecham, *The Letter of Aristeas* (Manchester: Manchester University Press, 1935), 135; John J. Collins, *Between Athens and Jerusalem: Jewish Identity in the Hellenistic Diaspora* (Biblical Resource Series; 2nd ed.; Grand Rapids: Eerdmans, 2000), 97–103.

[4] Victor Tcherikover, *Hellenistic Civilization and the Jews* (New York: Atheneum, 1970), 10, 16.

more plausible that the author is a Jew.[5] As in the Daniel court tales, therefore, readers are presented with a series of ahistorical details that challenge the Letter's value as a historical source while leaving intact its character as religious writing that creates a world rich with Jewish symbolism, imagery, and language for understanding the identity of God and God's people scattered abroad.[6]

As such, the Letter of Aristeas represents an ideological tour de force among diaspora-focused writings.[7] The value of the Letter is that it is a "self-conscious historical fiction" that exhibits particular sentiments emerging in Jewish circles outside Palestine during the Hellenistic period.[8] One discernible viewpoint the Letter projects is a theory about diaspora experience and life that names three themes as essential to Jewish cultic practice and identity abroad: law, temple, and land. Although these three are traditional symbolic pillars engrained in the consciousness of ancient Jews, the way the Letter casts them is striking. Instead of seeing them as possessions solely of ancient Palestinian Jewish people and the Judean homeland, the Letter designates them as shared entities. They are accessible to Jews and non-Jews who are located outside the land of Israel.

The Torah as an Instrument of Universalism

The Letter represents one of the oldest and best extant sources about the translation of the Hebrew Scriptures into Greek, although it

[5] Meecham, *Letter of Aristeas*, 92–93; André Pelletier, ed. and trans., *Lettre d'Aristeé à Philocrate* (SC 89; Paris: Cerf, 1962), 56; Robert J. H. Shutt, "Letter of Aristeas," *OTP* 2:7–34; Erich Gruen, *Heritage and Hellenism: The Reinvention of Jewish Tradition* (Berkeley: University of California Press, 1998), 210–11; Moses Hadas, *Aristeas to Philocrates* (New York: Ktav, 1973), 6.

[6] Günther Zuntz calls Aristeas "an imagined story." See Zuntz, "Aristeas Studies II: Aristeas in the Translation of the Torah," in *Studies in the Septuagint: Origins, Recensions, and Interpretations*, ed. Sidney Jellicoe (New York: Ktav, 1974), 208.

[7] Victor Tcherikover, "The Ideology of the Letter of Aristeas," *HTR* 51 (1958): 59–85; Sterling Tracy, "Aristeas and III Maccabees," *YCS* (1928): 239–52; George J. Howard, "The Letter of Aristeas and Diaspora Judaism," *JTS* 22 (1971): 337–48.

[8] Sara Raup Johnson, *Historical Fiction and Hellenistic Jewish Identity: Third Maccabees in Its Cultural Context* (Berkeley: University of California Press, 2004).

provides more legendary prose than historically accurate facts.[9] Indeed, the actual description of the translation process occupies only seven verses in the text (§§301–7). Consequently, the Letter's limited attention to the actual process of translation indicates that its literary purpose is different from the author's assertion in the opening.[10]

Yet one cannot deny that the law remains a ubiquitous image in the text, shaping readers' perceptions of Jewish as well as Ptolemaic Egyptian culture and religiosity. On the one hand, the author designates the law as entirely the possession and symbol of Palestinian Judaism although its value and imagery transcends the geographic border of Palestine. He says, "It was my devotion to the pursuit of religious knowledge that led me to undertake the embassy to the man [Eleazar] I have mentioned . . . who had in his possession documents of the highest value to the Jews in his own country and in foreign lands for the interpretation of the divine law" (§3). Here the law is cast as an enduring and valuable cultural and religious artifact both in the Jewish homeland and within the Jewish Dispersion. Likewise, the chief librarian, Demetrius, refers to the written law as documents in the possession of the rulers of Palestinian Judaism that inform Jewish populations living inside and outside the homeland (§§10, 11).

Interestingly, the original language of the law, Hebrew, distinguishes it as a Jewish text that "belongs to the whole Jewish race" (§15) and to which the Jews are devoted, although it appears Alexandrian

[9] David W. Gooding, "Aristeas and Septuagint Origins," *VTS* 13 (1963): 356; Albertus F. J. Klijn, "The Letter of Aristeas and the Greek Translation of the Pentateuch in Egypt," *NTS* 11 (1964): 154; Pelletier, *Lettre d'Aristeé à Philocrate*; George P. Howard, "Introduction to Septuagintal Studies," *Restoration Quarterly* 7 (1963): 138–42; Sylvie Honigman, *The Septuagint and Homeric Scholarship in Alexandria: A Study in the Narrative of the Letter of Aristeas* (London: Routledge, 2003), 142.

[10] There is an array of different scholarly rehearsals on the literary purpose of the Letter of Aristeas. For instance, Noah Hacham says its real purpose is "to offer a religious justification for the residence of Jews in Egypt." Hacham, "The Letter of Aristeas: A New Exodus Story?" *Journal for the Study of Judaism* 36 (2005): 1. Tcherikover argues the main purpose was not to give an accurate description of the origins of the LXX, but to glorify Judaism among Alexandrian Jews. Tcherikover, "Ideology," 60, 61. In contrast, Ronald Howard argues the Letter is an apology of Diaspora Judaism to Palestinian Judaism. Howard, "Letter of Aristeas," 341. Although scholars differ on the literary purpose of the letter, taken together they underscore the fact that its literary impact is different from the author's stated purpose.

Jews no longer speak the Semitic language (§30).[11] Yet the author devotes considerable literary space and rhetorical strategy to proving that the law of the Jews is as available to diaspora Jews and non-Jews as it is to Palestinian Jews. The author describes the law as an entity admired by Hellenistic Egyptian rulers, philosophers, and elites. Greek philosophers acknowledge its profundity as reliable and subscribe to its tenets (§31), and the leading intellectuals and book readers (or scroll readers) determine that the Jewish law, translated into the common Greek language, is as valuable as other royal books (§38).

Aristeas describes the law as an authoritative text that sets out practices, rituals, and observances that are entirely foreign to Alexandrian culture and ruling elites but nonetheless makes a demand on the lives of Jews abroad. One Jewish scribe says God "exhorts us in the Scripture, also, speaking thus: 'You will surely remember the Lord that performed among you those great and wonderful things'" (§155). Another scribe equates the law to Scripture and asserts it has a double purpose: to enable God's people to "practice righteousness" and to keep them "mindful of the God who rules" over all (§168). The law directs Jews to nurture a collective memory about God's actions among them and share a common devotion to this God. Behind Aristeas' mandate for a reciprocal relationship between God and God's people, one hears resonances of key texts like the Shema (LXX Deut 6:4; cf. 4:39; 7:7-11) that espouse a belief in a common history and shared fate, which are key elements in diaspora consciousness.

Another way the author describes the law as shaping the daily lives of its devotees is in dietary regulations (§5). Torah regulates Jewish dietary customs, some of which are different from those of the dominant culture. Eleazar addresses Jewish dietary regulations in his response to Aristeas' questions and designates it a mechanism that distances Jews from non-Jews (§§128–30): "So to prevent our being perverted by contact with others or by mixing with bad influences,

[11] The visible devotion of the Jews to the law, especially during the Hellenistic period, is attested by other primary sources. Josephus boasts of how Jews' devotion to the law inspires imitation among Greeks (Josephus, *C. Ap.* 2.283), whereas Juvenal criticizes Jews' devotion (Juvenal, *Sat.*14.96–106). Menahem Stern, *Greek and Latin Authors on Jews and Judaism* (vol. 2; Jerusalem: Israel Academy of Sciences and Humanities, 1974–1984), 301.

he hedged us in on all sides with strict observances connected with meat and drink and touch and hearing and sight, after the manner of the Law" (§142). The law prohibits the consumption of birds (§146), hoofed animals (§154), and rodents (§§144, 164). According to the Letter's conception of torah, food laws segregate Jews and limit the degree of integration and accommodation they make in foreign cultures without prohibiting it entirely. As in Daniel, food is a marker of culture and corporate identity. It is a subtle mechanism for cultural separation even abroad.

Using the law as the basis of their identity and practice abroad, Diaspora Jews inherit a measure for judging how Jewish or Alexandrian one can or should be. Not just religious observance and ritual but also identity and the staples of daily life are at stake. The Torah is an instrument crafting a particular kind of diaspora existence that envisions cultural coexistence as a feasible reality, which appears much more doable than what the Daniel court tales cast at times. Distinctions in dietary regimes are not viewed as suspicious and subversive, warranting censure as in LXX Daniel 1. Moreover, differences in cultic confessional practices, specific to the Jewish commitment to monotheism over and against pagan polytheism, are not grounds for alarm and concern on either the Jewish or Gentile side as is expressed in 1 Peter 4. The diaspora notion envisioned by Aristeas' descriptions of the law is one characterized by congenial and productive cultural coexistence.

Thus, as much as the Torah distances diaspora Jews from their foreign Greek environment, Aristeas demonstrates that its Greek translation and physical presence in Alexandria affiliates and aligns them too. The author illustrates that idea in the king's initial reception of the envoy from Palestine and its festive outcome. The king relaxes conventional procedures regarding the reception of foreigners into his imperial court (§§174–75). In commemoration of the presence of the Torah in their midst, the king institutes a national holiday (§180), asks to dine with his visitors, and orders a meal to be prepared in accordance to their dietary customs (§180). Moreover, he suspends his typical courtly rituals that signaled the beginning of imperial table fellowship in favor of carrying out "practices used by all his visitors from Judaea" (§184). This ritual practice was in the form of a priestly prayer to the "Almighty God" (§185).

Prior to the king's act of reverence and prostration, Eleazar had described pagan obeisance as misguided and unrighteous. He says, "For when they have made statues of stone and wood, they say that they are the images of those who have invented something useful for life and they worship them, though they have clear proof that they possess no feeling" (§135; cf. §§137–38; cf. LXX Ps 96:7). However, with the presence of the Torah and its signification of the one God and God's people, the king's response corresponds more so to a devout Jewish posture of worship than a pagan one.[12] When Philadelphus responds to the presence of the Torah with obeisance, worship, and festive honor, readers encounter a Jewish ally and friend, rather than a pagan antagonist. Aristeas portrays the king as a Jewish sympathizer, or God fearer, who subscribes to some Jewish ideals and cultic practices and represents a model worshiper of "the one Almighty God above all creations" (§139).[13]

In sum, Aristeas designates the Jewish law as the source of universalism. The God to whom the law attests is the same God in whom the Ptolemaic Egyptian rulers believe, although they call this God by a different name (§16). According to the Letter, the Torah becomes as much an esteemed aspect of the non-Jewish ruler's consciousness and an element in the life of the foreign culture of Alexandria as it is in the life and identity of Palestinian and diaspora Jews alike. Using the image of the Torah, Aristeas diminishes the distance between the religious sensibilities of the foreign environment and the conventional symbolic world and ritual life of Judaism. It creates a dialogue

[12] Compare §§176–77 to Moses' response to God in the giving of the law in LXX Exod 34:4-8. Sylvia Honigman, *Septuagint and Homeric Scholarship*, 37–63; Hacham, "Letter of Aristeas."

[13] The letter's portrayal of the king as one who responds appropriately by worshipping the "true God" (§§139–40) parallels its description of the seventy-two Jewish sages and the image of God fearers evident in NT texts such as Acts (Acts 16:15; 18:6-7). For information on God fearers or Gentile sympathizers of Jewish ideals, see T. M. Finn, "The God-Fearers Reconsidered," *CBQ* 47 (1985): 75–84; M. Wilcox, "The 'God-Fearers' in Acts—A Reconsideration," *JSNT* 13 (1981): 102–22. Some additional primary sources from the NT are Acts 10:2; 13:6, 26.

between Palestinian Judaism and Alexandrian Hellenism. Jewish Dispersion in Alexandria, therefore, is cast as a livable, even ideal, situation. This is not a context requiring divine intervention or remedying. Diaspora is an ancient context in which the cultural regulation of the marginal "other" (in this case Jews) can be positively received and integrated with dominant cultural values and rituals. One senses a substantive difference between Aristeas' imagining of what is possible in a diaspora and the conflict-ridden portrayals of the diaspora of a marginal and vulnerable "other" conveyed in the Daniel court tales and 1 Peter.[14] Indeed, readers of the Letter of Aristeas are presented with a world that appears more prone to celebrating multiculturalism than to suspicion and hostility toward a cultural "other."

The ease at which Jewish culture was absorbed and celebrated in the world of Ptolemaic Egypt, as portrayed by the Letter, reflects the text's diaspora Jewish origins and serves its ends, rather than servind the historic record. However, the cultural diversity and tolerance of Ptolemaic Egypt that makes such a positive Jewish outlook possible must not be underestimated. Under Hellenistic rule in Egypt, Jews were granted "equal privileges" to their Greek counterparts, forming their own *politeuma* and observing their religious customs. Subsequent Roman emperors honored and ratified such privileges.[15] Moreover, Alexandria Egypt served as a virtual melting pot of diversity and dispersion. As one scholar reports, "Alexandria was an assortment of ethnicities and social groups. Romans, Greeks, Jews, philosophers, sailors, indigenous Egyptians, transplanted Egyptians, pilgrims, military personnel, and governmental officials all interacted within its urban space."[16] The diverse peoples of Alexandria lived in proximity to each other, coexisting as discrete social groups with mutual aims and investment in their immediate surroundings rather than coalescing into a single homogenous body.[17] To be sure, the society was divided

[14] Charles, "Hybridity and the Letter of Aristeas," 252–53.

[15] *CPJ*, n.153 C.E., quoted in Louis Feldman and Meyer Reinhold, *Jewish Life and Thought among Greeks and Romans: Primary Readings* (Minneapolis, Fortress, 1996), 91. See also Josephus, *Ant.* 19.278-91.

[16] Brown, *The Lord's Prayer,* 105.

[17] Naphtali Lewis, *Greeks in Ptolemaic Egypt: Case Studies in the Social History of the Hellenistic World (*New York: Oxford University Press, 1986), 4.

into a two-tier structure of "haves" and "have-nots," with most of the population located in the lower classes. The social system, however, functioned primarily according to the patronage system in which the fate of both classes was inextricably linked to the other. It was a multicultural environment, which flourished because of its symbiotic workings. In this environment, an Egypt-based diaspora Judaism could imagine that accompanying its Greek translation of Scripture and its long-standing residence in Egypt was the rise of the Torah as an esteemed and reverenced artifact within dominant ruling circles and among its powerholders.

The Double Valence of the Torah in the Symposium

The Letter characterizes the situation of diaspora Judaism in Alexandria as a cultural negotiation between two sets of lawgivers and observers.[18] On the one hand, there is the law of the Jews and the Jewish people who uphold and observe it. On the other hand, there are the laws of Ptolemaic Egypt with its ruling powers and subordinates. The latter impact a wider spectrum of cultural peoples than does the Jewish law. Alexandrian diaspora Jews, therefore, have to navigate and balance foreign legal requirements as well as their native Jewish ones. Aristeas leaves the impression that in regard to the Torah, such action entails not only the integration of diaspora Jews into their foreign environment but also the concession of Alexandrian rulers that Judaism in general, and torah in particular, merit respect and recognition in their polyreligious environment.

One significant place readers encounter Aristeas' view that the Torah performs a double function in the context of the Alexandrian diaspora is in the symposium (§§187–294). Here, the Jewish sages provide answers to the Ptolemaic king's questions on a wide range of philosophical and political issues. They respond in terms that are at

[18] Another scholar concludes by summarizing the very point my analysis demonstrates—namely, that "the Letter offers a complex depiction of how a diasporic community could integrate and assimilate comfortably in the life of a host country without losing any of what constitutes the essence of its cultural and religious identity." Charles, "Hybridity and the Letter of Aristeas," 259.

once Hellenistic and yet thoroughly entrenched in the Torah. Aristeas devotes more attention to this section than he does to recounting the translation process. Literarily speaking, the Letter signals what dominates the author's topical commitments and interests, which is the complementary aspects of Hellenistic sensibilities and the divine law of the Jews.

One core Jewish tenet that recurs throughout the symposium is the claim that God is one and Almighty and that the law derives from that divine origin. Indeed, before the table talk begins and after it ends (§§187–294), positioned like literary bookends, the claim that the one God should be credited with the creation and establishment of the divine law is repeated by Hellenistic characters in the narrative. For instance, upon receiving the envoy from Jerusalem and viewing the Torah scrolls, the king says, "I thank you, good sirs, and him that sent you even more, but most of all I thank God whose holy words these are."[19] Likewise, Demetrius acknowledges the divine origin of the law when he responds to a question put by the king, saying, "the Law is holy and has come into being through God."[20] Similarly, immediately before the Socratic-style line of questioning commences, readers hear one of Jerusalem's own priests make the claim, in his stylized prayer, that God is Almighty (*ho pantokratōr theos*). The attribution of God as *pantokratōr* is frequent in the LXX and expresses a fundamental claim of Torah-based belief: that God alone is sovereign.[21] Within the Hellenistic court of the Ptolemaic king, the essential claim of Judaism regarding the oneness and sovereignty of God is not just made but embraced by its Gentile hosts, in a Hellenistic, pagan guise.

The author attests to the central role God plays even in Hellenistic issues of politics and justice (§209), philosophy and morality (§256), sociopolitical relationships (§228), and military tactics and standing

[19] See Josephus' version of this event in *Ant.* 12.90; Hadas, *Aristeas*, 169.

[20] Hadas, *Aristeas*, 223. Hadas correctly notes, "the insistence on the divine origin of the Law is an interesting foreshadowing of Philo." In the next chapter, we see how Philo develops this claim in his own work, particularly in regard to the lived experience of diaspora at the juncture between the Hellenistic world and Jewish sensibilities.

[21] For the specific phrase *pantokratōr theos*, in which God's sovereignty is underscored, see 2 Sam 7:25, 27; 1 Chr 17:24; 2 Macc 8:18; 3 Macc 6:2; Sir 50:17.

(§193).[22] Indeed, the topics discussed and content of the questions and answers is not overtly Jewish. The king does not ask specific questions about Judaism, its practices, and doctrines, nor do the priests respond with that as the content of their answers. The overt Jewishness of the priests' responses hinges on their constant reassertion, regardless of their answers, that their God is one and sovereign above all. The obvious indicator of this strong Jewish attitude appears in the second sage's answer. Here, the king inquired about "what was his best course in all his actions." The second sage provides a stock Jewish answer: "making your starting-point the fear of God" (§189, cf. §§200, 201). The intimation that the fear of God is the beginning of all knowledge and wisdom parallels similar claims made in Jewish wisdom literature (LXX Prov 1:7).

The notion that the Jews are more advanced than the Hellenistic philosophers because they place God in first position persists throughout the Letter and parallels a similar claim made in LXX Dan 1:20 about the four Jewish captives: "And in all matters of wisdom and understanding that the king inquired of them, he found them ten times better than all the magicians and enchanters that were in all his realm."[23] While the Daniel passage does not explicitly mention the Torah as the source of the diaspora Jews' acumen, Aristeas does. The pagan officials' and sages' assessment of the Jewish sages always includes a positive valuation of the Torah as the source of their knowledge and insight. For instance, after the first day of table talk, the king expresses his approval: "I think the virtue of these men is extraordinary and their understanding very great, for having questions of such a sort addressed to them they have given proper replies on the spur of the moment, all of them making God the starting-point of their reasoning" (§200).

Aristeas conveys the dual function of the Torah as both an instrument of Jewish identity and asset of Hellenistic culture by demonstrating its value as a source for Hellenistic political philosophy and militaristic strategizing. To questions regarding building political alliances and

[22] Josephus, *Ant.* 99; translation taken from Hadas, *Aristeas*, 173nn187–300.

[23] Hadas makes this connection and quotes the same Dan 1:20 passage as parallel to the Letter of Aristeas 235; Hadas, *Aristeas*, 192n235.

ensuring a stable imperial rule, the sages constantly appeal to God as model.[24] They make statements such as "by noticing how God acts" (§190) and "regard the methods of God" (§191). In fact, the eleventh Jewish respondent concludes his response to the king stating that God's "example must be followed" (§205). Likewise, in response to the king's various questions about securing military success and imperial succession, the sages tell him to "call always upon God" (§§193, 226), pray "always to God" (§196), and "entreat God" (§227). The reason for appealing to God is because, according to Aristeas' symposium, even for pagan rulers, "it is God who apportions fame and great wealth to all kings, and that no one is king by his own power" (§§224, 244).[25] Again, Aristeas asserts through the Jews' responses that God is the orchestrator of all history, both Jewish and Hellenistic.

In addition to Jewish elements and symbols, Aristeas' symposium exhibits contexts, symbols, and perceptions particular to Hellenism. In terms of literary context, like the symposia of Xenophon and Plato, Aristeas' scene is likely more a work of fiction than non-fiction. Both Xenophon and Plato recount Hellenistic banquet feasts in which Socrates and his companions are invited. Although their cast of characters and conversations are different, both accounts place Socrates at the center as a major interlocutor. Both Xenophon's and Plato's versions acknowledge overtly that the purpose of the banquet-styled dialogue is to entertain (Xen., *Symp.* 1.5) and provide a platform for "profound and lengthy discourse" (Xen., *Symp.* 1.6).[26] Similar to Xenophon's and Plato's versions, the purpose of Aristeas' banquet-style dialogue and philosophical discussion is explicitly merriment (Letter §186) and hearing from and considering the advice of wise and learned counsel beneficial to rulership (§286).[27]

Yet,the degree to which Aristeas' symposium mirrors Xenophon and Plato's versions is also limited. When compared to the latter, one is struck by the ways Aristeas' dialogue is a one-way exchange

[24] Günther Zuntz, "Aristeas Studies," *JSS* 4 (1959): 21–36.

[25] Hadas, *Aristeas*, 187.

[26] Marchant, LCL.

[27] Hadas, *Aristeas*, 212n286. This is opposed to what we see in Xenophon's *Symposium* where music provides the rhetorical situation and narrative frame through which the discussion unfolds.

between Hellenistic king and Jewish scribes. King Ptolemy Philadelphus asks a question to a single sage, and they respond with pithy and insightful truisms. In contrast, both Xenophon's and Plato's symposia unfold as a series of back-and-forth exchanges between Socrates and the other banquet participants. The conversations unfold as a combination of dialogues, statements, questions, and amplifications, not just quick question-and-answer sessions. Aristeas' inquiry and response session is closer in form to other Hellenistic banquet symposium-style accounts, such as Plutarch's *The Dinner of the Seven Wise Men*,[28] or the brief question-and-answer session between Alexander and the Gymnosophists narrated in *The Life of Alexander*,[29] or even Jewish portrayals of the exchange of wits between King Solomon and others in 1 Kings.[30]

In addition to resembling popular literary forms among pagan and Jewish Hellenistic literature, the Letter contains topoi prevalent in Hellenistic philosophy.[31] One set of questions and answers address stock themes, such as sleep (§213),[32] envy (§224),[33] friendship (§§225, 228, 265),[34] and grief (§232, 268).[35] The other set of topoi directly

[28] Plutarch, *The Dinner of the Seven Wise Men* (vol. 2; *Moralia*; LCL 222; Cambridge, Mass.: Harvard University Press, 1956), 270.

[29] Plutarch, *Alex.* 64.

[30] See King Solomon and Queen of Sheba (LXX 1 Kgs 10:1-3) or Josephus' description of the circumstances surrounding the exchanges between the King of Tyre and Solomon (Josephus, *Ap.* 1:114-120). These references and this point are indebted to Murray's observations. See Oswyn Murray, "Aristeas and Ptolemaic Kingship," *JTS* N.S. 18 (1967): 347.

[31] Murray, "Aristeas and Ptolemaic Kingship," 349.

[32] Cf. Sextus Empiricus, *Modes* 104; translated in Brad Inwood and Lloyd P. Gerson, *Hellenistic Philosophy: Introductory Readings* (Indianapolis: Hackett, 1988), 332.

[33] Cf. Plutarch, *On Envy and Hate* 536F (See also the article by Luke Timothy Johnson, "James 3:13–4:10 and the Topos Peri Phthonou," *Novum Testamentum* 25 (1983): 327–47. See also references and quotes of Thucydides 2.45 and Demosthenes 18.315 referenced in George Alexander Kennedy, *Progymnasmata: Greek Textbooks of Prose and Composition and Rhetoric* (SBLWGRW 10; Atlanta: SBL, 2003), 7.

[34] Cf. Plutarch, *Pleasant Life* 19; Aristotle, *Pol.* 1287B. See Luke Timothy Johnson, *Sharing Possessions: What Faith Demands* (2nd ed.; Grand Rapids: Eerdmans, 2011), 113, 118–20.

[35] Cf. Aristides, *Orations* 3.672; Cicero, *Tusc.* 3.76, referenced in J. Sihvola and T. Engberg-Pedersen, eds., *The Emotions in Hellenistic Philosophy* (The New Synthese

address the nature of kingship, particularly the nature of Hellenistic kingship, such as the qualifications of kings (§§209), the preservation of kingship (§§187, 245, 271), the goals of kingship (§§283, 291), and appropriate kingly action (§§267).[36] Whether the Jews are addressing general Hellenistic philosophical themes or Hellenistic kingship concerns, they constantly return, in some form and fashion, to a central tenet of Jewish thought: "God governs the whole world . . . [and] God's example, Your Majesty, you must follow."[37]

The constant fusion of Hellenistic imperial concerns and context with Jewish epistemology and symbols in the Letter demonstrates the Torah's relevance as well as the Letter writer's sensitivity to the situation of diaspora Judaism. The back and forth between Hellenistic king and Jewish sages in the symposium illustrates the Torah's double function. It both distinguishes Torah observers, Jewish or not, from the pagan world while also rooting them in that same world. The coalescence of Jewish monotheism and universal philosophy is epitomized when the king asks what the highest good for life is and the Jewish priest responds, "The realization that God rules all things, and that in our fairest achievements it is not we ourselves who accomplish our intentions, but God in His sovereignty consummates, and guides the actions of us all."[38] This is not an incidental expression. It represents the intersection between Hellenistic thought and Torah-based conviction.[39] Wielding the Torah as the chief image, Aristeas reportedly casts diaspora as synonymous with coexistence and mutuality. Instead of erasing the distinctions of discrete social groups and imagining a transformed homogenous population, the Letter presents the Torah as a point of unity, not uniformity, between complementary and symbiotic groups.

Historical Library 46; Dordrecht: Kluwer, 1998), 123.

[36] Erwin R. Goodenough, "The Political Philosophy of Hellenistic Kingship," *YCS* 1 (1928): 53–102; James L. O'Neal, "Royal Authority and City Law under Alexander and His Hellenistic Successors," *Classical Quarterly* 50 (2000): 424–31; J. Joel Farber, "The Cyropaedia and Hellenistic Kingship," *American Journal of Philology* 100 (1979): 497–514.

[37] Hadas, *Aristeas*, 201.

[38] Hadas, *Aristeas*, 177.

[39] Quoted by Honigman, *Septuagint and Homeric Scholarship*, 146.

Temple as a Symbol of Jewish Identity and Object of Ptolemaic Admiration

Another essential aspect of diaspora Judaism in Egypt, as conceived by Aristeas, is proper appreciation for the impressive image and necessary function the Jerusalem temple performs in the life of the Jew, whether local or abroad. In addition to being the site of the Jewish sacrificial system, the Letter goes to great lengths to portray the temple as the iconic symbol of the land of God's people as captured in the Torah. Forget the war-torn and tenuous political stability of Hasmonean Palestine. Aristeas calls the Alexandrian readers, whether Jew or Gentile, to see the Land of Israel as the Torah sees it: sacred, beneficent, and interminable.[40]

In an oddly shaped travelogue (§§83–119), Aristeas glorifies the temple in Jerusalem and expands its sphere of influence.[41] Rather than specific events occurring on the way to Jerusalem, Aristeas jumps ahead to describe what he observes upon reaching the city (§83). In his description, he treats only certain features of the temple. These features include its physical location (§§84–88), water supply and sewage system (§§88–91), priestly school and the high priest's vestments (§§96–99), the citadel and its garrison (§§100–104), ritual function (§§105–12), and the advantages of its larger geographic environs (§§113–18).[42] According to the author, not only does the image of the temple inspire awe and loyalty in Jews, but its renown and aesthetic evoke admiration and fidelity from non-Jews as well.

[40] Tcherikover, "Ideology," 78–79.

[41] In reference to the book of Acts, Dibelius provides a good rehearsal of the travelogue form in Hellenistic literature. Martin Dibelius, "Style Criticism and the Book of Acts," in *Studies in Acts of the Apostles*, ed. Heinrich Greeven, trans. Mary Ling (London: SCM Press, 1956), 6–7, 86. See 1 Cor 4:14-21; Gal 4:12-20; Philippians 2:19-30; Luke 9:52–19:10, Acts 20:1–21:17.

[42] Jonathan A. Goldstein, "The Message of Aristeas to Philokrates: In the Second Century B.C.E., Obey the Torah, Venerate the Temple of Jerusalem, but Speak Greek, and Put Your Hopes in the Ptolemaic Dynasty," in *Eretz Israel, Israel and the Jewish Diaspora Mutual Relation: Proceedings of the First Annual Symposium of the Philip M. and Ethel Klutznick Chair in Jewish Civilization Held on Sunday–Monday October 9–10, 1988*, ed. Menachem Mor (Studies in Jewish Civilization 1; Lanham, Md.: University Press of America, 1991), 2–3.

Aristeas' travelogue starts by treating the temple's location in Jerusalem. He describes it as situated "on the top of the hill" and "towering above all" (§84). For the author, the temple's spatial location indicates its pride of place in the Judean countryside as well as the Jewish imagination. Indeed, Aristeas' description of the temple represents an idealized vision of the temple and is reminiscent of prophetic descriptions in LXX Isaiah 2:2, Micah 4:1, and Ezekiel 47:1. When, for example, he describes the temple as a place with "an inexhaustible supply of water" and "an abundant natural spring" gushing up from within it (§89), Aristeas expresses a nostalgic view. In terms of its historicity, one scholar states, "There never was a natural spring within the Temple," denying the possibility that the text provides an accurate description.[43]

One aspect of the historical Jerusalem temple the text captures accurately is its cultic function. Aristeas continually reminds the reader that the temple is the location of Jewish cultic sacrifice (*thysion*). Through repeated references to temple sacrifice and its ritual and purity functions, Aristeas distances the form of Jewish sacrifice from pagan sacrifice.[44] The author states that accompanying the king's initial request for Eleazar's support of the translation endeavor is money from the king to support temple sacrifice (§§33, 44). Eleazar extols publically the king's gifts and, in turn, confirms the unique form of sacrifice performed in the Jewish temple. "We also showed them [local Jerusalemites] the vessels which you sent . . . and for the performance of the sacrifices and the furnishing of the Temple requirements one hundred talents of silver" (§42).

In the travelogue section, Aristeas also describes in a reverential manner the details of the temple's sacrificial space. For instance, the author says, "The entire floor is paved with stones and slopes down to the appointed places, that water may be conveyed to wash away

[43] Quoted and referenced in Tcherikover, "Ideology," 77n37.

[44] Other Greek texts attest to the distinction between Jewish and pagan sacrificial forms. For example, Diodorus Siculus, a contemporary text to the Letter of Aristeas, states, "But Moses so arranged the rites and ceremonies of the sacrifices, and the manner and nature of their customs, as that they should be wholly different from all other nations." Diodorus Siculus 40.3, referenced in Hadas, *Aristeas*, 134n88, but not quoted.

the blood from the sacrifices, for many thousand beasts are sacrificed there on the feast days" (§88). Likewise, in describing the temple guards, specifically the citadel garrison, the author says, "They were very reluctant to admit us—though we were but two unarmed men—to view the offering of the sacrifices" (§103). The image of the citadel garrison Aristeas provides is in stark contrast to the image of the citadel garrison Seleucid Antiochus IV supposedly stationed there around 164 BCE. First Maccabees 1:33-40 calls that contingency a "breed of sinners," who were "disloyal to Judaea and to the Torah."[45] Here, the Letter projects the idea that the Torah is observed and the sanctity of Jewish sacrifice protected by zealots of a militaristic order.

Within this literary context, where the author depicts the sacrificial space in the temple, he also references Jewish feast days (*heortoœn*, §§88, 102). In each case, the emphasis is on "the ceremonial character of the eating rather than upon the extent of what was eaten."[46] Although he never specifies the nature of the feasts or names particular holidays, Aristeas maintains that the temple is the environ for pious animal sacrifice and celebratory Jewish commemoration. Again, the historical veracity of his descriptions are questionable, but the image of the temple's function remains sound.

Yet Aristeas never refers to the temple as the "house of God" (*ho oikos tou theou*). This is striking given that it is a common attribution for the temple that other Hellenistic diaspora texts frequently employ (LXX Ezra 4:24; 5:2, 13; 6:7-8). This label, however, is more than just an alternate appellation. It signals another dimension—rather important dimension—of the temple's function: to house the presence of God. Observing sacrificial rites in the temple and Jewish pilgrimage holidays to Jerusalem are also about devotees being in the actual place where God resides. One provocative example of the correspondence between devout Jewish worship of God and the house of God is evident in David's response to the death of his child. In LXX 2 Samuel

[45] Quoted in Goldstein, "Message of Aristeas," 11; Goldstein, *II Maccabees* (vol. 41A; Garden City, N.Y.: Doubleday, 1983), 106–9.

[46] J. P. Louw and Eugene Albert Nida, *Greek–English Lexicon of the New Testament: Based on Semantic Domains* (New York: United Bible Societies, 1996 [1989]), 529.

12:20 he is said to have entered into the house of God and offered obeisance (*prosekynēsen*).

While the temple receives significant acclaim in the Letter of Aristeas, it is never portrayed as the sole place for which God is encountered and can be worshiped (*prosekynēsen*). As mentioned above, the king performs a similar act of worship (*prosekynēsen*) as the one David performed. In this case, however, the written Torah is the medium that mediates God's presence, not the temple edifice. With the presence of the Torah, God is accessible to diaspora Judaism and the pagans of foreign environs even though the rightful place of sacrificial offerings remains with the Jerusalem temple. Even as the Letter romanticizes the temple, it simultaneously diminishes the idea that it is the single location for the presence of God.

Lands of Multiple Attachments and Mutual Commitments

At the beginning of the letter, readers encounter a conventional category of diaspora life—namely, the attachment dispersed Jewish communities have to their original homeland. In the opening, Aristeas introduces the nature of his literary project as a "trustworthy narrative." He defines his aim to detail the exchange between Egyptian society and Palestinian Jews—embodied in the high priest figure, Eleazar. Initially, it appears the author juxtaposes Egyptian to Jew. He uses the pronoun "we" as an attribution for his Ptolemaic envoy as opposed to "they," which often refers to Palestinian Jews (§§11, 16). Moreover, the presence of "we-passages" in the Letter functions as a standard literary device of travelogues and is an ancient rhetorical mechanism for crafting compelling narrative events.[47]

However, as the narrative unfolds one realizes that the relationships Aristeas depicts are much more complex and varied than merely

[47] Stanley E. Porter, "Excursus: The 'We' Passages," in *The Book of Acts in Its Graeco-Roman Setting*, ed. David W. J. Gill and Conrad Gempf (Grand Rapids: Eerdmans, 1994), 545–74. Also in the same collection, see the essay by Brian M. Rapske, "Acts, Travel, and Shipwreck," 1–48. See also William S. Campbell, *The "We" Passages in the Acts of the Apostles: The Narrator as Narrative Character* (Studies in Biblical Literature; Atlanta: SBL, 2007), 4–10, 88.

Egyptian Jew dichotomies. The author describes a variety of social relationships or kinships, which exhibit varying concerns and different types of attachment to the land of Judea. Like in Daniel, the Greek term for diaspora—meaning a forcibly dislocated people by God's act—is not used in Aristeas. However, the negative connotation of diaspora as a forced dislocation and relocation is expressed. In §4 the author describes the current Jewish population in Egypt as descendants of Palestinian captives who were forcibly removed from Judea by Ptolemy II's father, Ptolemy I Lagus.[48] The author devotes sixteen sections to rehearsing the historical background of Jewish disenfranchisement and slavery in Egypt and the outcome of his petition for their liberation (§§12–27). Here the rationale for this forced and violent change is not God's decision or even Judea's failure to obey God. Forced dislocation and resettlement elsewhere is the result of human militaristic action. While diaspora is a reality for the author, Aristeas does not depict it as a punitive consequence of disobedience. From the vantage point of the Letter of Aristeas, diaspora is a type of sociopolitical predicament and not a divine initiative.

Consequently, land and the sociopolitical implications of it in antiquity are important to Aristeas. What region (or regions) signifies the essential identity of diaspora Judaism? The author once again foregoes historical accuracy in favor of literary effect. By mentioning the territories of Samaria and Idumaea (§107) and associating the harbors of Ashkelon, Jaffa, Gaza, and Ptolemais (§115), the author expands the Judean region beyond its historic geographic boundaries.[49] He also details the agricultural, commercial, and militaristic advantages of the terrain (§§113–18). Accordingly, Aristeas' literary strategy amplifies the Judean land in the imagination of the readers. His descriptions render the territorial scale of Jews' native homeland formidable.

As result of his creative treatment, the Palestinian region rivals Alexandria, Egypt, in scale and scope. Literarily speaking, the political friendship between Eleazar and Ptolemy II only makes sense if the two are depicted as heads of commensurate regions. A requisite

[48] Hadas, *Aristeas*, 94.

[49] Goldstein, "Message of Aristeas," 3.

of imperial friendship is mutuality and likeness.[50] In the symposium (§§182–300), the king asks "how he might keep his friends like-minded with himself" (§190). In these question and answer sessions, the Jewish elders often instruct the king to nurture political and social friendships as well (§§228, 231). The primary function of the king's friends, according to the Letter, is to secure political and financial prosperity (§45), ensure military protection (§225), and guarantee access to reliable advice and wisdom (§125).

Consequently, Aristeas embellishes the territorial boundaries of Judea in order to make it proportionate to Egypt, which makes the king's appeal to Eleazar to form a worthy friendship (*philias axion*, §40) valid. The "friendship" (*philia*) that emerges between Ptolemy II and Eleazar in the story, represents mutual sociopolitical commitments (§41). Eleazar's epistolary response to the king makes this very point: "Whatever is to your advantage, even if it be contrary to nature, we shall hearken; for to do so is a mark of friendship (*philia*) and affection. You too have vouchsafed our citizenry (*politēs*) great and unforgettable benefits (*euergeteō*) in many ways" (§44). Eleazar's statement is rich with overtones of political reciprocity, as well as undertones regarding kinship relations and citizenship responsibilities.

Aristeas often associates language of kinship and benefaction together in conversations about friendship and political relations. In the symposium, readers see this connection most clearly. The king asks the eleventh elder how he may keep peace even during periods of war. The response is, "By realizing that no wrong has been done to any of your subjects and that all will join in the struggle in return for benefits (*euergetēma*) received, knowing that even if they lay down their lives their dependents are in your tutelage" (§273). Repeatedly, Aristeas associates the function of benefactor to moral kingship practice (§249). Moreover, he characterizes the act of benefaction as a dimension of God's interactions with the people (§§190, 210).

[50] Johnson, *Sharing Possessions*, 111, 119; Johnson, *The Gospel of Luke* (Sacra Pagina 3; Collegeville, Minn.: Liturgical Press, 1991), 117. Some primary sources that depict friendship as political alliance include Luke 23:12; Josephus, *Ant.* 1.259; *Life* 3.16; 8.30.

In addition to weaving Hellenistic conceptions of friendship and benefaction into notions of land, Aristeas maintains a traditional understanding of the relationship between diaspora Jews and their homeland. According to Aristeas, diaspora Jews, even generations removed from the homeland, remain citizens of Jerusalem. The king's letter attests to this idea when he describes the nature of his imperial strategy: "Since we have assumed the throne, we meet all men in a very humane manner but your citizens to a special degree" (*politēs*, §36). Likewise, Eleazar designates the Alexandrian Jewry the citizenry of Jerusalem, even though they are residents of Egypt (§§44, 126). In fact, at the reading of the completed Greek translation, Aristeas refers to the corporate body of Alexandrian Jews as a *politeuma* (§310).[51] In the context of diaspora hubs like Alexandria, the label, *politeuma*, connoted "a recognized, semiautonomous body of residents in a city who, though not citizens, shared some specified rights with citizens."[52] Thus, Aristeas deploys language that depicts diaspora Jews as a community that possesses multiple political allegiances.

Conclusion

Aristeas constructs diaspora discourse from the symbolic world and traditional understandings of the ancient Jewish cult. Images and rhetoric related to law, temple, and land permeate the discourse. Focusing on these three images reveals what the author deems as the essential cultic rituals and tenets of diaspora Jewish life in general as well as the author's vision regarding the shape of kinship relations and the content of citizenship responsibilities in the Jewish diaspora, in Alexandria in particular.

The life of this diaspora community, according to Aristeas, is defined by the complementary nature of Jewish and Egyptian cultures. In terms of their religious sensibilities, Aristeas insinuates that both Jews *and* Egyptians worship the One Almighty God. The temple

[51] Hadas, *Aristeas*, 221n310.

[52] Wayne A. Meeks, *The First Urban Christians: The Social World of the Apostle Paul* (2nd ed.; New Haven, Conn.: Yale University Press, 2003), 35–36, and see nn. 69 and 70. Some other primary source material includes Josephus, *Ant.* 12.108.

becomes a space of cultural negotiation, affirmation, and concession. It signifies an immovable aspect of Jewish identity and practice—namely, ritual sacrifice. In terms of the political situation, the diaspora Jews' native land of Jerusalem and their place of permanent residence, Egypt, are political "friends." Thus, Jewish allegiance to both regions embodies the mutual sociopolitical commitments between the king and high priest and demonstrates that multiple regional attachments are feasible, even beneficial to the Jews living abroad. Ultimately, the Letter of Aristeas portrays diaspora as a space of multiple attachments with shared religious sensibilities, mutual sociopolitical commitments, and ongoing cultural negotiations.

Moreover, readers should remember that the diaspora life represented in the Letter is fictive. Although some historical figures and locations are mentioned, what is encountered in the narrative of Aristeas is not historiography in the positivistic sense. Rather, readers are confronted with the author's imaginings of Jewish diaspora life in Alexandria set in the third century BCE, under the rule of Ptolemy II Philadelphus (285/2–246 BCE).[53] It represents another literary portrayal of how the social anxieties and advantages envisioned as characteristic of Jewish diaspora life can be configured into their own unique system.

Unlike 1 Peter and the Daniel court tales, Aristeas has a positive viewpoint of diaspora life with its interregional and intergenerational relations. While the Letter alludes to the former history of tension between the ancestors of the current people of the diaspora and locals, Aristeas does not view that as a present reality. In fact, it is unclear whether Aristeas actually views those initial experiences of conquest and capture as a diaspora at all. From Aristeas' description, it appears that the prior war was a period of defeat and enslavement. That in itself is not diaspora life. Diaspora is not the moment of ancient colonial aims and invasion, but a life of acculturation and pluralism, conformity and nonconformity as well as double aims and dual epistemologies that complement, rather than compete with each other. The lifestyle of the scattered who live outside their homeland

[53] For dating possibilities, see Honigman, *Septuagint and Homeric Scholarship*, 2; Hadas, *Aristeas*, 3–5; Tcherikover, *Hellenistic Civilization*, 11, 15–16, 92.

is a reality that takes shape after that moment, even generations later when the offspring from that original homeland flourish outside of it. They know only the language of their birth land and not the original language of their people. Yet they embrace and observe the cultural rituals and beliefs that are actionable in the current context. They also esteem the stories of a homeland's beauty they have never seen, but to which they know they are eternally attached.

Another important contrast between Aristeas' construction of diaspora and what is presented in 1 Peter and the Daniel tales is the place the confessional life of the diaspora community has in its larger foreign environment. Whereas in 1 Peter the confessional life of diaspora is something they embody but do not share overtly with nonbelievers and in Daniel the Jewish confession of the one God in Babylon can appear as a verbal and public affront to the larger dominant culture, in Aristeas the Jewish confession in the Alexandrian diaspora is not antagonistic to Ptolemaic Egyptian sensibilities. In fact, there is much about diaspora Judaism in Egypt that complements and supports the life and cultural affinities of Ptolemaic Hellenism, including similar philosophical outlooks, appreciation of pluralistic modes of existence, as well as confirmation that other powers exist in the world, albeit with the Supreme God at the top.

In contrast to 1 Peter and Daniel, the Letter of Aristeas is confident that life abroad as Jews can be characterized as a peaceful and esteemed social situation that is safeguarded by both the diaspora community as well as their surrounding informed neighbors from the broader pagan setting. Diaspora life can be lived out in the open and publically embraced as a valuable asset to the larger multicultural ethos of the entire society in which it is situated as long as that society deliberately embraces and protects that cultural pluralism. Diaspora is cast as a mechanism for bridging difference, exercising hospitality and friendship to the foreign other, and encountering the heterogeneity of God's creation and manifestation within a diversity of human cultures, religious and philosophical postures, and social institutions and lifestyles.

6

Diaspora in Alexandria

Philo

Respectively, the First Letter of Peter, the Daniel court tales, and the Letter of Aristeas present visions of what diaspora life is like with its many issues and challenges, rewards and benefits, prescriptions and proscriptions. Each one represents religious writing that addresses, to varying degrees, the sociohistorical and anthropological realities of a population living in the land of another. Their literary contexts are set in the aftermath of conquest and their target populations and audiences are depicted as largely subordinates and slaves who are managing the fears and grievances of a subjugated community living at the mercy of mercurial dominant powers. Yet one major point of convergence is that each writing up to this point crafts a fictive diaspora situation, rather than describing, in historically positivistic terms, an actual diaspora community existing at the time the writing was penned. This is where Philo's contribution becomes important. Philo's writings, especially *The Embassy to Gaius* (*Embassy*) and *Against Flaccus* (*Flaccus*), are nonfictional sources. Although written in hindsight and shaped for rhetorical effect, Philo's compositions detail recent events and offer glimpses into realities of diaspora life at one particular Jewish center in the early first century CE, Alexandria.

While the other writings are preoccupied with the origins and purpose of dispersion in some form, an examination of Philo's treatises reveals that he is not. According to Philo, Jews outside of Palestine have both a mother city—Jerusalem—as well as a fatherland—the land of their birth. Philo states, "it is the holy city where the sacred temple of the Most High God stands, that they regard as their mother city (*metropolis*), but the regions they obtained from their fathers, grandfathers, great-grandfathers, and even more remote ancestors, to live in, (they regard) as their fatherland (*patris*) where they were born and brought" (*Flaccus* 45–46).[1] Philo's mantra of dual allegiance seems characteristic of Jewish literature arising from Hellenistic Alexandria. Like Aristeas, Philo asserts that there exists among Jews an intense and complementary attachment to two lands: the adopted and native lands of their ancestors.[2] Also like Aristeas, Philo distinguishes Jews from non-Jews by deploying language and imagery rooted in notions of torah, temple, land, ancestral customs, and imperial benefaction. Moreover, like 1 Peter (and Aristeas to a lesser degree), he galvanizes Jewish kinship, characterizing it as both a local and global connection that spans the entire Roman Empire.

Yet Philo is not just another iteration of Alexandrian Jewish diaspora thinking akin to the constructions put forward by the Letter of Aristeas. Philo provides a novel conception that stands on its own. In Philo's estimation, the Jews are one people among multiple peoples with their own set of convictions and practices. They are not displaced or dislocated any more or any less than all humanity. In broad terms, Philo describes the state of affairs of Judaism in Alexandria and across the empire without conceiving of its situation as a "diaspora." This is not to say that diaspora thinking is wholly absent from Philo's thought. Indeed, Philo conceives of diaspora and even deploys the technical term, albeit sparingly. Even in these rare cases, Philo's understanding of diaspora is entirely different from the interpretations depicted in the other writings. As such, Philo is representative of yet another position regarding diaspora life and identity.[3]

[1] All translations of *Flaccus* are taken from or informed by Pieter W. van der Horst's translation in *Philo's Flaccus: The First Pogrom* (Philo of Alexandria Commentary Series; Leiden: Brill, 2003).

[2] Erich Gruen, *Diaspora: Jews amidst Greeks and Romans* (Cambridge, Mass.: Harvard University Press, 2002), 243.

[3] A. Mendelson, *Philo's Jewish Identity* (BJS 161; Atlanta: Scholars Press, 1988).

Locating Philo: His Life and Literary Works

Historical Background

Not much is known about the specifics of Philo's life.[4] Most details are inferred from his historical context and the various comments he makes across his dozens of extant writings.[5] From Philo's self-designation as an "old man" in *Embassy* 1, scholars date Philo's life from about 20 BCE to 41 CE.[6] According to Josephus, Philo's family was privileged and connected to the Jewish leadership in Alexandria, sometimes referred to as the *politeuma* and other times the *gerousia*.[7] Josephus says one of Philo's brothers, Alexander, was a high-

[4] This background information draws on some of the standard overviews as well as special studies. See Gregory E. Sterling, "Philo," in *Dictionary of New Testament Background*, ed. C. A. Evans and S. E. Porter (Downers Grove, Ill.: InterVarsity, 1992); John J. Collins, *Between Athens and Jerusalem: Jewish Identity in the Hellenistic Diaspora* (Biblical Resource Series; 2nd ed.; Grand Rapids: Eerdmans, 2000); E. Birnbaum, *The Place of Judaism in Philo's Thought: Israel, Jews, and Proselytes* (Atlanta: Scholars Press, 1996).

[5] Kenneth Schenck, *A Brief Guide to Philo* (Louisville, Ky.: Westminster John Knox, 2005), 14–23.

[6] Elsewhere, Philo defines an "old man" as someone over fifty-seven (*Creation* 105); Schenck, *A Brief Guide to Philo*, 23n1. Moreover, the single historical event by which scholars date Philo is the 38 CE Alexandrian pogrom. Philo's treatises, *Flaccus* and *Embassy* were written not long after the initial eruption, with the former predating the latter work. This puts Philo's ambassadorial trip to Rome at around 39–41 CE. This is prior to the emperor's assassination and Claudius' succession, in which Claudius eventually makes a statement about the status of Alexandrian Jews in the city and the empire and reinstates their religious liberty. *CPJ* II.153.73, quoted in Margaret Williams, *The Jews among the Greeks and Romans: A Diasporan Sourcebook* (London: Duckworth Press, 1998), 133–34. H. S. Jones, "Claudius and the Jewish Question in Alexandria," *Journal of Roman Studies* 16 (1926): 26–29.

[7] The meaning of *politeuma* as a word connoting the organizational and governing structure of diaspora Jewish communities is highly contested and ambiguous, although Philo uses it in some of his writings (*Creation* 143; *Husbandry* 81; *Confusion* 109; *Joseph* 69; *Laws* 2.45). The *Letter of Aristeas* alleges a Jewish *politeuma* existed in Alexandria (*Letter of Aristeas* §§308–10). It could refer to the entire Jewish community at particular diaspora hubs, especially those built around military settlements (as may be the case in Alexandria and/or Leontopolis). Or, it could refer to a smaller, more elite group within the diaspora Jewish community. After evaluating archaeological and literary sources, Sandra Gambetti compellingly defines the Alexandrian *politeuma* as the latter, saying it "is institutionally close to, but separate from the rest of the Jewish community." Having evaluated primarily Philo's writings

ranking official in Alexandria, known as an "alabarch" (Josephus, *Ant.* 18.259). Alexander donated two hundred thousand drachmas to Herod Agrippa I for the plating of the Jerusalem gates (Josephus, *Ant.* 18.159–160).[8] The affluence of Philo's family likely contributed to their extended citizenship rights. Although Roman citizenship among Jews was rare, it is highly likely that Philo and his family were examples of this exception.[9] With the exception of Philo's nephew who eventually apostatizes from Judaism and ascends the ranks of Roman administration (Josephus, *Ant.* 18.259; 20.100), Philo and his family appear to have successfully reconciled their Judaism and Hellenism.[10] Furthermore, the wealth of Philo's family afforded him the opportunity to devote much of his time to leisurely contemplation and philosophy.[11] As such, Philo was well educated in both Jewish law and Hellenistic philosophy and rhetoric, as his corpus of writings attests.[12]

---

and other related historical documents, Schenk also asserts it is a smaller powerful group within the larger body. He defines *politeuma* as "a smaller political unit within a city, usually a particular ethnic group allowed limited authority to self-govern according to its own customs. Sometimes such a body was directed by an ethnarch (a single ethnic leader), as the Alexandrian Jews were until the time of the emperor Augustus. After Augustus, the Jews had this limited self-governance by way of a *gerousia* (a council of elders)." Schenk, *Brief Guide to Philo*, 12, 141; Sandra Gambetti, *The Alexandrian Riots of 38 C.E. and the Persecution of the Jews: A Historical Reconstruction* (Leiden: Brill, 2009), 49; C. Zuckermann, "Hellenistic Politeuma and the Jews: A Reconsideration," *SCI* 8–9 (1985–88): 175–76, 181.

[8] *CPJ* 1:78–79; Schenck, *Brief Guide to Philo*, 23n6, 7.

[9] What remains unclear is the meaning of Philo's citizenship. Is he just an elevated citizen of the Jewish *politeuma*, or is he also a citizen of Rome? The former seems certain, but the latter remains obscure. Tiberius Claudius' letter to the Alexandrians in 41 CE, after Philo's writings, suggests some Jewish citizens existed. "To all who have become *ephebi* down to my principate, I secure and confirm the Alexandrian citizenship (*poleiteian*) withal the privileges and amenities enjoyed by the city, except only to such as may have intruded themselves among you and contrived, though born of servile mothers, to become *ephebi*." Quoted in Harry A. Wolfson, "Philo on Jewish Citizenship in Alexandria," *JBL* 63 (1944): 165–68; H. I. Bell, *Jews and Christians in Egypt* (London: Oxford University Press, 1924), 14; Tessa Rajak, "Was There a Roman Charter for the Jews?" *Journal of Roman Studies* 74 (1984): 109.

[10] *CPJ* 1:78-79.

[11] Philo, *Laws* 3.1-6.

[12] *Embassy*, 182. Kenneth Schenck says, "From comments scattered throughout his writings, we know that Philo's education covered all the subjects of what became the medieval trivium (grammar, rhetoric, dialectic) and quadrivium (arithmetic,

Philo's eclectic educational background bespeaks his dual cultural orientation. On the one hand, Philo appears to be an observant and devout Jew. In his writings, he advocates Jewish dietary regulations, circumcision, Sabbath observance, holy festivals, and temple loyalty (*Migration* 91–92). He is clearly learned in Jewish interpretation. On the other hand, Philo seems to have frequented the Greek gymnasium (*Laws* 2.229-230) and Greek theater (*Drunkenness* 117).[13] His writings, therefore, suggest he was a learned and cultivated man of two worlds: Judaism and Hellenism.[14] While Philo observes his Jewish customs, he also participates in the affluent life and culture of Alexandria, eventually receiving a hearing from the emperor himself.

The double life of Philo is, perhaps, on greatest display in his civic service. He was nominated as one of the leaders of the Alexandrian Jewry and served as an envoy to the emperor on behalf of the beleaguered Alexandrian *politeuma*. While Philo served in this political capacity, it does not appear that he did so willingly. He compared his political adventures to a drunken man in *Dreams* 2.104. In *Laws* 3.3,

geometry, music, astronomy)." Schenck, *Brief Guide to Philo*, 11, 24nn14–15. The "scattered" references to which Schenck refers are *Prelim. Studies* 11, 16–18, 75–76, 148; *Dreams* 1.205.

[13] The possibility that Philo was a member of the local gymnasium is additional evidence that those in Philo's family were probably Roman citizens since members had to, at least, be citizens of the city to participate. Schenck, *Brief Guide to Philo*, 12. Some primary source evidence includes 2 Macc 4:7-14; Williams, *Jews among the Greeks and Romans*, 113–14.

[14] This orientation raises questions regarding Jewish particularism and Jewish universalism in the Hellenistic diaspora. See Schenk, *Brief Guide to Philo*, 46. On the spectrum between total rejection of the outside world (sectarianism like the Essenes) and complete accommodation to the point of apostasy like Philo's nephew, Philo seems to model a sort of middle ground that formed specifically outside of Palestine. Scholars have long recognized that by the time Philo wrote, there were more Jews living outside Palestine than within it. Compare the covenantal nomism posited by E. P. Sanders and the diversity of Jewish forms argued by Alan F. Segal. See Sanders, *Paul and Palestinian Judaism: A Comparison of Patterns of Religion* (Philadelphia: Fortress, 1977); Segal, *The Other Judaisms of Late Antiquity* (BJS; Atlanta: Scholars Press, 1987).

Philo says, "'envy' forced him into the great sea of civic concerns."[15] Indeed, one finds in Philo's exegetical treatment of Joseph the tension he seems to embody in his own experience. What is the role and place of political activity in the life of a philosopher and devout contemplative Jew? Is it a virtue or a vice? In *Joseph*, Philo argues political activity is necessary, even laudable when done in the service of the community to regulate an orderly civil society.[16] Here, Philo equates Joseph's administrative skill to the work of a governor and counts that virtuous. However, in *Dreams*, Philo gives a completely different vision of Joseph, the politician, which is negative and dismissive. In this treatise, Philo suggests Joseph's political life contributed to his lack of virtue rather than being representative of it.[17] Although two different audiences were in view for these treatises, Philo's own dilemma and changing sensibilities may still be discerned. According to Philo's multiple descriptions, living in the cultural and political worlds of both Judaism and Rome invites a conundrum of warring ideals and clashing values that appear difficult to fully reconcile.

Shape and Significance of Philo's Literary Corpus

One of the many portraits of Philo that emerges from careful study of his works and other evidence is that Philo was a biblical interpreter.[18] Philo's corpus of writings is dominated by works in which he engages and appropriates Jewish Scripture, particularly the books of

[15] Schenck aptly notes that the word Philo uses to identify why he entered the political realm *phthonos* (envy) is the same word he uses to describe the Alexandrian reaction to Herod Agrippa in the city (*Flaccus* 29). Schenck, *Brief Guide to Philo*, 24n17.

[16] *Flight* 33–35; *Joseph* 37–39.

[17] *Dreams* 1.219–220 and book 2. In fact, a comparison between how Philo describes Joseph's coat of many colors in the former and how he describes it in *Joseph* 32–34 speaks volumes to the contrast and tension.

[18] For a brief summary of the various portraits scholars have produced for Philo, see Schenck, *Brief Guide to Philo*, 3–6. Some of the more prominent portraits put forward include Philo the devout Jew, proposed by Peder Borgen; Philo the Platonic philosopher, proposed by John Dillon; and Philo the mystic, proposed by Erwin Goodenough. Borgen, *Philo of Alexandria: An Exegete of His Time* (Leiden: Brill, 1997); Borgen, *Early Christianity and Hellenistic Judaism* (London: A&C Black, 1998); Dillon, *The Middle Platonists: 80 B.C. to A.D. 220* (Ithaca, N.Y.: Cornell

Moses. Consistently, Philo exercises masterful exegetical skill, producing both allegorical treatments and literal sense readings of the Pentateuch (*Migration* 89–91).[19]

Exegetical skill, however, is not the only characteristic of Philo's thinking and work that is on display in his extant writings. Philo's large corpus conveys degrees of Jewish accommodation of Hellenistic philosophy as well as Jewish sectarian sensibility. In particular, *Embassy* and *Flaccus* are two treatises most likely written for a Roman imperial audience to persuade them that the empire benefits from preserving and protecting its historical Jewish presence. Written for outsiders of the Jewish community, Philo argues that Judaism embodies the highest values of Rome—namely, honoring imperial authority—while simultaneously remaining a distinct people because of their religious convictions and practices. None of these pose a threat to the Romans, unless they attack the Jews first. The point Philo makes clear is that God defends His people, the Jews (*Embassy* 4).

In addition to providing insight about Philo's political leanings and theological outlook, his two political tracts provide glimpses into Philo's self-understanding as one who lives in two worlds: as an Alexandrian Jew and as a Hellenistic sophisticate. More so in *Embassy* and *Flaccus* than other writings, Philo speaks in the first person and passionately shares his view of those non-Jews who malign Jewish character and discount the Jewish presence in the empire. Philo's conception of the world informed by the historic realities of Roman imperialism, Hellenistic Judaism, and social conflict in the form of anti-Semitism is more visible in these two texts than others. Cultural patterns of kinship and citizenship, which 1 Peter closely connects to Christian diaspora experience, Philo identifies as normative aspects of Hellenistic Jewish life in Alexandria and abroad. Philo's position is that allegiance to the Jewish *politeuma* (*Flaccus* 53, *Embassy* 157, 194)

University Press, 1977); Erwin Goodenough, *By Light, Light: The Mystic Gospel of Hellenistic Judaism* (New Haven, Conn.: Yale University Press, 1935).

[19] See Goodenough's chapter called "Philo's Writings," where he lays out the basic framework of the writings and their condition. Erwin Ramsdell Goodenough, *An Introduction to Philo Judaeus* (2nd ed.; Oxford: Basil Blackwell, 1962), 30–51.

and devotion to Jerusalem is entirely compatible with life everywhere in the Roman Empire, even if one is critical of the empire.[20]

Philo's writings are some of the best primary source material contemporary readers have about Alexandrian Judaism in the early Roman period.[21] A literary examination of Philo's description of Judaism within and outside of Alexandria and his conception of diaspora provide yet another rendering of diaspora thinking extant among Hellenistic Jewish writings. As a historical source, what is the meaning of Jewish life outside of Jerusalem according to Philo? What is the content—in terms of convictions and practices—of the Alexandrian Jewry? Finally, from Philo's descriptions, what can one discern as his meaning and understanding of diaspora?

Response to Crisis: *Embassy to Gaius* and *Against Flaccus*

As detailed in part I, the First Letter of Peter was written in response to crisis. Diaspora Christians, as 1 Peter conceives of them, were targets of social ostracism, civic ridicule, and public defamation. Philo narrates a similar crisis—but more immediately and vividly than 1 Peter. In his two historical and apologetic works, *Embassy to Gaius* and *Against Flaccus*, Philo recounts the circumstances surrounding the recent disenfranchisement of the Alexandrian Jewry. By the commands of imperial agents and rulers who had been charged to protect them, Alexandrian Jews faced mob violence, military oppression, tortuous deaths, the rescinding of their civic privileges and religious liberties, and the desecration of their sacred edifices—synagogues and the temple (*Flaccus* 33, 41, 43; *Embassy* 132). Similar to 1 Peter's view of Christianity in the Roman world, Philo does not think Judaism is overtly antagonistic to Rome, although the Roman world remains a threat to Judaism.

[20] Gruen, *Diaspora*, 135. Gruen elaborates further, saying, "Jews of the Second Temple period did not perceive themselves as victims of a diaspora. That fact alone arrests attention" (*Diaspora*, 136).

[21] Collins, *Between Athens and Jerusalem*, 131.

In the earliest available accounts of overt anti-Semitic attitudes and violence, Philo details the suffering Jews experienced in the 38 CE anti-Jewish pogrom in Alexandria, Egypt. In contrast to 1 Peter, which advocates a kind of passive and submissive posture in the face of overt and unmerited attack and violence (see 1 Pet 1:6; 2:18–19; 4:12), Philo verbally disparages Egyptian attackers of Alexandrian Jews and invites readers to share his attitude. One reason for the acute difference in tone is a difference in situation. Whereas 1 Peter's Christian readers are primarily small household communities populated by slaves, women, and men not occupying positions of significant power or wielding enormous political and economic capital (1 Pet 2:11, 17–18; 3:1–7); the social status of Philo's community is quite the opposite. The membership of Philo's community spans the entire socioeconomic spectrum, from slaves to aristocracy, shopkeepers, and elders of the *politeuma* (*Joseph* 69; *Flaccus* 74).[22] He numbers the Alexandrian Jews at almost one-half the population (*Flaccus* 55, 62) and constantly reminds readers of the large numbers of Jews settled across the entire Roman Empire. He says, "for no one country can contain the whole Jewish nation, by reason of its populousness" (*Flaccus* 45; cf. *Embassy* 214, 226). The diverse and dispersed Jewish kinship, according to Philo, constitute, a formidable and unified body across the empire.

According to Philo's sketch, the Alexandrian Jewish community is not only large, but tight knit. Even under duress, Philo says the community remains committed to its members, attempting to meet their resource needs. "When, finally, they could no longer endure their privation, some of them, quite contrary to what they had been used to, went to the houses of their relatives and friends to beg for the basic necessities of life, as a loan. Others, whose consciousness of their standing meant they could not endure the condition of beggars, which they saw as fitter for slaves than for the free, went to the market-place for no other reason than to buy food for their relatives and themselves" (*Flaccus* 64). Philo insisted that Jewish unity and kinship undermined social stratification that divided the membership into distinct economic groups. At the arrest of Flaccus, Philo

[22] See Josephus, *Ant.* 14.117; Williams, *Jews among the Greeks and Romans*, 48.

describes the beleaguered community as "crowded in their houses" at nightfall (*Flaccus* 119)[23] and pouring through the Alexandrian gates at daybreak in jamboree as a unified body (*Flaccus* 121).[24] Internal commitment to the preservation of the community persisted in times of peace, conflict, and jubilant celebration.

Whereas 1 Peter's community is fairly young, existence of the Alexandrian Jewry extends back centuries to the founding of the city and has deep roots in Alexandrian culture and history.[25] In fact, Philo indirectly commends the Alexandrian Jewry for this long history, suggesting that even the Gentile founders of the city found great "pleasure" in the presence and prospective contributions of the Jewish community to the new city (*Flaccus* 46).

First Peter entertains the possibility that by being "zealous for what is right" (1 Pet 3:13) pagan aggressors of diaspora Christians can recognize the merits of Christian character and presence and accept them, but Philo does not extend that courtesy to Egyptian Alexandrians. His rhetoric is inflamed with vitriol directed toward indigenous and Greek Egyptians. He uses acerbic language when he calls them "a wicked seed," "infected with the poison and bad temper like that of crocodiles and asps" (*Flaccus* 166), and a "rancorous people (*Flaccus* 19).[26] When Philo is not decrying the collective Egyptian Gentile population, he directs his animus toward specific individuals from that body, particularly those he identifies as chief agitators. For example, he names Helicon as an initial accuser of the Alexandrian Jews. Philo pronounces him a "damnable and abominable slave" (*Embassy* 166), "rascal" (*Embassy* 177), and "scorpion-like slave" (*Embassy* 205).[27]

[23] Van der Horst, *Philo's Flaccus*, 75.

[24] Van der Horst, *Philo's Flaccus*, 76.

[25] Rajak, "Was There a Roman Charter for the Jews?" references Josephus, *Ant.* 12.199.

[26] It is important to note that Philo does not think all native Alexandrians and Egyptians are this way. He acknowledges outright that the attack was by a select group. "The crowd perceived this—I do not refer to the peaceful and decent inhabitants, but to the rabble that is always intent on creating confusion and turmoil" (*Flaccus* 41).

[27] All translations from *Embassy* taken from E. Mary Smallwood, *Philonis Aleaxandrini: Legatio Ad Gaium* (2nd ed.; Leiden: Brill, 1970).

Readers sense that hidden just below the surface of his libel against Helicon are the realities of Philo's privileged social status, even as an Alexandrian Jew. His constant restatement of Helicon's basic social rank as "slave" (*doulos* in *Embassy* 203 and *andrapodon* in *Embassy* 205) suggests Philo's elevated rank as a citizen of the Jewish *politeuma*, and possibly a citizen of Rome. Consequently, Philo appears to exhibit elite Hellenistic sensibilities concerning social arrangements. At the very least, he is an informed storyteller and apologist unconcerned about the broad social matrix of master, slave, freedman, and so forth, at work in his world. On more than one occasion he unceremoniously names classes of Hellenistic population as realities of Jewish life. For instance, when Agrippa recovers from fainting after hearing Gaius' intention to erect an image of himself in the temple, his servants say, "It is all right. You are in your own house. . . . Look at the people here. They are all your own people, the most respected of your friends, freedmen, and servants, and those who most respect you" (*Embassy* 272). Philo is thoroughly acclimated to Greco-Roman social arrangements and status. For him, there is no conflict between Jewish life and belief and the social arrangements of the Roman social world in which they find themselves members. Like all other peoples of that world, Jews occupy all levels of the social pyramid.

For Philo, the fact that Jews are subject to Roman rulers is also not an overt problem. Life outside Palestine is just a state of affairs, not a divine act or statement, and it does not have to be oppositional to the Roman Empire.[28] The bone of contention for Philo (and the Jewish bodies he represents) in both letters is twofold: a concern regarding the maintenance of their religious liberty and their exemption from participating in the imperial cult and the preservation of their civic

[28] Katell Berthelot, "Philo's Perception of the Roman Empire," *Journal for the Study of Judaism* 42 (2011): 166–87. Berthelot says that "Philo, while appreciating the *pax romana* and the religious freedom generally enjoyed by Jews in the Roman Empire, was nevertheless critical of Rome." She is expanding on Goodenough's original claim that Philo "loved the Romans no more than the skipper of a tiny boat loves a hurricane" (quoted by Berthelot in "Philo's Perception," 176). See Erwin R. Goodenough and Howard L. Goodhart, *The Politics of Philo Judaeus: Practice and Theory, with a General Bibliography of Philo* (New Haven, Conn.: Yale University Press, 1938), 7; Goodenough, *Introduction*, 62.

rights (*Embassy* 366, *Flaccus* 53, 54). Although *Flaccus* seems to emphasize the latter and *Embassy* the former, both aspects—the eradication of religious liberty and the violation of civic rights—are present to some degree in each treatise.

In *Flaccus*, the apex of these violations occurs when Flaccus declared Alexandrian Jews "foreigners (*xenos*) and aliens (*epēlus*)" (*Flaccus* 54) and dissolves the rights of their *politeuma* (*politeias anairesin*, *Flaccus* 53).[29] By expunging their civic rights, the Jews themselves can be physically removed from the land and, in terms of the law or legal recourse, are rendered an invisible nonentity. Like the author of 1 Peter, who rejects the notion of diaspora Christians being rendered homeless by their foreign civil environs, Philo seems to take a similar position. Philo rejects the notion that Alexandria Jews are displaced and homeless. He argues that political maneuvering to make Jewish displacement a reality encroaches on both their civil (human authority) and providential (divine authority) rights.

Consequently, Philo suggests that the Alexandrian conflict between indigenous Egyptians and native Jews was much more complex and involved than just fomenting ethnic tension. The ethnic antagonism was informed and exacerbated by perceptions regarding social station and place as well as assumptions regarding territorial access. For instance, Philo puts on the lips of Helicon this self-confession: "You have false charges made against the Jews and Jewish customs, charges among which you grew up; you learnt them right from your cradle, not from a single individual but from the most garrulous section of the Alexandrian population" (*Embassy* 170). Through Helicon's declaration, Philo pinpoints the origin of Helicon's prejudice. Helicon did not invent disdain for Jews. Rather, he leveraged frustration with Jewish prosperity and success ubiquitous among certain segments of the indigenous and Greek Alexandrians. These segments perceived Egypt to be *their* homeland, not the Jews'. That public bias, Philo suggests, shaped and informed Helicon's perceptions and contributed to

[29] Van der Horst, *Philo's Flaccus*, 156n54.

the misinformation about Jewish practice and conviction shared with Gentile rulers.[30]

Moreover, Philo responds to questions of Jewish civic rights throughout the treatises. Are Alexandrian Jews, with the status of Roman citizenship, legitimate citizens of Rome? Philo answers in the affirmative (*Embassy* 155). Do Jews living in Alexandria have a right to be there and call it home? Yet again Philo answers in the affirmative (*Flaccus* 46). Can Jews live as Jews in both character and practice and be loyal subjects, even agents of Rome? Philo responds with a resounding yes and names the Jewish King Agrippa as his exemplar.

Indeed, it was the Jewish King Agrippa I's visit to Alexandria that triggered the violent attack against the Jews (*Flaccus* 25–35). According to Philo, Egyptians "were vexed by the idea that a Jew has become a king, which was to them as if each of them had been deprived of an ancestral kingdom" (*Flaccus* 29). In the larger rhetorical drama of both *Embassy* and *Flaccus*, Agrippa represents the quintessential assimilated Jew. He is one who is both devoted to Judaism and loyal to the empire while the empire and Judaism are rendered loyal to him. In other words, at work in Agrippa's career, at least as Philo presents it, is the reciprocal nature of political benefaction (*Flaccus* 25–26; *Embassy* 272). Agrippa represents a double-conscious Jew—one who in Philo's narratives has successfully fused Hellenism and Judaism together for his personal ends, as well as the benefit of the entire Jewish kinship. Philo made an intentional literary effort to underscore Agrippa's double cultural devotion. Philo states that Agrippa's fidelity to Judaism

[30] Philo names Capito as yet another example of Gentile envy and attack on thriving Jewish communities and commerce, except this occurs in their homeland, Judea. Capito, like Helicon, had the ear of Gaius and was a trusted agent of Roe. But like Helicon, he too had a deep-rooted resentment for the Jews, stemming from his socioeconomic background. Philo says, "Capito is the collector of revenues of Judaea, and he has a grudge against its inhabitants. He arrived a poor man, but by robbery and embezzlement he amassed a large and varied fortune" (*Embassy* 199). Although focused on the circumstances in Alexandria, Philo's treatise constantly connects the acts of anti-Semitism and the violation of Jewish civic rights in Alexandria to the experiences of Jewish settlements in other parts of the empire. He constantly, therefore, indirectly reminds his readers that the Alexandrian Jewry is only one of many dispersed all over the world, thereby, in turn, insulating the potential domino effect such unrest can have in other places.

was perceivable not only by the public but by the emperor himself (*Embassy* 268).[31] He calls the relationship between Agrippa and Gaius one of close friends (*Flaccus* 40). As such, Philo does not think Judaism, in its many iterations, is overtly antagonistic to Rome, although Alexandrian accusers claim it is.

In contrast, *Embassy* highlights the strain the imperial cult placed on Jewish religious liberty. Instead of Flaccus being the antagonist, Philo depicts the Emperor Gaius as the prime adversary to the Jews. "It was only of the Jews that Gaius was suspicious, on the grounds that they were the only people who deliberately opposed him and had been taught from their very cradles, as it were, by their parents, tutors, teachers—and more than that—by their holy Laws and even by their unwritten customs, to believe that the Father and creator of the universe is one God" (*Embassy* 115; cf. *Embassy* 119). While the explicit issue is Jewish worship of the emperor, the issue right below the surface is a question of Jewish character and their political loyalties. Can devout Jews actually pledge loyalty to their pagan, foreign ruler?

Jewish Customs in Alexandria through Philo's Eyes

According to Philo, the fundamental elements constituting Jewish character and cultic practice, particularly in Alexandria, are observance of imperial authority and its legislative matrix and obedience to their ancestral traditions. Philo says, "When we are dead let this be our epitaph: "Even God would not reproach us for having striven to attain two ends—respect for the Emperor and obedience to our hallowed Laws" (*Embassy* 236). In his first point—the declaration of Jewish deference for the emperor—Philo states the sociopolitical situation of Judaism. The Jews are subjects to foreign rulers. He even refers to the emperor repeatedly, without contention or disdain, as the Jews' master (*despotēs*, *Embassy* 183, 222). Moreover, Philo places on the lips

[31] According to Philo, Gaius even confesses Agrippa's loyalty to Judaism: "He said, 'If my closest and dearest friend, Agrippa, who is under great obligations to me is such a slave of his national customs that he cannot bear to hear a word spoken against them but faints and even almost dies, what must one expect of the other Jews, who have no powerful incentives for acting otherwise?'" (*Embassy* 268).

of the Judean protesters an affirmation of the relationship between their foreign master and their status as slaves, "We know that cavalry and infantry forces have been prepared against us in case we should oppose the dedication. No one is so senseless as to oppose his master when he is himself only a slave. We readily and gladly offer our throats" (*Embassy* 233).

Philo insists repeatedly that the Alexandrian Jewry is loyal to the emperor and that they demonstrate that resolve publicly and repeatedly. In both treatises, he adduces proof after proof to demonstrate that they honor the emperor and acknowledge his role as benefactor of the empire (*euergetēs*, *Embassy* 22), although it is not practiced in the form of the Hellenistic imperial cult. As Agrippa pens in his letter, Jews "do not merely say that they are friends of Caesar, but really are his friends" (*Embassy* 280). In describing Jewish orientation toward the Roman emperor, Philo says the Jews drafted a letter of congratulations and a decree of loyalty to the emperor, which Flaccus never delivered. "For we had decreed by our votes and carried out by our actions all possible honors to Gaius as far as they were allowed by our laws, and we delivered the decree to Flaccus, begging him that it might be forwarded by him. . . . Flaccus, however, disregarded all our intentions and also his own words and promises, and he retained the decree in his possession" (*Flaccus* 97, 101).

Although their special imperial privileges excuse them from worshipping idol images of the emperor, this does not mean they do not participate in any type of public demonstration of their deference for their foreign ruler. In another example from *Flaccus*, Philo points out that by attacking Jewish synagogues, the mob is also attacking public honors to the emperor. "You do not realize that for the Jews all over the world it is their synagogues that clearly form the basis for their piety towards the imperial family. If these are destroyed, what other place or method is left to us for paying this homage?'" (*Flaccus* 48, 49).[32] Likewise, in *Embassy*, Philo's delegation details their forms of honoring the emperor in response to Isidorus' accusation that they are

[32] Van der Horst, *Philo's Flaccus*, 63.

disloyal (*Embassy* 355). They say, "Lord Gaius, we are being maligned. We did sacrifice and hecatombs at that" (*Embassy* 356).

Throughout both treatises Philo references "ancestral customs" (*patrios* or *ethos*)[33] as the core of Jewish conviction and practice, which makes them visibly distinct from their foreign neighbors. Specifically, Philo names liturgical hymns and songs as common elements in the worship life of diaspora Jews. When he describes Alexandrian Jews' initial celebratory response to Flaccus' arrest, he describes their singing as a statement of fact. It is just a manifestation of the corporate worship life of the community. Likewise, Philo refers to prayer as a staple of Jewish cultic life, both through his repeated references to synagogues as Jewish houses of prayer (*Flaccus* 47–49)[34] and through references to specific moments of corporate prayer ("answer our prayers," *Flaccus* 123, 124). Other components of Jewish life include recognition of the Jerusalem temple (*Flaccus* 46), temple sacrifice (*Embassy* 278–80), the annual temple collection (*Embassy* 156; *Laws* 1.77-78), Sabbath observance and synagogue meetings (*Embassy* 156, 158), and festival pilgrimages like the Festival of Booths (*Flaccus* 116; cf. *Laws* 2.204; *Migration* 92).[35]

According to Philo, the situation of Jewish life in Alexandria and across the Roman Empire was complicated. His account of the violence and persecution the Jews faced under Flaccus' rule is not written as a neutral historical report. Rather, it expresses a particular social memory—an emic consciousness. In rehearsing the events leading up

[33] BDAG defines *patrios* broadly as a subset of *patris*, meaning "of one's fathers," and it largely restricts the connotation, defining the term as a particular geographic area or locale identified as the origin of a people's ancestors (BDAG, 788–89). The accuracy of this definition is questionable, particularly in the case of Philo, who seems less concerned with ancestral lands and location and more focused on ancestral traditions and customs. Often, it is practices, not territory, that Philo is focused on delineating as characteristic of Jewish identity, at least in *Flaccus* and *Embassy*. This may well be the reason why Philo frequently couples *patrios* with *ethos* (*Flaccus* 43, 52, 53; *Embassy* 300; cf. *Hypothetica* 7.11). Since the basic meaning of ethos is "custom" or "habit," it sharpens his meaning of *patrios* (BDAG, *ethos*, 277; cf. Josephus, *Ant.* 15.286-88). Philo uses the terms together to clarify he means action, not location, as markers of Jewish conviction.

[34] Van der Horst, *Philo's Flaccus* 63.

[35] *Decalogue* 96–101; *Embassy* 158.

to the pogrom, Philo says, "What then did the governor of the country do? He knew that the city, as the rest of Egypt, has two kinds of inhabitants, us and them" (*Flaccus* 43). As outsiders, current readers hear an assessment of Jewish diaspora life from *within* the social group. Philo's division of the Alexandria population into "them" and "us" or "attackers" and "the attacked" (also known as "victims," *Flaccus* 52) appears to parallel his own lived duality being both Jew and Hellenized. Yet Philo's Jewish identity eclipses the latter. Furthermore, his rhetoric—particularly in the opening and closing verses of the treaties—invites readers to share his position.[36] Philo's own personal experience has proven that life in the diaspora can bring great prosperity and advancement (as is the case with his brother, nephew, and Agrippa I), but that the danger remains—namely, the attitude of Roman authorities and local environments can shift unfavorably against its Jewish populace.

Ultimately, Philo's response to Jewish persecution in Alexandria is characterized by sharp, direct rhetoric. It is a corrective written for hostile Gentiles in authority, who are, in Philo's view, misinformed about Jewish convictions and practice and who also question Jews' place and role in the empire. Philo responds by enumerating the violations against Jews and characterizing them as the unfounded suspicions of Gentile opportunists and imperial arrogance. What is perhaps most striking about Philo's response to the crisis facing Alexandrian Jews is that he depicts it as a crisis confronting the entire Jewish population, locally and abroad, as well as the entire Roman Empire with its diverse cultures and peoples. "For it was more than clear that the rumor of the destruction of the synagogues that started in Alexandria would spread immediately to the districts of Egypt and spread from Egypt eastwards to the oriental nations, and from the coastal strip and Mareia, which are the borders of Libya, westwards to the nations living there. For there is not one country that can contain all the Jews, so numerous are they" (*Flaccus* 45, 49). With this statement, Philo warns that there are worldwide consequences for Jewish persecution. As such, the universal implications of the Jewish

[36] Compare the rhetorical force (particularly its *pathos*) of *Embassy's* opening (1–7) and closing (370–73) to *Flaccus'* opening (1) and closing (91).

predicament points in the direction of Philo's conception of diaspora. In Philo's mind, there is no Jewish diaspora predicament, but there is a human diaspora condition.

Philo's Novel Construction of Diaspora (*Confusion of Tongues*, *On Rewards & Punishments*, and Other Writings)

Even though diaspora does not appear in Philo's political treatises, he is familiar with the Hellenistic Jewish term and deploys it sparingly elsewhere—only twice (*Confusion* 197; *Rewards* 115). He associates "diaspora" and its conventional Hellenistic meaning in the Jewish Scripture (a punishing act of God that scatters people from a single territorial origin to multiple locations) to a specific narrative account: the Tower of Babel in LXX Genesis 11. In the allegorical treatise called *On the Confusion of Tongues*, Philo deploys both the noun and verb forms of diaspora (*diaspora* and *diaspeirō*) in the last verses to describe the scattering of all humanity, not just Jews (*Confusion* 196–98). The significance of this difference cannot be overstated and warrants a full quotation:

> That is why he adds—The Lord dispersed (*diaspeirō*) them thence (Gen 11:8), that is He caused them to be scattered (*skedannumi*), to be fugitives, to vanish from sight . . . For when these are scattered, those who have been living in exile for many a day under the ban of folly's tyranny, shall receive their recall under a single proclamation, even the proclamation enacted and ratified by God, as the oracles shew, in which it is declared that "if thy dispersion (*diaspora*) be from one end of heaven to the other he shall gather thee from thence" (Deut 30:4).[37]

Since Abraham is not introduced until LXX Gen 12, the Babel story precedes the establishment of a specific people. Philo leverages the law's narrative structure in this case to set the proper noun. Diaspora

[37] *Confusion* 196–97. Colson, LCL.

outside the specific history of Israel. Philo's rewriting is even more striking given that Philo imports the term "diaspora" in his interpretation of the Babel event. In the Septuagint version, the proper noun Diaspora does not appear in Genesis 11, while the verb form *diaspeirō* does.

Like the Daniel court tales, Philo describes the dispersion of God's people as a punishing action of God. Unlike the Daniel court tales, however, Philo does not link the Babylonian or Hellenistic Dispersion of Jews to this conception. Rather, Philo uses diaspora very carefully. He limits its meaning and shapes it into a unique Philonic technical term and concept that conveys God's action in scattering all humankind across the world, before the selection of an elect group of people. In this way, Philo broadens diaspora conceptualization to denote everyone, not just Jews. It signifies the condition of all humanity as a creation distributed across the world, living according to customs and laws that suit each distinct settlement, rather than a narrowly defined designator of Israel's people spread across the Roman world.

The usefulness of the term for Philo is that it captures the origins and journeys of all nations, not just Israel. Moreover, Philo's thinking around diaspora shapes his interpretations of specific Torah passages that are normally understood solely in terms of Israel's history. For example, Philo's interpretation of LXX Deuteronomy 32:7-9 departs from the Torah, which uses the poem to speak specifically about Israel's failings. Philo maintains diaspora is a punitive consequence of unfaithfulness to God, but contrary to it he asserts it is not a punishment solely doled out to Jews. In another text, *On the Preliminary Studies*, Philo interprets LXX Deuteronomy 32:8 stating that diaspora is the consequence meted out to anyone, Jew or Gentile, who denies or ignores God and God's sovereignty. "When the Highest divided the nations, when He dispersed (*diaspeirō*) the sons of Adam. . . . For none of the wicked have preserved for them home or city, nor aught else that tends to fellowship, but they are scattered without settlement, driven about on every side, ever changing their place, nowhere able to hold their ground . . ." (*Prelim. Studies* 58).[38] If diaspora is punishment

[38] Colson, LCL. See also *Prelim. Studies* 56.

for mass human irreverence, Philo consigns the end of diaspora as the turning of all humanity to the one God. "I believe that each nation would abandon its peculiar ways, and, throwing overboard their ancestral customs, turn to honouring our laws alone." (*Moses* 2.44).[39]

Philo deploys the term "diaspora" in one other text, *On Rewards and Punishments*. Here, he uses it as an allegorical metaphor for discussing the journey of the soul. Philo states, "And therefore those who would imitate these examples of good living so marvelous in their loveliness, are bidden not to despair of changing for the better or of a restoration to the land of wisdom and virtue from the spiritual dispersion (*diaspora*), which vice has wrought" (*Rewards* 115).[40] When Philo describes biblical understandings of Israelite movements, diaspora is not his conventional term, and the treatise *On Rewards and Punishments* is instructive. When he details the movements and dissemination of the Israelites in this treatise, Philo uses terms such as fleeing (*pheugō*, *Rewards* 17, 148), captivity (*aichmalōtos*, *Rewards* 164), and scattered (*sporas*, *Rewards* 165). Although his allegorical discourse in this passage echoes and interprets LXX Deuteronomy 30:1-7, he is not using the term "diaspora" here in the strict sense of the physical and geographic movements of the Israelites. In this text, the term is reserved and deployed in service to his higher allegorical interpretation of the transience of the soul.

By deploying the term in a very limited fashion, Philo expresses a different kind of sensibility concerning diaspora than Daniel, Aristeas, or even 1 Peter. The experience of diaspora—particularly as Philo deploys it in service to interpreting Deuteronomy—is not limited to a single people. Dispersion is emblematic of the condition of the entire

[39] Colson, LCL. Berthelot makes a similar point about Deut 30 when describing Philo's understanding of exile in the Torah. "This discourse [*Rewards* 169–70] clearly echoes passages from Deuteronomy (30:1-7 in particular). More generally, it reflects the biblical understanding of exile as a temporary punishment, and of the nations as an instrument in the hands of God to castigate Israel. Ultimately, the divine purpose remains to save people, if they agree to repent and return to God." Berthelot, "Philo's Perception," 186. The drawback to Berthelot's description, however, is that it duplicates the fallacy challenged throughout this book. Namely, she collapses biblical conceptions of exile, diaspora, and wandering into the same category. Nonetheless, her summative point is helpful.

[40] Colson, LCL.

human race. The human condition of dispersion evokes an array of representations for Philo, including massive population movements, divine punishment, and physical violence in the form of dismemberment and persecution at the hands of other human beings (*Moses* 1.128; *Flaccus* 71). Consistently, Philo wields diaspora as scriptural proof that Gentiles will ultimately turn to the Jewish God. The conclusion of the diaspora is not the return of Jews to their original homeland. Rather, the summation of diaspora is the affirmation of a single claim: the oneness of God and the successful journey of the human soul to God. Thus, Philo's opening claim in *Embassy* represents his conception of diaspora in general: "even though some people have become skeptical about God's providential care for all mankind, and especially for 'the race of suppliants' which is the particular concern of the Father and King of the world, the Origin of all things, yet surely the present critical time and the many important questions now being settled should serve to convince them of it" (*Embassy* 3).

Conclusion

In terms of diaspora consciousness and the fortunes and misfortunes of displacement and dislocation, Philo's novel perspective shares some commonalities with the other writings. Similar to Aristeas, Philo's political treatises depict social dislocation instead of a religious experience. Jewish dislocation is the outcome of human militaristic ends and misplaced feelings of entitlement and prejudice. It represents the denigration of the human spirit into one that produces the mentality of "wild animals" (*Flaccus* 66). In the liturgical hymn of gratitude the Alexandrian Jews offer to God on the beach after learning of Flaccus' arrest, Philo makes this very point when he narrates the people describing themselves as "cityless and homeless because of the malice of their governor" (*Flaccus* 123).[41] While Jews are aware of their contingent positions in Alexandria and remain mindful of their native land, there is no pressure to return to and readopt that land.

Philo's notion resembles 1 Peter's theological narrative underpinning diaspora-Christian identity. For 1 Peter, God and Jesus Christ

[41] Van der Horst, *Philo's Flaccus*, 76.

are in heaven and diaspora Christians are the portion of humanity moving toward heaven as their ultimate destination. For Philo, God is in heaven and *all of humanity* can choose to journey toward God's heavenly abode only if they confess God's sovereignty. In allegorical fashion in *On Dreams*, Philo states that the "city of God" has become an otherworldly mystical destination suited for all peoples (*Dreams* 2.250). Unlike 1 Peter, where Christian confession of messianism and monotheism requires total abandonment of polyreligious practices, Philo's diaspora sensibility does not demand the same. Dispersion is the experience of the entire human race, and Philo's single requirement is that the One God is confessed as the Supreme Deity.

Philo's construction of diaspora is unique, =because he *reckons it a condition of humanity as a whole.* Philo does not want it to be associated with Jews living outside of Palestine. Nor does he want to imply that it will end with a massive Jewish return to that homeland. His careful and limited appropriation of the term suggests that he is, to some degree, aware of one line of thought related to diaspora and rejects it. For Philo, as long as diaspora means divine punishment and divine redress in the form of regathering all Jewish peoples to a central location, it is not a well-matched label for Jewish realities across the Greco-Roman world but a perfect descriptor for all humankind.

CONCLUSION

Liberating 1 Peter's Diaspora Vision

What is a thirty-something-year-old southern African American woman, a great-granddaughter and granddaughter of tenant horse farmers and housemaids, doing giving an appreciative reading of 1 Peter? After all, the letter is filled with language of subordination, servitude, oppression, inequity, ageism, and xenophobia. Four times it calls for the underdogs of society—foreigners, slaves, women, youth—"to submit" to government authorities and household superiors that render them servile and invisible (1 Pet 2:13; 2:18; 3:1; 5:5). It never calls for organized retaliation or militant action against provincial autocrats and local adversaries. Nor does it enjoin its readers to abandon conventional society altogether and establish alternate communities outside its precincts. On the contrary, 1 Peter encourages its readers to stay and "endure" maltreatment and exploitation as faithful followers of Christ who may win some of their persecutors over to the faith. Indeed, these aspects made 1 Peter an attractive text for bolstering colonial imperatives, especially in America.

First Peter was one of the biblical books used by southern evangelical proslavery and antiwomen proponents.[1] They argued the Bible in

[1] J. Albert Harril, "The Use of the NT in the American Slave Controversy: A Case History in the Hermeneutical Tension between Biblical Criticism and Christian Moral Debate," *Religion and American Culture* 10, no. 2 (2000): 149–86; Brad R. Braxton, *No Longer Slaves: Galatians and African American Experience* (Collegeville,

general, and 1 Peter in particular, endorse slavery and reckon women inferiors and African peoples uncivilized.[2] In an 1860 collection of proslavery essays, Thornton Stringfellow, a Virginia Baptist minister and staunch defender of slavery, comments on a series of passages from the Old Testament to the New Testament.[3] His task is simple: to prove that the American institution of slavery "is full of mercy" because God ordains it and Jesus Christ ratifies it.[4] He describes 1 Peter as a proslavery text by saying, "It is worthy of remark that he [Peter] says much to secure civil subordination to the State, and hearty and cheerful obedience to the masters, on the part of servants; yet he says nothing to masters in the whole letter. It would seem from this, that danger to the cause of Christ was on the side of *insubordination among the servants*, and a *want of humility with inferiors*, rather than *haughtiness among superiors* in the church." Stringfellow designates 1 Peter a vital Christian witness to the merits and necessity of slavery and the subordination of women in America, declaring, "What an important document is this!"[5]

Stringfellow's reading is disquieting and flawed on many fronts. One error in his approach that is most glaring is his denial (or perhaps ignorance) of the sociohistorical context that gave rise to 1 Peter. Before 1 Peter was collected with the other books of the Bible and

---

Minn.: Liturgical Press, 2002); Wayne A. Meeks, "'The Haustafeln' and American Slavery: A Hermeneutical Challenge," in *Theology and Ethics in Paul and His Interpreters: Essays in Honor of Victor Paul Furnish*, ed. Eugene Lovering Jr. and Jerry L. Sumney (Nashville: Abingdon, 1996), 245–52; Mitzi J. Smith, "Slavery in the Early Church," in *True to Our Native Land: An African American New Testament Commentary*, ed. Brian Blount and Cain Hope Felder (Minneapolis: Fortress, 2007), 11–22; Demetrius K. Williams, "The Bible and Models of Liberation in African American Experience," in *Yet with a Steady Beat: Contemporary U.S. Afrocentric Biblical Interpretation*, ed. Randall C. Bailey (Leiden: Brill, 2003), 37–40.

[2] For background information and source material on the proslavery and antislavery debate in the 18th and 19th centuries, see Curtis Evans, *The Burden of Black Religion* (Oxford: Oxford University Press, 2008).

[3] E. N. Elliott, ed., *Cotton Is King and Pro-slavery Arguments: Comprising the Writings of Hammond, Harper, Christy, Stringfellow, Hodge, Bledsoe, and Cartwright on This Important Subject* (Augusta, Ga.: Pritchard, Abbott & Loomis, 1860).

[4] Thornton Stringfellow, "The Bible Argument: Or, Slavery in the Light of Divine Revelation," in Elliott, *Cotton Is King*, 462.

[5] Stringfellow, "Bible Argument," 483, emphasis in original.

designated Christian Scriptures and before it was misused to legitimate an American brand of slavery and patriarchy, 1 Peter strategized survival for a scattered population facing real threats of verbal attack, physical harm, and the looming chance of genocide.[6] Although the proslavery master class of the United States, as embodied by Stringfellow's reading, wielded 1 Peter as a righteous Christian justification for disenfranchising minority populations based on race, gender, and class, it was not written originally as the master's text. First Peter is, in fact, the writing of the slave. It is writing from the underclass for the underclass, not the overlord. The First Letter of Peter was originally intended as an insider correspondence for an incipient group in need of a new perspective on their precarious circumstances and a vision of their status as a collective bearing the stigma "Christian" (1 Pet 4:16).

First Peter is not a divine mandate defining a hierarchal social order that places white American males on top and female physiology and brown bodies at the bottom. Rather, it is a private prescription, supplying multicultural and vulnerable Christian populations with a strategy for functioning and surviving in environments prone to violent and aggressive reprisals for cultural difference and social deviance. The author of 1 Peter was not persuading his Christian sisters and brothers to see their plight as domestic slaves, inferior people, and subjects of imperial control as God's created order. Rather, the First Letter of Peter conveys just *one* out of several options available to a leader of a dispersed population that is exposed, vulnerable, and defenseless. The author commands submission not because it was God's way but because it was his way of mitigating the conspicuousness of his community and keeping members alive. The writer of 1 Peter did not want Christian sisters and brothers to die any more than he wanted them to abandon the faithful community altogether. Yet he recognized that they were targets for verbal assault, social ostracism, and even susceptible to random or systematic acts of capital punishment.

Even if it could not be entirely remedied or avoided, the intention of the letter is to lessen the suffering the communities experienced by offering a reimagined way of life in the form of a Christian diaspora.

[6] In this case, the Pliny–Trajan correspondence is helpful in appreciating the author of 1 Peter's grasp of reality. Pliny, *Ep.* 10.96.

First Peter expresses a new perspective and vision of Christian identity and practice through a divergent understanding of what diaspora means. Up to the moment the letter was penned, a dominant conception of diaspora was that it is a punitive action taken by God. It was a theological rationale for the geographic displacement and dispersion of Israel across the ancient Mediterranean world. Yet as the select writings of part II display, that is not the only understanding of diaspora circulating in Hellenistic Jewish literary circles. First Peter takes up the task of conceiving and reconceiving dispersion anew in light of social and historical realities. Positionality, not theology, becomes the defining characteristic of diaspora thinking for which 1 Peter is an exemplar.

The idea of positionality rings true in 1 Peter on two levels. At one level, it is the social position of the letter's community that drives the author to write the letter in the first place. The community's position left the letter writer with a limited set of options and outcomes—namely, accommodate and live or defy and die. While there may have been more opportunities or options available to strategize, the author apparently did not find those nuanced alternatives (if he conceived of them at all) as appealing enough to put forward. This gives rise to the second level of positionality at work in 1 Peter. In light of the sociohistorical positions 1 Peter is assessing and responding to, the position of the proper noun "Diaspora" in the discourse is essential. By positioning the noun form of diaspora after the label "elect-foreigner" and before the list of five Roman provinces in 1 Peter 1:1, the author designates diaspora as the principal situation of the intended addressees. Diaspora is not punishment for followers of Christ but reward for their unwavering commitment to the practices and basic beliefs of Christianity. First Peter's diaspora vision is not Philo's version where all humanity is cast as scattered and journeying, but it is an essential feature of Christian confession and community. Diaspora, in the letter, represents not the destruction of a people but the making of a new, more pluralistic and tolerant kinship in ways akin to the Letter of Aristeas. It inaugurates the constitution of a new and unconventional fellowship (*koinōneō*, 1 Pet 4:13) composed of mixed ethnic, territorial, and cultural backgrounds.

The image of diaspora illustrates how this new ethnic group is to function in its native locales while simultaneously existing separate from it. First Peter deploys the image of diaspora at the beginning of the letter only to retool it throughout the rest. Indeed, the letter portrays a double literary motive in which it advocates neither a fully conformist position nor a nonconformist position in relation to Christian life and its larger non-Christian environs. The letter puts forward a social strategy that consists of a diaspora form of double consciousness in which the author makes his readers aware of two aspects of their Christian existence. On the one hand, the letter describes the distinctive features of Christian social identity, narrative history, and ritual practice. On the other hand, it addresses how Christians should expect to be perceived and received by their local surroundings and domestic spaces given their "Christian" affiliation.

The insights about diaspora and 1 Peter provided in this book have purchase for at least two different types of readers. The first are Christians interested in grappling with 1 Peter's social propositions on their own terms. It is a resource for those compelled to divorce the rhetoric of 1 Peter from American history and policies, personal inclinations and ideologies, and contemporary concerns about the maltreatment of women, various ethnicities, and foreigners. The study corrects readings of 1 Peter that argue it reflects God's divine arrangement of the household and government and divine gradation of different classes of people. Rather, the book depicts the real life-and-death decision that the letter writer had to make because of the larger political-economic system, characterized as a limited-good society, that early Christians had to survive.

Having read this book, many contemporary Christians should feel some form of maladjustment because 1 Peter appears to be making a radical demand on us in a form we rarely, if ever, contemplate. Diversity should not be a reality that we are moving toward and trying to achieve in our respective congregations, neighborhoods, organizations, and bible study cell groups. *Through the eyes of the author of 1 Peter, we discern that the basic makeup of Christianity is that we begin in diversity.* Seeking and embracing diversity that is most radical and deviant from our current social norm is the necessary first step in ensuring that the formation of our Christian communities is aligned to an authentic Christian vision of radical fellowship and transformed group identity. If diversity that transgresses social and cultural boundaries of gender, class, ethnicity, age, and cultural difference were not a priority at the initial stages of our respective faith communities, 1 Peter and the other literary witnesses in this book would urge us to reassess the very foundation upon which our local neighborhoods and churches, denominational connections and associations, and friendships and alliances were founded.

The second readership that I hope finds this book instructive are investigators of historic population movements—diasporas, emigrations, exiles, resettlements, and so forth. This book has much to offer those concerned about contemporary rhetoric around global population movements and those seeking to understand the dynamics of navigating foreignness in changing and unpredictable environments. Notions regarding the process of moving from one place to another and living as kinship groups on the borders of multiple sociopolitical regimes and balancing numerous regional attachments are not new. Concerns about citizenship, social allegiances, and multilingualism (to name a few) are apprehensions that have plagued humanity for ages, and different groups have maneuvered these dynamics in different ways. By returning to some of the earliest renderings of diaspora and marginality available to us in Hellenistic Jewish literature, contemporary readers confront their own biases and narrow frameworks regarding what hospitality and kinship to strangers look like. The face of "the stranger" and "the foreigner" in our midst changes as quickly as political power changes hands. It is not a static interaction. Each new generation and distinct context must revisit old notions related to diaspora, immigration, and foreignness and consider them anew in light of what makes sense and is ethical and hospitable in their particular sociohistorical setting.

Instead of approaching this New Testament letter with suspicion and skepticism, there is reason to appreciate the strategic maneuvering 1 Peter exhibits. It precipitates a different kind of liberation ethic—one that may make modern interpreters of the letter, especially those of us committed to social activism and aggressive acts of social transformation, cringe. Yet its liberative ethic or idea is no less significant. The liberative decision the author of 1 Peter makes, leveraging diaspora as its dominant image, is to tell communities to stay alive. They have no major resources. They have no real systemic power in the governing systems around them. All they have is a future hope that a time of triumph, retribution, and restitution will come. But in order to see that they must navigate the world they inhabit and live in—not die in—now. In other words, 1 Peter should be read and appreciated for the particular liberation moment it captures in the life of a marginal, oppressed, and disenfranchised community. No matter how much I want it to be, it is not the community's time to revolt, rebel, attack, challenge, and defy the status quo. It is a time to survive the system despite the system.

My truth rings clear this moment. As much as I am a daughter of those who fought and declared openly their full humanity and rights as God's creation, I am also the daughter of those who made an honest assessment of their odds and decided it was more expedient in the moment for them to survive the ungodly, inhumane, and evil systems forced on them. I am as much the daughter of those who survived the Middle Passage and auction blocks as I am the daughter of those who fought for civil rights and continue to fight for equal access and fair treatment for all in the current movements of Black Lives Matter and others. Many of us are indebted to both decision makers: those who confronted evil disparities as well as those who concealed their critique in the mask of social compliance, cultural performance, and verbal niceties so that their progeny could live to fight another day. Therefore, here we are, continuing this dance between hidden and public resistance or affirmation. Some of us are the product of both choices—to survive and to challenge in varying degrees and at different moments as strangers and family, whose plights are linked one to the other.

BIBLIOGRAPHY

Achtemeier, Paul J. "The Christology of 1 Peter: Some Reflections." Pages 140–54 in *Who Do You Say That I Am? Essays on Christology in Honor of Jack Dean Kingsbury*. Edited by Mark A. Powell and David R. Bauer. Louisville, Ky.: Westminster John Knox, 1999.

———. *1 Peter*. Hermeneia. Philadelphia: Fortress, 1996.

Albertz, Rainer. "The Social Setting of the Aramaic and Hebrew Book of Daniel." Pages 171–204 in *The Book of Daniel: Composition and Reception*. Edited by John J. Collins and Peter W. Flint. Vetus Testamentum Supplement 83. Leiden: Brill, 2001.

Alter, Robert. *The Art of Biblical Narrative*. London: Allen & Unwin, 1981.

Anderson, Cheryl. *Ancient Laws and Contemporary Controversies: The Need for Inclusive Biblical Interpretation*. London: Oxford University Press, 2009.

Arichea, Daniel C., and Eugene A. Nida. *Handbook on the First Letter from Peter*. New York: United Bible Societies, 1980.

Aristotle. *The "Art" of Rhetoric*. Translated by John Henry Freese. Loeb Classical Library. Vol. 22. Cambridge, Mass.: Harvard University Press, 1994.

———. *Politics*. Translated by H. Rackham. Loeb Classical Library. Vol. 21. Cambridge, Mass.: Harvard University Press, 1990.

———. *The Politics*. Translated by Carnes Lord. Chicago: University of Chicago Press, 1984.

Avalos, Hector. "The Comedic Function of the Enumerations of Officials and Instruments in Daniel 3." *Catholic Biblical Quarterly* 53, no. 4 (1991): 580–88.

Avis, Paul. *God and the Creative Imagination: Metaphor, Symbol and Myth in Religion and Theology*. London: Routledge, 1999.

Balch, David. "Hellenization/Acculturation in 1 Peter." In Talbert, *Perspectives on First Peter*, 79–101.

———. "Household Codes." Pages 25–50 in *Greco-Roman Literature and the New Testament: Selected and Forms and Genres*. Edited by David E. Aune. Society of Biblical Literature Sources for Biblical Study 21. Atlanta: Scholars Press, 1988.

———. *Let Wives Be Submissive: The Domestic Code in 1 Peter*. Society of Biblical Literature Monograph Series 26. Atlanta: Scholars Press, 1981.

Baltzer, Klaus. *Deutero-Isaiah: A Commentary on Isaiah 40–55*. Edited by Peter Machinist. Translated by Margaret Kohl. Hermeneia 23C. Minneapolis: Fortress, 2001.

Bammel, Ernst. "The Commands in 1 Peter II.17." *New Testament Studies* 11 (1964–1965): 279–81.

Barclay, John M. G. *Jews in the Mediterranean Diaspora: From Alexander to Trajan (323 BCE–117 CE)*. Edinburgh: T&T Clark, 1996.

———. *Negotiating Diaspora: Jewish Strategies in the Roman Empire*. The Library of Second Temple Studies 45. New York: T&T Clark, 2004.

———. "Universalism and Particularism: Twin Components of Both Judaism and Early Christianity." Page 207–24 in *A Vision for the Church: Studies in Early Christian Ecclesiology in Honour of J. P. M. Sweet*. Edited by Markus Bockmuehl and Michael B. Thompson. Edinburgh: T&T Clark, 1997.

Barclay, William. *New Testament Words*. Philadelphia: Westminster, 1974.

Barreto, Eric. *Ethnic Negotiations: The Function of Race and Ethnicity in Acts 16*. Wissenschaftliche Untersuchungen zum Neuen Testament 2. Tübingen: Mohr Siebeck, 2010.

Barth, Fredrik, ed. *Ethnic Groups and Boundaries: The Social Organization of Culture Difference*. Boston: Little, Brown, 1969.

Bauckham, Richard J. "James, 1 and 2 Peter, Jude." Pages 303–17 in *It Is Written: Scripture Citing Scripture*. Edited by Don A. Carson and Hugh G. M. Williams. Cambridge: Cambridge University Press, 1988.

Bauer, Walter, Frederick William Danker, William F. Arndt, and F. Wilbur Gingrich, eds. *A Greek–English Lexicon of the New Testament and)ther Early Christian Literature*. 3rd ed., version 1.5. Chicago: University of Chicago Press, 2000.

Bauman-Martin, Betsy J. "Speaking Jewish: Postcolonial Aliens and Strangers in First Peter." In Webb and Bauman-Martin, *Reading First Peter with New Eyes*, 144–77.

———. "Women on the Edge: New Perspectives on Women in the Petrine Haustafel." *Journal of Biblical Literature* 123, no. 2 (2004): 253–79.

Baur, Ferdinand Christian. *Das Christentum und die christliche Kirche der drei ersten Jahrhunderte.* 2nd ed. Tübingen: Friedrich Frommann, 1966 [1860].

Beale, G. K. "A Reconsideration of the Text of Daniel in the Apocalypse." *Bib* 67 (1986): 539–43.

Beare, Francis W. *The First Epistle of Peter: The Greek Text with Introduction and Notes.* 3rd ed. Oxford: Blackwell, 1970 [1947].

———. "The Text of 1 Peter in Papyrus 72." *Journal of Biblical Literature* 80 (1961): 253–60.

Bell, H. I. *Jews and Christians in Egypt.* London: Oxford University Press, 1924.

Benko, Stephen. *Pagan Rome and the Early Christians.* Bloomington: Indiana University Press, 1985.

Berquist, Jon L., and Claudia V. Camp. *Constructions of Space I. Theory, Geography, and Narrative.* New York: T&T Clark, 2007.

———. *Constructions of Space II: The Biblical City and Other Imagined Spaces.* New York: T&T Clark, 2008.

Berthelot, Katell. "Philo's Perception of the Roman Empire." *Journal for the Study of Judaism in the Persian, Hellenistic, and Roman Periods* 42 (2011): 166–87.

Best, Ernest. "1 Peter and the Gospel Tradition. *New Testament Studies* 16 (1970): 95–113.

———. *1 Peter.* New Century Bible. London: Marshall, Morgan & Scott, 1982.

Bevan, A. A. *A Short Commentary on the Book of Daniel.* Cambridge: Cambridge University Press, 1892.

Bhabha, Homi K. "Cultural Diversity and Cultural Differences." Pages 155–57 in *The Post-colonial Studies Reader.* 2nd ed. Edited by Bill Ashcroft et al. London: Routledge, 2006 [1988].

———. *The Location of Culture.* London/New York: Routledge, 1994.

Bickerman, Elias J. *The Jews in the Greek Age.* Cambridge, Mass.: Harvard University Press, 1988.

———. "The Name of Christians." *Harvard Theological Review* 42 (1949): 109–24.

———. "Trajan, Hadrian and the Christians." *Rivista di filogia e di instruzione classica* 96 (1968): 290–315.

Birnbaum, E. *The Place of Judaism in Philo's Thought: Israel, Jews, and Proselytes.* Atlanta: Scholars Press, 1996.

Blount, Brian K., and Cain Hope Felder, eds. *True to Our Native Land: An African American New Testament Commentary*. Minneapolis: Fortress, 2007.

Boismard, M. E. *Quatre hymnes baptismales dans la première épître de Pierre*. Lectio Divina 30. Paris: Cerf, 1961.

Borgen, Peder. *Early Christianity and Hellenistic Judaism*. London: A&C Black, 1998.

———. *Philo of Alexandria: An Exegete of His Time*. Leiden: Brill, 1997.

Boring, M. Eugene. "First Peter in Recent Study." *Word and World* 24 (2004): 358–67.

———. "Narrative Dynamics in First Peter: The Function of Narrative World." In Webb and Bauman-Martin, *Reading First Peter with New Eyes*, 7–40.

———. *1 Peter*. Abingdon New Testament Commentaries. Nashville: Abingdon, 1999.

Boyarin, Daniel. *Dying for God: Martyrdom and the Making of Christianity and Judaism*. Stanford: Stanford University Press, 1999.

Boyarin, Daniel, and Jonathan Boyarin. "Diaspora: Generation and the Ground Jewish Identity." *Critical Inquiry* 19 (1993): 693–725.

Braxton, Brad R. *No Longer Slaves: Galatians and African American Experience*. Collegeville, Minn.: Liturgical Press, 2002.

———. "Paul and Racial Reconciliation: A Postcolonial Approach to 2 Corinthians 3:12–18." Pages 411–28 in *Scripture and Traditions: Essays on Early Judaism and Christianity in Honor of Carl R. Holladay*. Edited by Patrick Gray and Gail R. O'Day. Leiden: Brill, 2008.

Braziel, Jana Evans, and Anita Mannur. *Theorizing Diaspora*. Malden, Mass.: Blackwell, 2006.

Briant, Pierre. *From Cyrus to Alexander: A History of the Persian Empire*. Paris: Eisenbrauns, 2002.

Brown, Jeannine K. "Just a Busybody? A Look at the Greco-Roman Topos of Meddling for Defining ἀλλοτριεπίσκοπος in 1 Peter 4:15." *Journal of Biblical Literature* 125 (2006): 549–68.

Brown, Michael Joseph. *The Lord's Prayer Through North African Eyes: A Window into Early Christianity*. London: T&T Clark, 2004.

Brubaker, Rogers. "The 'Diaspora' Diaspora." *Ethnic and Racial Studies* 28, no. 1 (2005): 1–19.

———. *Nationalism Reframed: Nationhood and the National Question in the New Europe*. Cambridge: Cambridge University Press, 1996.

Brubaker, Rogers, and Frederick Cooper. "Beyond 'Identity.'" *Theory and Society* 29, no. 1 (2000): 1–47.

Brueggemann, Walter. *Biblical Perspectives on Evangelism: Living in a Three-Storied Universe*. Nashville: Abingdon, 1993.

Burr, Vikto. *Tiberius Julius Alexander*. Bonn: Habelt, 1955.

Burt, Sean. *The Courtier and the Governor: Transformations of Genre in the Nehemiah Memoir*. Göttingen: Vandenhoeck & Ruprecht, 2014.

Butler, Kim D. "Defining Diaspora, Refining a Discourse." *Diaspora* 10, no. 2 (2001): 189–219.

Campbell, R. Alastair. *The Elders: Seniority within Earliest Christianity*. Studies of the New Testament and Its World. London: T&T Clark, 1994.

Campbell, William S. *The "We" Passages in the Acts of the Apostles: The Narrator as Narrative Character*. Studies in Biblical Literature. Atlanta: Society of Biblical Literature, 2007.

Charles, Robert H. *A Critical and Exegetical Commentary on the Book of Daniel*. Oxford: Clarendon, 1929.

Charles, Ronald. "Hybridity and the Letter of Aristeas." *Journal for the Study of Judaism in the Persian, Hellenistic, and Roman Periods* 40, no. 2 (2009): 242–59.

Chatman, Seymour. *Story and Discourse: Narrative Structure in Fiction and Film*. Ithaca, N.Y.: Cornell University Press, 1978.

Cherry, David. *The Roman World: A Sourcebook*. Malden, Mass.: Blackwell, 2001.

Cicero, Marcus Tullius. *Cicero on Oratory and Orators: With His Letters to Quintus and Brutus*. Translated by John Selby Watson. Bohn's Classical Library. London: R. Clay Printer, 1855.

Clifford, James. "Diasporas." *Cultural Anthropology* 9, no. 3 (1994): 302–38.

Cohen, Naomi. "The Names of the Translators in the Letter of Aristeas: A Study in the Dynamics of Cultural Tension." *Journal for the Study of Judaism in the Persian, Hellenistic, and Roman Periods* 15 (1984): 32–64.

Cohen, Robin. "Diaspora." Pages 3642–45 in *International Encyclopedia of the Social and Behavioral Sciences*. Edited by Neil J. Smelser and Paul B. Baltes. Amsterdam: Elsevier, 2001.

———. "Diasporas and the Nation-State: From Victims to Challengers." *International Affairs* 72, no. 3 (1996): 507–20.

———. *Global Diasporas: An Introduction*. London: UCL Press, 1997.

Collins, Adela Yarbro. "The Son of Man Tradition and the Book of Revelation." Pages 536–68 in *The Messiah: The First Princeton Symposium on*

Judaism and Christian Origins. Edited by James H. Charlesworth. Minneapolis: Fortress, 1992.

Collins, John. *Apocalypse, Prophecy, and Pseudepigraphy: On Jewish Apocalyptic Literature*. Grand Rapids: Eerdmans, 2015.

———. *The Apocalyptic Imagination: An Introduction to Jewish Apocalyptic Literature*. 2nd ed. Grand Rapids: Eerdmans, 1998.

———. *Between Athens and Jerusalem: Jewish Identity in the Hellenistic Diaspora*. 2nd ed. Biblical Resource Series. Grand Rapids: Eerdmans, 2000.

———. *Daniel: A Commentary on the Book of Daniel*. Hermeneia 27. Minneapolis: Fortress, 1993.

Cone, James. *A Black Theology of Liberation*. 20th anniv. ed. Maryknoll, N.Y.: Orbis Books, 2001 [1970].

Coser, Lewis. *The Functions of Social Conflict*. London: Routledge & Kegan Paul, 1956.

Counihan, Carole, and Penny Van Esterik, eds. *Food and Culture: A Reader*. 2nd ed. New York: Routledge, 2013.

Cranfield, C. E. B. *The First Epistle of Peter*. London: SCM Press, 1950.

Crawford, Sidnie White. "The Book of Esther." In vol. 3 of *The New Interpreter's Bible*. Edited by L. Keck et al. Nashville: Abingdon, 1999.

Cross, Frank Leslie. *1 Peter: A Paschal Liturgy*. 2nd ed. London: Mowbray, 1957.

Cullmann, Oscar. *Salvation in History*. London: SCM Press, 1967.

Dahl, Nils Alstrup. "The One God of Jews and Gentiles (Romans 3:29-30)." Pages 178–91 in *Studies in Paul: Theology for the Early Christian Mission*. Edited by Nils Alstrup Dahl. Minneapolis: Augsburg, 1977.

Dalton, William Joseph. *Christ's Proclamation to the Spirits: Study of 1 Peter 3:18–4:6*. Analecta Biblica 23. Rome: Editrice Pontificio Istituto Biblico, 1989.

———. "The Interpretation of 1 Peter 3:19 and 4:6: Light from 2 Peter." *Biblica* 60 (1979): 547–55.

Davids, Peter H. *The First Epistle of Peter*. New International Commentary on the New Testament. Grand Rapids: Eerdmans, 1990.

Davidson, J. *Courtesans and Fishcakes: The Consuming Passions of Classical Athens*. New York: St. Martin's, 1998.

Deissmann, Adolf. *Light from the Ancient East*. Translated by Lionel R. M. Strachan. 4th ed. Grand Rapids: Baker, 1978.

deSilva, David A. *Honor, Patronage, Kinship and Purity: Unlocking New Testament Culture*. Downers Grove, Ill.: InterVarsity, 2000.

De Ste. Croix, Geoffrey E. M. "Why Were the Early Christians Persecuted?" *Past and Present* 26 (1963): 6–38.

Dewald, Carolyn. "Greek Education and Rhetoric." Pages 1077–1107 in vol. 2 of *Civilization of the Ancient Mediterranean: Greece and Rome*. Edited by Michael Grant and Rachel Kitzinger. New York: Scribner's Sons, 1988.

Dibelius, Martin. "Style Criticism and the Book of Acts." Pages 1–25 in *Studies in Acts of the Apostles*, edited by Heinrich Greeven, translated by Mary Ling. London: SCM Press, 1956.

———. *Urchristentum und Kultur*. Heidelberg: Carl Winters Universitätsbuchhandlung, 1928.

Dillon, John. *The Middle Platonists: 80 B.C. to A.D. 220*. Ithaca, N.Y.: Cornell University Press, 1977.

Doering, Lutz. "Apostle, Co-elder, and Witness of Suffering: Author Construction and Peter Image in First Peter." Pages 645–81 in *Pseudepigraphie und Verfasserfiktion in frühchristlichen Briefen*. Edited by J. Frey et al. Wissenschaftliche Untersuchungen zum Neuen Testament 246. Tübingen: Mohr Siebeck, 2009.

Donaldson, Terence L. *Judaism and the Gentiles: Jewish Patterns of Universalism (to 135 CE)*. Waco, Tex.: Baylor University Press, 2007.

Doran, Robert. "The Martyr: A Synoptic View of the Mother and Her Seven Sons." Pages 189–221 in *Ideal Figures in Ancient Judaism: Profiles and Paradigms*. Edited by George W. E. Nickelsburg and John J. Collins. Society of Biblical Literature Sources for Biblical Study 12. Chico, Calif.: Scholars Press, 1983.

Downing, F. Gerald. "Pliny Prosecutions of Christians: Revelation and 1 Peter." *Journal for the Study of the New Testament* 34 (1988): 105–23.

Dubis, Mark. *1 Peter: A Handbook on the Greek Text*. Baylor Handbook on the Greek New Testament. Waco, Tex.: Baylor University Press, 2010.

———. "Research on 1 Peter: A Survey of Scholarly Literature Since 1985." *Currents in Biblical Research* 4 (2006): 199–239.

Du Bois, W. E. B. *The Souls of Black Folk*. New York: Dover, 1994.

Dufoix, Stephane. *Diasporas*. Berkeley: University of California Press, 2008.

Duncan-Jones, Richard. *The Economy of the Roman Empire: Quantitative Studies*. 2nd ed. Cambridge: Cambridge University Press, 1982 [1974].

———. *Structure and Scale in the Roman Economy*. Cambridge: Cambridge University Press, 1990.

Dunning, Benjamin Harrison. *Aliens and Sojourners: Self as Other in Early Christianity*. Philadelphia: University of Pennsylvania Press, 2009.

———. "Strangers and Aliens No Longer: Negotiating Identity and Difference in Ephesians 2." *Harvard Theological Review* 99 (2006): 1–16.

Edwards, Brent Hayes. "The Uses of Diaspora." *Social Text* 19, no. 66 (2001): 45–73.

Elazar, Daniel. "The Jewish People as the Classic Diaspora: A Political Analysis." Pages 212–57 in *Modern Diasporas in International Politics*. Edited by Gabriel Sheffer. London: Croom Helm, 1986.

Elliott, E. N., ed. *Cotton Is King and Pro-slavery Arguments: Comprising the Writings of Hammond, Harper, Christy, Stringfellow, Hodge, Bledsoe, and Cartwright on This Important Subject*. Augusta, Ga.: Pritchard, Abbott & Loomis, 1860.

Elliott, John H. *Conflict, Community, and Honor: 1 Peter in Social-Scientific Perspective*. Cascade Companions. Eugene, Ore.: Cascade Books, 2007.

———. "Disgraced yet Graced: The Gospel according to 1 Peter in the Key of Honor and Shame." *Biblical Theology Bulletin* 25 (1995): 166–78.

———. "Elders as Leaders in 1 Peter and the Early Church." *Harvard Theological Studies* 28 (2001): 549–59.

———. *The Elect and the Holy: An Exegetical Examination of 1 Peter 2:4–10 and the Phrase* basileion hierateuma. Supplements to Novum Testamentum 12. Leiden: Brill, 1996.

———. *A Home for the Homeless: A Social-Scientific Criticism of 1 Peter, Its Situation and Strategy*. 2nd ed. Minneapolis: Fortress 1990 [1981].

———. "1 Peter, Its Situation and Strategy: A Discussion with David Balch." In Talbert, *Perspectives on First Peter*, 61–78.

———. *1 Peter: A New Translation with Introduction and Commentary*. Anchor Bible 37B. New York: Doubleday, 2000.

———. "Peter, Silvanus and Mark in 1 Peter and Acts: Sociological-Exegetical Perspectives on a Petrine Group in Rome." Pages 250–67 in *Wort in der Zeit: Neutestamentliche Studiend. Festgabe für Kar Heinrich Rengstorff zum 75. Geburtstag*. Edited by W. Haubeck and M. Bachmann. Leiden: Brill, 1980.

———. "The Rehabilitation of an Exegetical Step-Child: 1 Peter in Recent Research." *JBL* 95 (1976): 243–54. Reprinted in Talbert, *Perspectives on First Peter*, 3–16.

———. "The Roman Provenance of 1 Peter and the Gospel of Mark: A Response to David Dungan." Pages 181–94 in *Colloquy on New Testament Studies: A Time for Reappraisal and Fresh Approaches*. Edited by Bruce Corley. Macon, Ga.: Mercer University Press, 1983.

———. *What Is Social-Scientific Criticism?* Minneapolis: Fortress, 1993.

Elliott, J. K. *The Apocryphal New Testament: A Collection of Apocryphal Christian Literature in an English Translation*. Oxford: Clarendon, 1993.

Elliott, Neal, and Mark Reasoner. *Documents and Images for the Study of Paul*. Minneapolis: Fortress, 2011.

Epictetus. *Enchiridion and Selections from the Discourses of Epictetus*. Translated by George Long. Stilwell, Kans.: Digireads, 2005.

Evans, Curtis. *The Burden of Black Religion*. Oxford: Oxford University Press, 2008.

Fagbemi, Stephen Ayodeji A. *Who Are the Elect in 1 Peter? A Study in Biblical Exegesis and Its Application to the Anglican Church of Nigeria*. Studies in Biblical Literature 104. New York: Lang, 2007.

Farber, J. Joel. "The Cyropaedia and Hellenistic Kingship." *American Journal of Philology* 100 (1979): 497–514.

Feldman, Louis H. *Jew and Gentile in the Ancient World: Attitudes and Interactions from Alexander to Justinian*. Princeton, N.J.: Princeton University Press, 1993.

———. *Jewish Life and Thought among Greeks and Romans: Primary Readings*. Minneapolis: Augsburg Fortress, 1996.

Feldmeier, Reinhard. *Die Christen als Fremde: Die Metapher der Fremde in der antiken Welt, im Urchristentum und im ersten Petrusbrief*. Wissenschaftliche Untersuchungen zum Neuen Testament 64. Tübingen: Mohr Siebeck, 1992.

———. *Der erste Brief des Petrus*. Theologischer Handkommentar zum Neuen Testament 15, no. 1. Leipzig: Evangelische Verlagsanstalt, 2005.

———. *The First Letter of Peter: A Commentary on the Greek Text*. Translated by Peter H. Davids. Waco, Tex.: Baylor University Press, 2008.

———. "The 'Nation' of Strangers: Social Contempt and Its Theological Interpretations in Ancient Judaism and Early Christianity." Pages 240–70 in *Ethnicity and the Bible*. Edited by Mark G. Brett. Biblical Interpretation. Leiden: Brill, 1996.

———. "Salvation and Anthropology in First Peter." In Niebuhr and Wall, *Catholic Epistles and Apostolic Tradition*, 203–13, 437–41.

Finn, T. M. "The God-Fearers Reconsidered." *Catholic Biblical Quarterly* 47 (1985): 75–84.

Flusser, David. "The Four Empires in the Fourth Sibyl and in the Book of Daniel." *Israel Oriental Studies* 2 (1972): 148–75.

Fornberg, Tord. *An Early Church in a Pluralistic Society: A Study of 2 Peter*. Lund: Gleerup, 1977.

Foucault, Michel. "Of Other Spaces." *Diacritics* 16 (1986): 22–27.

Gager, John G. *Moses in Greco-Roman Paganism*. Nashville: Abingdon Press, 1972.

Gambetti, Sandra. *The Alexandrian Riots of 38 C.E. and the Persecution of the Jews: A Historical Reconstruction*. Leiden: Brill, 2009.

Gill, David W. J., and Conrad Gempf, eds. *The Book of Acts in Its Graeco-Roman Setting*. Grand Rapids: Eerdmans, 1994.

Gilroy, Paul. *The Black Atlantic: Modernity and Double Consciousness*. Cambridge, Mass.: Harvard University Press, 1993.

———. "Diaspora." *Paragraph* 17, no. 1 (1994): 207–12.

Goffman, Erving. *Stigma: Notes on the Management of Spoiled Identity*. London: Penguin, 1990 [1963].

Goldstein, Jonathan A. "The Message of Aristeas to Philokrates: In the Second Century B.C.E., Obey the Torah, Venerate the Temple of Jerusalem, but Speak Greek, and Put Your Hopes in the Ptolemaic Dynasty." Pages 1–23 in *Eretz Israel, Israel and the Jewish Diaspora Mutual Relation: Proceedings of the First Annual Symposium of the Philip M. and Ethel Klutznick Chair in Jewish Civilization Held on Sunday–Monday October 9–10, 1988*. Edited by Menachem Mor. Studies in Jewish Civilization-1. Lanham, Md.: University Press of America, 1991.

———. *II Maccabees*. Anchor Bible 41A. Garden City, N.Y.: Doubleday, 1983.

Gomez, Michael. *Reversing Sail: A History of the African Diaspora*. Cambridge: Cambridge University Press, 2005.

Gonzalez, Catherine Gunsalus. *1 & 2 Peter, and Jude. Belief: A Theological Commentary on the Bible*. Louisville, Ky.: Westminster John Knox, 2010.

Good, E. M. "Apocalyptic Comedy: The Book of Daniel." *Semeia* 32 (1984): 41–70.

Goodenough, Erwin R. *By Light, Light: The Mystic Gospel of Hellenistic Judaism*. New Haven, Conn.: Yale University Press, 1935.

———. *An Introduction to Philo Judaeus*, 2nd ed. Oxford: Basil Blackwell, 1962.

———. "The Political Philosophy of Hellenistic Kingship." *Yale Classical Studies* 1 (1928): 53–102.

Goodenough, Erwin R., and Howard L. Goodhart. *The Politics of Philo Judaeus: Practice and Theory, with a General Bibliography of Philo*. New Haven, Conn.: Yale University Press, 1938.

Gooding, David W. "Aristeas and Septuagint Origins." *Vetus Testamentum* 13 (1963): 357–79.

Goppelt, Leonhard. *A Commentary on 1 Peter*. Grand Rapids: Eerdmans, 1993.

Goulder, Michael D. "Did Peter Ever Go to Rome?" *Scottish Journal of Theology* 57 (2004): 377–96.

Green, Joel B. "Living as Exiles: The Church in the Diaspora in 1 Peter." Pages 311–25 in *Holiness and Ecclesiology in the New Testament*. Edited by Kent E. Brower and Andy Johnson. Grand Rapids: Eerdmans, 2007.

———. *1 Peter*. Two Horizons New Testament Commentary. Grand Rapids: Eerdmans, 2007.

Grieb, A. Katherine. *The Story of Romans: A Narrative Defense of God's Righteousness*. Louisville, Ky.: Westminster John Knox, 2002.

Gross, Carl D. "Are the Wives of 1 Peter 3:7 Christians?" *Journal for the Study of the New Testament* 35 (1989): 89–96.

Grudem, Wayne A. *1 Peter*. TNTC. Downers Grove, Ill.: InterVarsity, 1988.

Gruen, Erich. "Diaspora and Homeland." In Wettstein and Soussloff, *Diasporas and Exiles*, 18–25.

———. *Diaspora: Jews amidst Greeks and Romans*. Cambridge, Mass.: Harvard University Press, 2002.

———. *Heritage and Hellenism: The Reinvention of Jewish Tradition*. Berkeley: University of California Press, 1998.

Gunn, D. M., and P. M. McNutt. *Imagining Biblical Worlds: Studies in Spatial, Social and Historical Constructs in Honor of James W. Flanagan*. New York: Sheffield Academic, 2002.

Haas, Christopher. *Alexandria in Late Antiquity: Topography and Social Conflict*. Baltimore: Johns Hopkins University Press, 1997.

Hacham, Noah. "The Letter of Aristeas: A New Exodus Story?" *Journal for the Study of Judaism in the Persian, Hellenistic, and Roman Periods* 36 (2005): 1.

———. "3 Maccabees and Esther: Parallels, Intertextuality, and Diaspora Identity." *Journal of Biblical Literature* 126 (2007): 765–85.

Hadas, Moses. *Aristeas to Philocrates*. New York: Ktav, 1973.

Haines-Eitzen, Kim. *Guardians of Letters: Literacy, Power, and the Transmitters of Early Christian Literature*. Oxford: Oxford University Press, 2000.

Hall, Jonathan. *Ethnic Identity in Greek Antiquity*. Cambridge: Cambridge University Press, 2000.

Hall, Stuart. "Cultural Identity and Diaspora." Pages 223–37 in *Identity: Community, Culture, Difference*. Edited by Jonathan Rutherford. London: Lawrence & Wishart, 1990.

———. "Thinking the Diaspora: Home-Thoughts from Abroad." *Small Axe* 6 (1999): 1–18.

Hanson, K. C. "BTB Readers Guide: Kinship." *Biblical Theology Bulletin* 24 (1994): 183–94.

———. "The Herodians and Mediterranean Kinship, Part 3." *Biblical Theology Bulletin* 20, no. 1 (1990): 10–21.

Harland, Philip A. *Associations, Synagogues, and Congregations: Claiming a Place in Ancient Mediterranean Society*. Minneapolis: Fortress, 2003.

———. *Dynamics of Identity in the World of the Early Christians: Associations, Judeans, and Cultural Minorities*. London: T&T Clark, 2009.

Harnack, Adolf von. *The Expansion of Christianity in the First Three Centuries*. Vol. 1. London: Williams & Norgate, 1905.

———. *The Expansion of Christianity in the First Three Centuries*. Vol. 2. London: Williams & Norgate, 1905.

Harril, J. Albert. "Paul and Empire: Studying Roman Identity after the Cultural Turn." *Early Christianity* 2 (2011): 281–311.

———. "The Use of the NT in the American Slave Controversy: A Case History in the Hermeneutical Tension between Biblical Criticism and Christian Moral Debate." *Religion and American Culture* 10, no. 2 (2000): 149–86.

Harris, Joseph E., ed. *Global Dimensions of the African Diaspora*. 2nd ed. Washington, D.C.: Howard University Press, 1993.

Hegedus, Tim. "Naming Christians in Antiquity." *Studies in Religion* 32 (2004): 173–90.

Hemer, Colin J. "The Address of 1 Peter." *Expository Times* 89 (1978): 239–43.

Hengel, Martin. "Early Christianity as a Jewish-Messianic, Universalistic Movement." Pages 1–41 in *Conflicts and Challenges in Early Christianity*. Edited by Donald A Hagner. Harrisburg, Pa.: Trinity International, 1999.

———. *Judaism and Hellenism: Studies in Their Encounter in Palestine during Early Hellenistic Period*. 2 vols. Eugene, Ore.: Wipf & Stock, 1974.

———. *Saint Peter: The Underestimated Apostle*. Grand Rapids: Eerdmans, 2010.

———. "Salvation History." Pages 229–44 in *Reading Texts, Seeking Wisdom: Scripture and Theology*. Edited by David Ford and Graham Stanton. Grand Rapids: Eerdmans, 2003.

Henning, Meghan. *Educating Early Christians through the Rhetoric of Hell: Weeping and Gnashing of Teeth as Paideia in Matthew and the Early Church*. Wissenschaftliche Untersuchungen zum Neuen Testament 2. Tübingen: Mohr Siebeck, 2014.

Hill, David. "'To Offer Spiritual Sacrifices' (1 Peter 2:5): Liturgical Formulations and Christian Paraenesis in 1 Peter." *Journal for the Study of the New Testament* 16 (1982): 45–63.

Holladay, Carl R. *Fragments from Hellenistic Jewish Authors*. 2 vols. Atlanta: Society of Biblical Literature, 1983, 1989.

Holloway, Paul A. *Coping with Prejudice: 1 Peter in Social-Psychological Perspective*. Wissenschaftliche Untersuchungen zum Neuen Testament 244. Tübingen: Mohr Siebeck, 2009.

Holt, Thomas. "The Political Uses of Alienation: W. E. B. Du Bois on Politics, Race, and Culture, 1903–1940." *American Quarterly* 42 (1990): 301–23.

Honigman, Sylvie. *The Septuagint and Homeric Scholarship in Alexandria: A Study in the Narrative of the Letter of Aristeas*. London: Routledge, 2003.

Horrell, David G. *Becoming Christian: Essays on 1 Peter and the Making of Christian Identity*. The Library of New Testament Studies 394. London: T&T Clark, 2013.

———. "'Becoming Christian': Solidifying Christian Identity and Content." Pages 309–35 in *Handbook of Early Christianity: Social Science Approaches*. Edited by Anthony J. Blasi et al. Walnut Creek, Calif.: AltaMira Press, 2002.

———. "Between Conformity and Resistance: Beyond the Balch-Elliott Debate towards a Postcolonial Reading of First Peter." In Webb and Bauman-Martin, *Reading First Peter with New Eyes*, 111–43.

———. *The Epistles of Peter and Jude*. London: Epworth, 1998.

———. "The Label Χριστιανός: 1 Peter 4:16 and the Formation of Christian Identity." *Journal of Biblical Literature* 126 (2007): 361–81.

———. *1 Peter*. New Testament Guides. London: T&T Clark, 2008.

———. *Solidarity and Difference: A Contemporary Reading of Paul's Ethics*. London: T&T Clark, 2005.

Horsley, Richard, ed. *Hidden Transcripts and the Arts of Resistance: Applying the Work of James C. Scott to Jesus and Paul*. Semeia Studies 48. Atlanta: Society of Biblical Literature, 2004.

Horst, Pieter W. van der, trans. *Philo's Flaccus: The First Pogrom*. Philo of Alexandria Commentary Series. Leiden: Brill, 2003.

Hort, F. J. A. *The First Epistle of St. Peter I.1–II.17: The Greek Text with Introductory Lecture, Commentary, and Additional Notes*. London: Macmillan, 1898. Reprint, Eugene, Ore.: Wipf & Stock, 2005.

Howard, George E. "The Letter of Aristeas and Diaspora Judaism." *Journal of Theological Studies* 22 (1971): 337–48.

Howard, George P. "Introduction to Septuagintal Studies." *Restoration Quarterly* 7 (1963): 138–42.

Humphreys, W. Lee. "Life-Style for Diaspora: A Study of the Tales of Esther and Daniel." *Journal of Biblical Literature* 92 (1973): 211–23.

Hunzinger, Claus-Junno. "Babylon als Deckname für Rom und die Datierung des 1. Petrusbriefes." Pages 67–77 in *Gottes Wort und Gottes Land.* Edited by Henning Graf Reventlow. Hertzberg: Vandenhoeck & Ruprecht, 1965.

Inwood, Brad, and Lloyd P. Gerson. *Hellenistic Philosophy: Introductory Readings.* Indianapolis: Hackett, 1988.

Isaac, Benjamin. *The Invention of Racism in Classical Antiquity.* Princeton, N.J.: Princeton University Press, 2004.

James, Leslie R. "The African Diaspora as Construct and Lived Experience." Pages 11–18 in *The Africana Bible: Readings Israel's Scriptures from Africa and the African Diaspora.* Edited by Hugh R. Page Jr. et al. Minneapolis: Fortress, 2010.

Jeffers, James S. *The Greco-Roman World of the New Testament Era: Exploring the Background of Early Christianity.* Downers Grove, Ill.: InterVarsity, 1999.

Jellico, Sidney. "The Occasion and Purpose of the Letter of Aristeas: A Reexamination." *New Testament Studies* 12 (1966): 144–50.

———. "Septuagint Origins: The Letter of Aristeas." Pages 29–58 in *The Septuagint and Modern Study.* Edited by Sidney Jellicoe. Oxford: Oxford University Press, 1968.

Jobes, Karen H. *1 Peter.* Baker Exegetical Commentary on the New Testament. Grand Rapids: Baker, 2005.

Johnson, Luke Timothy. *Among the Gentiles: Greco-Roman Religion and Christianity.* Anchor Yale Bible Reference Library. New Haven, Conn.: Yale University Press, 2009.

———. *The Gospel of Luke.* Sacra Pagina 3. Collegeville, Minn.: Liturgical Press, 1991.

———. "Imagining the World Scripture Imagines." *Modern Theology* 14 (1998): 165–80.

———. "James 3:13–4:10 and the *Topos Peri Phthonou.*" *Novum Testamentum* 25 (1983): 327–47.

———. *Sharing Possessions: What Faith Demands.* 2nd ed. Grand Rapids: Eerdmans, 2011.

———. *The Writings of the New Testament.* 3rd ed. Minneapolis: Fortress, 2010.

Johnson, Sara Raup. *Historical Fiction and Hellenistic Jewish Identity: Third Maccabees in Its Cultural Context.* Berkeley: University of California Press, 2004.

Jones, E. E., et al. *Social Stigma: The Psychology of Marked Relationships.* New York: Freeman, 1984.

Jones, H. S. "Claudius and the Jewish Question in Alexandria." *Journal of Roman Studies* 16 (1926): 26–29.

Joseph, Abson Predestin. *A Narratological Reading of 1 Peter.* The Library of New Testament Studies 440. London: T&T Clark, 2012.

Josephus. Translated by H. St. J. Thackeray et al. Loeb Classical Library. 10 vols. Cambridge, Mass.: Harvard University Press, 1926–1965.

Judge, Edwin A. *The Social Pattern of Early Christian Groups in the First Century: Some Prologomena to the Study of the New Testament Ideas of Social Obligation.* London: Tyndale, 1960.

Judge, Edwin A., and James R. Harrison. *The First Christians in the Roman World: Augustan and New Testament Essays.* Wissenschaftliche Untersuchungen zum Neuen Testament 229. Tübingen: Mohr Siebeck, 2008.

Judge, Edwin A., and G. S. R Thomas. "The Origin of the Church at Rome: A New Solution?" *Reformed Theological Review* (1966): 81–94.

Juvenal. *Satires.* Translated by G. G. Ramsey. Loeb Classical Library. Cambridge, Mass.: Harvard University Press, 1999.

Kahl, Brigitte. *Galatians Re-imagined: Reading with the Eyes of the Vanquished.* Minneapolis: Fortress, 2010.

Kagan, Donald. *The End of the Roman Empire: Decline or Transformation.* 3rd ed. Lexington, Mass.: D. C. Heath, 1992.

Kelly, J. N. D. *A Commentary on the Epistles of Peter and Jude.* Black's New Testament Commentaries. London: A&C Black, 1969.

Kennedy, George Alexander. *Progymnasmata: Greek Textbooks of Prose and Composition and Rhetoric.* Writings from the Greco-Roman World 10. Atlanta: Society of Biblical Literature, 2003.

Kenny, Kevin. *Diaspora: A Very Short Introduction.* Oxford: Oxford University Press, 2013.

Klauck, Hans-Josef. *The Religious Context of Early Christianity: A Guide to Graeco-Roman Religions.* Minneapolis: Fortress, 2003.

Klijn, Albertus F. J. "The Letter of Aristeas and the Greek Translation of the Pentateuch in Egypt." *New Testament Studies* 11 (1964): 154–58.

Knox, John. "Pliny and 1 Peter: A Note on 1 Pet 4:14-16 and 3:15." *Journal of Biblical Literature* 72 (1953): 187–89.

Konradt, Matthias. "The Historical Context of the Letter of James in Light of Its Traditio-Historical Relations with First Peter." In Niebuhr and Wall, *Catholic Epistles and Apostolic Tradition*, 101–25, 403–25.

Kraabel, A. T. "The Disappearance of the 'God-Fearers.'" *Numen* 28 (1981): 113–26.

Kraftchick, Steven J. "1 Peter." Pages 455–58 in *Theological Bible Commentary*. Edited by David L. Petersen and Gail R. O'Day. Louisville, Ky.: Westminster John Knox, 2009.

———. "Reborn to a Living Hope: A Christology of 1 Peter." Pages 83–97 in *Reading 1–2 Peter and Jude: A Resource for Students*. Edited by Eric F. Mason and Troy W. Martin. Atlanta: Society of Biblical Literature, 2014.

Kuhl, Curt. *Die drei Männer im Feuer*. Beihefte zur Zeitschrift für die neutestamentliche Wissenschaft 55. Giessen: Töpelmann, 1930.

Lacocque, André. *The Book of Daniel*. Translated by D. Pellauer. Atlanta: Westminster John Knox, 1979.

Lake, Kirsopp, and Henry Cadbury. *Acts: English Translation and Commentary*. Vol. 4 of *The Beginnings of Christianity, Part I: The Acts of the Apostles*. Edited by F. J. Foakes Jackson and Kirsopp Lake. London: Macmillan, 1933.

Lapham, F. *Peter: The Myth, the Man and the Writings*. Journal for the Study of the New Testament Supplement Series 239. Sheffield: Sheffield Academic, 2003.

Lefkowitz, Mary R., and Maureen B. Fant. *Women's Life in Greece and Rome: A Sourcebook in Translation*. 3rd ed. Baltimore: Johns Hopkins University Press, 2005.

Levinskaya, I. A. "The Inscription from Aphrodisias and the Problem of God-Fearers." *Tyndale Bulletin* 41 (1990): 312–18.

Lévi-Strauss, Claude. *The Origin of Table Manners*. Chicago: University of Chicago Press, 1968.

Levitt, Peggy. "Redefining the Boundaries of Belonging: The Institutional Character of Transnational Religious Life." *Sociology of Religion* 65, no. 1 (2004): 1–18.

Liddell, H. G., and Robert Scott, eds. *An Intermediate Greek–English Lexicon*. Accordance electronic ed., version 2.1. New Haven, Conn.: Yale University Press, 1996.

Lewis, Naphtali. *Greeks in Ptolemaic Egypt: Case Studies in the Social History of the Hellenistic World*. New York: Oxford University Press, 1986.

Lieu, Judith M. *Christian Identity in the Jewish and Graeco-Roman World.* Oxford: Oxford University Press, 2004.

———. *Neither Jew nor Greek? Constructing Early Christianity.* London: T&T Clark, 2002.

———. "'The Parting of the Ways': Theological Construct or Historical Reality?" *Journal for the Study of the New Testament* 56 (1994): 101–19.

———. "The Race of the God-Fearers." *Journal of Theological Studies* 46 (1995): 483–501.

Linder, Amnon. *The Jews in Roman Imperial Legislation.* Detroit and Jerusalem: Wayne State University Press and the Israel Academy of Sciences and Humanities, 1987.

Livy. *History of Rome.* Translated by Evan T. Sage. Loeb Classical Library. Cambridge, Mass.: Harvard University Press, 1997.

Llewellyn-Jones, Lloyd. *King and Court in Ancient Persia 559 to 331 BCE.* Edinburgh: Edinburg University Press, 2013.

Lohr, Joel. *Chosen and Unchosen: Conceptions of Election in the Pentateuch and Jewish-Christian Interpretation.* Siphrut 2. Winona Lake, Ind.: Eisenbrauns, 2009.

Longenecker, Bruce W., ed. *Narrative Dynamics in Paul: A Critical Assessment.* Louisville, Ky.: Westminster John Knox, 2002.

Louw, J. P., and Eugene Albert Nida. *Greek–English Lexicon of the New Testament: Based on Semantic Domains.* New York: United Bible Societies, 1996 [1989].

Lovejoy, Paul E. "The African Diaspora: Revisionist Interpretations of Ethnicity, Culture and Religion and Slavery." *Studies in the World History of Slavery, Abolition, and Emancipation* 2, no. 1 (1977): 1–21. Online: http://ejournalofpoliticalscience.org/diaspora.html. Accessed December 12, 2015.

Lull, Timothy F., ed. *Luther's Basic Theological Writings.* Minneapolis: Augsburg Fortress, 2005.

Lust, Johan. "Daniel 7:13 and the Septuagint." *Ephemerides Theologicae Lovanienses* 54 (1978): 62–69.

MacDonald, Margaret Y. "Beyond Identification of the *Topos* of Household Management: Reading the Household Codes in Light of Recent Methodologies and Theoretical Perspectives in the Study of the New Testament." *New Testament Studies* 57 (2011): 65–90.

MacMullen, Ramsay. *Paganism in the Rome Empire.* New Haven, Conn.: Yale University Press, 1981.

Malherbe, Abraham. *Social Aspects of Early Christianity.* 2nd ed. Philadelphia: Fortress, 2003.

Malina, Bruce J. *The New Testament World: Insights from Cultural Anthropology.* Louisville, Ky.: Westminster John Knox, 2001.

Malina, Bruce J., and Jerome Neyrey. "Honor and Shame in Luke-Acts: Pivotal Values of the Mediterranean World." Pages 35–66 in *The Social World of Luke–Acts: Models for Interpretation.* Edited by Jerome Neyrey. Peabody, Mass.: Hendrickson, 1991.

Malina, Bruce J., and Richard Rohrbaugh. *Social-Science Commentary on the Synoptic Gospels.* Philadelphia: Fortress, 1992.

Mann, T. *Deuteronomy.* Word Biblical Commentary. Louisville, Ky.: Westminster John Knox, 1995.

Marshall, I. Howard. *1 Peter.* IVP New Testament Commentary Series. Downers Grove, Ill.: InterVarsity, 1991.

Martin, Clarice. "The *Haustafel* (Household Codes) in African American Biblical Interpretation: 'Free Slaves' and 'Subordinate Women.'" Pages 206–31 in *Stony the Road We Trod.* Edited by Cain Hope Felder. Minneapolis: Fortress, 1991.

Martin, Dale B. "Ancient Slavery, Class, and Early Christianity." *Fides et Historia* 23 (1991): 105–13.

———. *Slavery as Salvation: The Metaphor of Slavery in Pauline Christianity.* New Haven, Conn.: Yale University Press, 1990.

Martin, Troy W. *Metaphor and Composition in 1 Peter.* Society of Biblical Literature Dissertation Series. Atlanta: Scholars Press, 1992.

McKim, Donald K. *Westminster Dictionary of Theological Terms.* Louisville, Ky.: Westminster John Knox, 1996.

McLay, Tim. *The OG and Th Versions of Daniel.* Atlanta: Scholars Press, 1996.

Meecham, Henry G. *The Letter of Aristeas.* Manchester: Manchester University, 1935.

———. *The Oldest Version of the Bible: "Aristeas" on Its Traditional Origin.* London: Holborn, 1932.

Meeks, Wayne A. *The First Urban Christians: The Social World of the Apostle Paul.* 2nd ed. New Haven, Conn.: Yale University Press, 2003.

———. "'The Haustafeln' and American Slavery: A Hermeneutical Challenge." Pages 232–53 in *Theology and Ethics in Paul and His Interpreters: Essays in Honor of Victor Paul Furnish.* Edited by Eugene Lovering Jr. and Jerry L. Sumney. Nashville: Abingdon, 1996.

———. "The Social World of Early Christianity." *Council on the Study of Religion Bulletin* 6 (1975): 1–5.

Méléze-Modrzejewski, Joseph. *The Jews of Egypt from Rameses II to Emperor Hadrian*. Translated by Robert Cornman. Jerusalem: The Jewish Publication Society, 1995.

Mendels, Doron. "The Five Empires: A Note on a Propagandistic Topos." *American Journal of Philology* 102 (1981): 330–37.

Mendelson, Alan. *Philo's Jewish Identity*. Brown Judaic Studies 161. Atlanta: Scholars Press, 1988.

Michaels, J. Ramsey. "Eschatology in 1 Peter III.17." *New Testament Studies* 13 (1967): 394–401.

———. *1 Peter*. Word Biblical Commentary 49. Waco, Tex.: Word Books, 1988.

Monera, Arnold T. "The Christian's Relationship to the State according to the New Testament: Conformity or Non-conformity?" *Asia Journal of Theology* 19 (2005): 106–42.

Moss, Candida. *The Myth of Persecution: How Early Christians Invented a Story of Martyrdom*. New York: HarperCollins, 2013.

Murray, Oswyn. "Aristeas and Ptolemaic Kingship." *Journal of Theological Studies*, n.s. 18 (1967): 337–71.

Neill, Stephen. *The Interpretation of the New Testament 1861–1961*. London: Oxford University Press, 1964.

Newman, Carey C., ed. *Jesus and the Restoration of Israel: A Critical Assessment of N. T. Wright's* Jesus and the Victory of God. Downers Grove, Ill.: InterVarsity, 1999.

Newsom, Carol A. "Daniel." Pages 293–98 in *Women's Bible Commentary*. 3rd ed. Edited by Carol A. Newsom, Sharon H. Ringe, and Jacqueline E. Lapsley. Louisville, Ky.: Westminster John Knox, 2012.

———. *Daniel: A Commentary*. Old Testament Library. Louisville, Ky.: Westminster John Knox, 2014.

———. "God's Other: The Intractable Problem of the Gentile King in Judean and Early Jewish Literature." Pages 31–48 in *The "Other" in Second Temple Judaism: Essays in Honor of John J. Collins*. Edited by Daniel C. Harlow, Karina Martin Hogan, Matthew Goff, and Joel S. Kaminsky. Grand Rapids: Eerdmans, 2011.

———. "Why Nabonidus? Excavating Traditions from Qumran, the Hebrew Bible, and Neo-Babylonian Sources." Pages 57–80 in *The Dead Sea Scrolls: Transmission of Traditions and Production of Texts*. Edited by Sarianna Metso, Hindy Najman, and Eileen M. Schuller. Studies on the Texts of the Desert of Judah 92. Leiden: Brill, 2010.

Niditch, Susan. *Folklore and the Hebrew Bible.* Eugene, Ore.: Wipf & Stock, 2004.

———. *A Prelude to Biblical Folklore: Underdogs and Tricksters.* 2nd ed. San Francisco: Harper & Row, 2000 [1987].

Niditch, Susan, and Robert Doran. "Success Story of the Wise Courtier: A Formal Approach." *Journal of Biblical Literature* 96 (1977): 179–93.

Niebuhr, Karl-Wilhelm, and Robert W. Wall, eds. *The Catholic Epistles and Apostolic Tradition: A New Perspective on James to Jude.* Waco, Tex.: Baylor University Press, 2009.

Nikiprowetzky, Valentin. *Le commentaire de l'écriture chez Philon d'Alexandrie.* Leiden: Brill, 1977.

Norlin, George. *Isocrates with an English Translation in Three Volumes.* Cambridge, Mass.: Harvard University Press, 1980.

O'Neal, James L. "Royal Authority and City Law under Alexander and His Hellenistic Successors." *Classical Quarterly* 50 (2000): 424–31.

Orlinsky, Harry M. "The Septuagint as Holy Writ and the Philosophy of the Translators." *Hebrew Union College Annual* 46 (1975): 89–114.

Osiek, Carolyn. "The Family in Early Christianity: 'Family Values' Revisited." *Catholic Biblical Quarterly* 58 (1996): 1–25.

Osiek, Carolyn, and David L. Balch. *Families in the New Testament World: Households and House Churches.* Louisville, Ky.: Westminster John Knox, 1997.

Palmer, Colin A. "Defining and Studying the Modern African Diaspora." *Perspectives* 39, no. 6 (1998): 27–32.

Parpola, Simo. "The Forlorn Scholar." Pages 257–78 in *Language, Literature, and History: Philological and Historical Studies Presented to Erica Reiner.* Edited by Francesca Rochberg-Halton. New Haven, Conn.: American Oriental Society, 1987.

Patterson, Richard D. "Holding on to Daniel's Court Tales." *Jounal of Evangelical Theological Society* 36 (1993): 445–54.

Patterson, Tiffany Ruby, and Robin D. G. Kelley. "Unfinished Migrations: Reflections on the African Diaspora and the Making of the Modern World." *African Studies Review* 43, no. 1 (2000): 11–45.

Pelletier, André, ed. and trans. *Lettre d'Aristée a Philocrate.* Sources chrétiennes 89. Paris: Cerf, 1962.

Perdelwitz, Richard. *Die Mysterienreligion und das Problem des 1. Petrusbriefes.* Religionsversuche und Vorarbeite 11. Giessen: Töpelmann, 1911.

Person, Raymond. *The Deuteronomic School: History, Social Setting, and Literature.* Studies in Biblical Literature 2. Atlanta: Society of Biblical Literature, 2002.

Philo. Translated by F. H. Colson and G. H. Whitaker. 10 vols. Loeb Classical Library. Cambridge, Mass.: Harvard University Press, 1937.

Pliny the Younger. *Letters and Panegyricus.* Translated by Betty Radice. 2 vols. Loeb Classical Library. Cambridge, Mass.: Harvard University Press, 1969.

Plutarch. *The Dinner of the Seven Wise Men.* Vol. 2, *Moralia.* Loeb Classical Library 222. Cambridge, Mass.: Harvard University Press, 1956.

———. *Moralia.* Translated by Frank Cole Babbit. 15 vols. Loeb Classical Library. Cambridge, Mass.: Harvard University Press, 1927–1969.

———. *The Parallel Lives.* Translated by Bernadotte Perrin. 11 vols. Loeb Classical Library. Cambridge, Mass.: Harvard University Press, 1914–1926.

Porteous, Norman W. *Daniel: A Commentary.* Old Testament Library. Philadelphia: Westminster, 1965.

Porter, Stanley E. "Excursus: The 'We' Passages." In Gill and Gempf, *Book of Acts in Its Graeco-Roman Setting*, 545–74.

Pritchard, James B., ed. *Ancient Near Eastern Texts Relating to the Old Testament.* 3rd ed. Princeton, N.J.: Princeton University Press, 1969.

Rae, Murray. *History and Hermeneutics.* London: T&T Clark, 2005.

Rajak, Tessa. "Was There a Roman Charter for the Jews?" *Journal of Roman Studies* 74 (1984): 107–23.

Ramsey, W. M. *The Social Basis of Roman Power in Asia Minor.* Aberdeen: Aberdeen University Press, 1941.

Rappaport, Uriel. "The Letter of Aristeas Again." *Journal for the Study of the Pseudepigrapha* 21 (2012): 285–303.

Rapske, Brian M. "Acts, Travel, and Shipwreck." In *The Book of Acts in Its Graeco-Roman Setting.* Vol. 2 of *The Book of Acts in Its First Century Setting.* Edited by David W. J. Gill and Conrad Gempf, 1–47. Grand Rapids: Eerdmans, 1994.

Reasoner, Mark. *Roman Imperial Texts: A Sourcebook.* Minneapolis: Fortress, 2013.

Redding, Ann Holmes. "The Christian Family and the Household Codes." *Living Pulpit* 8 (1999): 36–37.

———. "Not Again: Another Look at the Household Codes." In *Eve & Adam*, edited by Kristen E. Kvam et al., 456–63. Bloomington: Indiana University Press, 1999.

———. "Together, Not Equal: The Rhetoric of Unity and Headship in the Letter to Ephesians." Ph.D. diss., Union Theological Seminary, 1999.

Reid, Stephen Breck. "The Theology of the Book of Daniel and the Political Theory of W. E. B. Du Bois." Pages 37–49 in *The Recovery of Black Presence: An Interdisciplinary Exploration: Essays in Honor of Dr. Charles B. Copher.* Edited by Randall C. Bailey and Jacquelyn Grant. Nashville: Abingdon Press, 1995.

Res gestae divi Augusti. Translated by Frederick W. Shipley. Loeb Classical Library. London: W. Heinemann, 1924.

Richard, Lucien. *Living the Hospitality of God.* New York: Paulist Press, 2000.

Robbins, Vernon K. *Exploring the Textures of Texts.* Harrisburg, Pa.: Trinity International, 1996.

———. *Jesus the Teacher: Socio-rhetorical Interpretation of Mark.* Minneapolis: Fortress, 1984.

———. "Socio-Rhetorical Interpretation." Pages 192–219 in *The Blackwell Companion to the New Testament.* Edited by David E. Aune. Chichester: Wiley-Blackwell, 2010.

———. *The Tapestry of Early Christian Discourse: Rhetoric, Society, and Ideology.* London: Routledge, 1996.

Roberts, Michelle Voss. *Dualities: A Theology of Difference.* Louisville, Ky.: Westminster John Knox, 2010.

Russell, Letty M., and J. Shannon Clarkson, eds. *Dictionary of Feminist Theologies.* Louisville, Ky.: Westminster John Knox, 1996.

Safran, William. "Diasporas in Modern Societies: Myths of Homeland and Return." *Diaspora* 1, no. 1 (1991): 83–99.

Sanders, E. P. *Judaism: Practice and Belief 63 BCE–66 CE.* London: SCM Press, 1992.

———. *Paul and Palestinian Judaism: A Comparison of Patterns of Religion.* Philadelphia: Fortress, 1977.

Santos, Narry F. "Diaspora in the New Testament and Its Impact on Christian Mission." *Torch Trinity Journal* 13, no. 1 (2010): 3–18.

Savage, Barbara Dianne. "Biblical and Historical Imperatives: Toward a History of Ideas about the Political Role of Black Churches." Pages 367–88 in *African Americans and the Bible: Sacred Texts and Social Textures.* Edited by Vincent L. Wimbush. New York: Continuum, 2000.

Schäfer, Peter. *The History of the Jews in the Greco-Roman World.* New York: Routledge, 2003.

Schenck, Kenneth. *A Brief Guide to Philo.* Louisville, Ky.: Westminster John Knox, 2005.

Schneider, Johannes. "*timē*." *Theological Dictionary of the New Testament* 8:172–75.

Schürer, Emil. *The History of the Jewish People in the Age of Jesus Christ (175 BCE–AD 135)*. Translated by Geza Vermes and Fergus Miller. 3 vols. Edinburgh: T&T Clark, 1986.

Scott, James C. *Domination and the Arts of Resistance: Hidden Transcripts*. New Haven, Conn.: Yale University Press, 1990.

———. *Weapons of the Weak: Everyday Forms of Peasant Resistance*. New Haven, Conn.: Yale University Press, 1985.

Segal, Alan F. *The Other Judaisms of Late Antiquity*. Brown Judaic Studies. Atlanta: Scholars Press, 1987.

Seland, Torrey. *Strangers in the Light: Philonic Perspectives on Christian Identity in 1 Peter*. Biblical Interpretation Series 76. Leiden: Brill, 2005.

———, ed. *Reading Philo: A Handbook to Philo of Alexandria*. Grand Rapids: Eerdmans, 2014.

Seneca. *Moral Essays*. Translated by John W. Basore. 3 vols. Loeb Classical Library. Cambridge, Mass.: Harvard University Press, 1964–1970.

Seow, Choon-Leong. *Daniel*. Westminster Bible Companion. Louisville, Ky.: Westminster John Knox, 2003.

Septuaginta: id est, Vetus Testamentum graece iuxta LXX interpretes. Edited by Alfred Rahlfs. 2 vols. 6th ed. Stuttgart: Württembergishe Bibelanstalt, 1959.

Schaefer, Hans. "Paroikoi." *Paulys Real-Encyclopädie der classischen Altertumswissenschaft* 18, no. 4 (1949): 1695–1701.

Sheffer, Gabriel. *Diaspora Politics: At Home Abroad*. New York: Cambridge University Press, 2003.

Shelton, Jo-Ann. *As the Romans Did: A Sourcebook in Roman Social History*. 2nd ed. Oxford: Oxford University Press, 1998.

Shepperson, George. "The African Abroad or the African Diaspora." *African Forum* 2 (1966): 76–93.

Sherk, Robert K. *The Roman Empire: Augustus to Hadrian*. Translated Documents of Greece and Rome. Vol. 6. Cambridge: Cambridge University Press, 1988.

Sherwin-White, Susan, and Amelie Kuhrt. *From Samarkhand to Sardis: A New Approach to Seleucid Empire*. London: Duckworth, 1993.

Shutt, Robert J. H. "Letter of Aristeas." *Old Testament Pseudepigrapha* 2:7–34.

———. "Letter of Aristeas." Pages 7–34 in vol. 2 of *The Apocrypha and Pseudepigrapha of the Old Testament*. Edited by J. D. Charlesworth. Garden City, N.Y.: Doubleday, 1985.

———. "Notes on the Letter of Aristeas." *Bulletin of the International Organization for Septuagint and Cognate Studies* 10 (1977): 22–30.

Sihola, J., and T. Engberg-Pedersen, eds. *The Emotions in Hellenistic Philosophy*. New Synthese Historical Library 46. Dordrecht: Kluwer, 1998.

Smallwood, E. Mary. *The Jews under Roman Rule: From Pompey to Diocletian*. Leiden: Brill, 1976.

———. *Philonis Alexandrini: Legatio ad Gaium*. 2nd ed. Leiden: Brill, 1970.

Smart, Ninian. "The Importance of Diasporas." Pages 288–97 in *Gilgul: Essays on Transformation, Revolution, and Permanence in the History of Religions*. Edited by Shauel Shaked et al. Leiden: Brill, 1987.

Smith, Abraham. "'It Seems to Me We Do Agree,' Said Booker T. and W. E. B.: Structures of Oppression in the Hermeneutics of *Up from Slavery* and *The Souls of Black Folk*." Pages 163–83 in *Reading Communities, Reading Scripture*. Edited by Daniel Patte et al. Harrisburg, Pa.: Trinity International, 2002.

Smith, Mitzi J. "Slavery in the Early Church." Pages 11–22 in *True to Our Native Land*. Edited by Brian Blount et al. Minneapolis: Fortress, 2007.

Smith-Christopher, Daniel. *A Biblical Theology of Exile*. Overtures to Biblical Theology. Minneapolis: Fortress, 2002.

———. "The Book of Daniel: Introduction, Commentary, and Reflections." Pages 17–152 in vol. 7 of *The New Interpreter's Bible*. Edited by Leander Keck. Nashville: Abingdon Press, 1996.

———. *The Religion of the Landless: The Social Context of the Babylonian Exile*. Bloomington: Meyer-Stone, 1989.

Snyder, S. "Participles and Imperatives in 1 Peter: A Re-examination in the Light of Recent Scholarly Trends." *Filologia Neotestamentaria* 8 (1995): 187–98.

Sterling, Gregory E. *Historiography and Self-Definition: Josephus, Luke–Acts and Apologetic Historiography*. Leiden: Brill, 1992.

———. "Philo." Pages 789–93 in *Dictionary of New Testament Background*. Edited by C. A. Evans and S. E. Porter. Downers Grove, Ill.: InterVarsity, 1992.

Stern, Elsie R. "Esther and the Politics of Diaspora." *Jewish Quarterly Review* 100 (2010): 25–53.

Stern, Menahem. *Greek and Latin Authors on Jews and Judaism*. Vol. 2. Jerusalem: Israel Academy of Sciences and Humanities, 1974–1984.

Sugirtharajah, R. S. *Exploring Postcolonial Biblical Criticism: History, Method, Practice*. Oxford: Blackwell, 2012.

Swain, Joseph W. "The Theory of the Four Monarchies: Opposition History under the Roman Empire." *Classical Philology* 35 (1940): 1–21.

Tacitus. *The Histories and The Annals*. Translated by C. H. Moore and J. Jackson. 4 vols. Loeb Classical Library. Cambridge, Mass.: Harvard University Press, 1937.

Talbert, Charles H., ed. *Perspectives on First Peter*. Macon, Ga.: Mercer University Press, 1986.

Tanzer, Sarah J. "Ephesians." Pages 325–48 in vol. 2 of *Searching the Scriptures: A Feminist Commentary*. Edited by E. Schüssler Fiorenza. New York: Crossroad, 1995.

Tcherikover, Victor. *Hellenistic Civilization and the Jews*. New York: Atheneum, 1970.

———. "The Ideology of the Letter of Aristeas." *Harvard Theological Review* 51 (1958): 59–85.

Thatcher, Tom. "Philo on Pilate: Rhetoric or Reality?" *Restoration Quarterly* 37 (1995): 215–18.

Thiselton, Anthony C. *New Horizons in Hermeneutics: The Theory and Practice of Transforming Biblical Reading*. Grand Rapids: Zondervan, 1997.

Thuren, Lauri. *Argument, and Theology in 1 Peter: The Origins of Christian Paraenesis*. Sheffield: Sheffield Academic, 1995.

Tinsley, Annie. *A Postcolonial African American Re-reading of Colossians: Identity, Reception, and Interpretation under the Gaze of Empire*. Postcolonialism and Religions. New York: Palgrave Macmillan, 2013.

Tölölyan, Khachig. "Rethinking Diaspora(s): Stateless Power in Transnational Moment." *Diaspora* 5 (1996): 3–36.

Tracy, Sterling. "Aristeas and III Maccabees." *Yale Classical Studies* (1928): 239–52.

Traina, Giusto. *428 AD: An Ordinary Year at the End of the Roman Empire*. Princeton, N.J.: Princeton University Press, 2009.

Unnik, Willem Cornelis van. *Das Selbstverständnis der jüdischen Diaspora in der hellenistisch-römischen Zeit*. Leiden: Brill, 1993.

———. "The Teaching of Good Works in 1 Peter." Pages 83–105 in *Sparsa Collecta: The Collected Essays of W. C. van Unnik: Part 2*. Edited by C. K. Barrett. Supplements to Novum Testamentum 30. Leiden: Brill, 1980.

Verner, D. C. *The Household of God: The Social World of the Pastoral Epistles*. Chico, Calif.: Scholars Press, 1983.

Volf, Miroslav. "Soft Difference: Theological Reflections on the Relation between Church and Culture in 1 Peter." *Ex Auditu* 10 (1994): 15–30.

von Harnack, Adolf. *Die Geschichte der altchristlichen Literatur bis Eusebius.* Leipzig: Hunrichs, 1904.

Vos, Craig S. de. "Popular Graeco-Roman Responses to Christianity." Pages 869–89 in *The Early Christian World*, edited by Philip F. Esler. London: Routledge, 2000.

Wall, Robert W. "The Canonical Function of 2 Peter." *Biblical Interpretation* 9 (2001): 64–81.

Webb, Robert L. "Intertexture and Rhetorical Strategy in First Peter's Apocalyptic Discourse: A Study in Sociorhetorical Interpretation." In Webb and Bauman-Martin, *Reading First Peter with New Eyes*, 72–110.

———. "The Petrine Epistles: Recent Developments and Trends." Pages 373–90 in *The Face of New Testament Studies: A Survey of Recent Research.* Edited by Scot McKnight and Grant R. Osborne. Grand Rapids: Baker, 2004.

Webb, Robert L., and Betsy Bauman-Martin, eds. *Reading First Peter with New Eyes: Methodological Reassessments of the Letter of First Peter.* The Library of New Testament Studies 364. London: T&T Clark, 2007

Weber, Max. *Economy and Society: An Outline of Interpretative Sociology.* Vol. 1. Berkeley: University of California Press, 1968.

———. *The Sociology of Religion.* Boston: Methuen, 1965.

Webster, Jane, and Nicholas J. Cooper, eds. *Roman Imperialism: Postcolonial Perspectives.* Leicester Archaeology Monograph 3. Leicester: School of Archaeological Studies, University of Leicester, 1996.

Weidinger, Carl. *Die Haustafeln: Ein Stuck urchristlicher Paranese.* Hamburg: Heinrich Bauer, 1928.

Wellhausen, Julius. *Prolegomena to the History of Israel: With a Reprint of the Article "Israel" from the "Encyclopedia Britannica."* Translated by J. Sutherland Black and Allan Menzies. Edinburgh: A&C Black, 1885.

Wettstein, Howard. "Coming to Terms with Exile." Pages 47–59 in *Diasporas and Exiles: Varieties of Jewish Identity.* Edited by Howard Wittstein. Berkeley: University of California Press, 2002.

Wettstein, Howard, and Catherine Soussloff, eds. *Diasporas and Exiles: Varieties of Jewish Identity.* Berkeley: University of California Press, 2002.

Wilcox, M. "The 'God-Fearers' in Acts—A Reconsideration." *Journal for the Study of the New Testament* 13 (1981): 102–22.

Williams, Delores. *Sisters in the Wilderness: The Challenge of Womanist God-Talk.* Maryknoll, N.Y.: Orbis Books, 1993.

Williams, Demetrius K. "The Bible and Models of Liberation in African American Experience." Pages 33–59 in *Yet with a Steady Beat:*

Contemporary U.S. Afrocentric Biblical Interpretation. Edited by Randall C. Bailey. Leiden: Brill, 2003.

Williams, Margaret. *The Jews among the Greeks and Romans: A Diasporan Sourcebook*. London: Duckworth, 1998.

Williams, Travis B. *Persecution in 1 Peter: Differentiating and Contextualizing Early Christian Suffering*. Supplements to Novum Testamentum 145. Leiden: Brill, 2012.

———. "Reconsidering the Imperatival Principle in 1 Peter." *Westminster Theological Journal* 73 (2011): 59–78.

Wills, Lawrence M. *Ancient Jewish Novels: An Anthology*. Oxford: Oxford University Press, 2002.

———. *The Jew in the Court of the Foreign King: Ancient Jewish Court Legends*. Harvard Dissertations in Religion 26. Minneapolis: Fortress, 1990.

———. *The Jewish Novel in the Ancient World*. Ithaca, N.Y.: Cornell University Press, 1995.

———. *Not God's People: Insiders and Outsiders in the Bible World*. Religion in the Modern World. Plymouth: Rowman & Littlefield, 2008.

Wimbush, Vincent L., ed. *African Americans and the Bible: Sacred Texts and Social Textures*. New York: Continuum, 2003.

———. *Bible and African Americans: A Brief History*. Minneapolis: Fortress, 2003.

———. "The Bible and African Americans: An Outline of an Interpretative History." Pages 81–97 in *Stony the Road We Trod*. Edited by Cain Hope Felder. Minneapolis: Fortress, 1991.

———. ". . . Not of This World . . . : Early Christianities as Rhetorical and Social Formation." Pages 23–36 in *Reimagining Christian Origins*. Edited by Elizabeth A. Castelli, Burton L. Mack, and Hal Tassig. Valley Forge, Pa.: Trinity International, 1996.

———. "We Will Make Our Own Future Text: An Alternate Orientation to Interpretation." Pages 43–53 in *True to Our Native Land*. Edited by Brian Blount et al. Minneapolis: Fortress, 2007.

Windisch, Hans. *Die Katholischen Briefe*. 2nd ed. Handbuch zum Neuen Testament 15. Tübingen:: Mohr Siebeck, 1930 [1911].

Winkler, John. *The Constraints of Desire*. New York: Routledge, 1990.

Winter, Bruce W. "The Public Honouring of Christian Benefactors: Romans 13:3-4 and 1 Peter 2:14-15." *Journal for the Study of the New Testament* 34 (1988): 87–103.

———. *Roman Wives, Roman Widows: The Appearance of New Women and the Pauline Communities*. Grand Rapids: Eerdmans, 2003.

———. *Seek the Welfare of the City: Christians as Benefactors and Citizens.* Grand Rapids: Eerdmans, 1994.

Wire, Antoinette C. "Review Essay on Elliott. Home for the Homeless, and Balch, Let Wives Be Submissive." *Religious Studies Review* 10 (1984): 209–16.

Witherington, Ben. *Letters and Homilies for Hellenized Christians.* Vol. 2, *A Socio-rhetorical Commentary on 1–2 Peter.* Downers Grove, Ill.: InterVarsity, 2007.

Woan, Sue. "The Psalms in 1 Peter." Pages 213–29 in *The Psalms in the New Testament.* Edited by Steve Moyise and Maarten J. J. Menken. London: T&T Clark, 2004.

Wolfson, Harry A. "Philo on Jewish Citizenship in Alexandria." *Journal of Biblical Literature* 63 (1944): 165–68.

Wright, David F. "A Race Apart? Jews, Gentiles, Christians." *Bulletin de la Société d'archéologie copte* 160 (2003): 131–41.

Wright, N. T. *Jesus and the Victory of God: Christian Origins and the Question of God.* Vol. 2. Minneapolis: Augsburg Fortress, 1996.

Yarbrough, O. Larry. "Paul, Marriage, and Divorce." Pages 404–28 in *Paul in the Greco-Roman World: A Handbook.* Edited by J. Paul Sampley. Harrisburg, Pa.: Trinity Press, 2003.

Yonge, C. D. *The Works of Philo, Completed and Unabridged.* New updated ed. Peabody, Mass.: Hendrickson, 1993.

Xenophon. *Memorabilia, Oeconomicus, Symposium, Apology.* Translated by E. C. Marchant and O. J. Todd. Loeb Classical Library. Vol. 168. Cambridge, Mass.: Harvard University Press, 1923.

Zadok, Ran. *The Earliest Diaspora: Israelites and Judeans in Pre-Hellenistic Mesopotamia.* Tel Aviv: Diaspora Research Institute, 2002.

Zeleza, Paul Tiyambe. "Diaspora Dialogues: Engagements between Africa and its Diasporas." Pages 31–60 in *The New African Diaspora.* Edited by Isidore Okpewho and Nkiru Nzegwu. Bloomington and Indianapolis: Indiana University Press, 2009.

Zerubavel, Yael. *Recovered Roots: Collective Memory and the Making Israeli National Tradition.* Chicago: University of Chicago Press, 1995.

Ziegler, Joseph. *Susanna; Daniel; Bel et Draco Bible.* Old Testament, 2nd ed. Rev. Olivier Munnich. Septuaginta 16, no. 2. Göttingen: Vandenhoeck & Ruprecht, 1999.

Zuckermann, C. "Hellenistic Politeuma and the Jews: A Reconsideration." *Scripta Classica Israelica* 8–9 (1985–88): 171–85.

Zuntz, Günther. "Aristeas Studies." *Journal of Semitic Studies* 4 (1959): 21–36, 109–26.

———. "Aristeas Studies II: Aristeas in the Translation of the Torah." Pages 208–25 in *Studies in the Septuagint: Origins, Recensions, and Interpretations*. Edited by Sidney Jellicoe. New York: Ktav, 1974.

Index